The Pocket History of Kerry

First published in 2007 by Polymath Press,
Courthouse Lane,
Tralee, County Kerry, Ireland

Copyright © Gerald O'Carroll

ISBN 978-0-9547902-1-9

Printed in Ireland by Alphaset, Limerick

Tomb of Sir Edward Denny and wife Margaret Edgecombe
(courtesy Waltham Abbey)

For Michael and Mary,
and for my late mother who was a great reader of the
old church records

Preface

This book was begun in May 2006 as an attempt to introduce Kerry to the visitor. Then I identified another readership, among professionals who studied very little history at school and who appeared to me to be in the dark about key episodes of the past, as well as the Christian legacy.

My job was relatively easy. Kerry has been very well served by historians like Rev. A.B. Rowan, Mary Agnes Hickson and H.L.L. Denny, who did valuable spadework research before our Irish record office was burned during the Civil War of the early twentieth century. Of more recent research, I have drawn heavily on the journals of the Kerry Archaeological and Historical Society, and those of the Thomond and Cork Societies, as well as my own researches on Justice Robert Day.

Some very valuable work has been done abroad in recent years by historians of the Irish Colleges and the Irish Jacobites in exile. Until recently we have had only an impression of what lies in European archives. This has begun to change with greater research opportunities and easier travel by air, with the result that scholars have been able to appreciate the work of Irish missionaries who conserved Irish manuscripts in Europe during the Middle Ages, and those who conserved Irish history and scholarship in Europe after the defeat at Kinsale (1601).

My approach has been to follow the histories of leading families and individuals (Gaelic and foreign), with less emphasis on castles and battles and complicated clan rivalry; and I have tried to incorporate the viewpoint of the settlers, some of them very influential figures like William Petty and the Great Earl of Cork. Such an approach imposes strict conditions, however, which is why I have tried to remind readers of the sufferings, including religious persecution, endured by our ancestors during colonisation, insurrection and the long era of landlordism.

Two eras are of seminal importance in an account of the broad constitutional tradition in Kerry's history: the Jacobite era and the era of the French Revolution and Napoleon. Nineteenth-century historians understood the participation of all communities in the arguments of those times, which is why the rehabilitation of that understanding, with the assistance of the pedigrees, is one of the purposes of this book.

Acknowledgments

I owe a great debt of gratitude to Canon Albert Stokes and Russell MacMorran, both of whom provided inspirational assistance, particularly with the seventeenth century. The Knight of Kerry, Sir Adrian FitzGerald, and Enid O'Toole of Australia assisted with advice on pedigrees. Breandán O Cíobhán made valuable corrections to chapters on the later Middle Ages and the Irish lords and sub-lords; any remaining errors are my own. More recently I have availed of the assistance of the Kerry Diocesan Archives who supplied lists of our Kerry martyrs. I have used Sean Ó Liatháin's thesis on the Great Famine. I have benefited from the considerable enthusiasm and support of Eamon Browne and Michael Lynch at the Kerry County Library, not forgetting the Kerry Archaeological and Historical Society and members too numerous to mention, and Mike Maguire in the Limerick City Library (the Granary). Among leading historians whose approach has raised the bar for historians of the regions, I have learned much from A.T.Q. Stewart and J.C. Beckett, and, more recently, David Dickson.

Table of Contents

List of illustrations

484   Birth of St Brendan (d.577): founds Ardfert, Clonfert and Annaghdown (Co. Galway).

824   Viking (Norse) attack on the Sceilig (922 foundation of the Viking kingdom of Limerick).

1111   Synod of Rathbrassil divides Ireland into dioceses.

1169   Norman ("Old English") arrival at Bannow Bay, Wexford.
c.1200 Norman arrival in Kerry; principal family FitzGerald (the Munster Geraldines), future earls of Desmond.
c.1215-c.1330 Writing of the Annals of Innisfallen (named after a monastic island in a Killarney lake).

1243   Foundation of the Dominican house in Tralee by the Geraldines, who choose it as their burial place.

1261   Battle of Callan (near Kilgarvan), defeat of the Geraldines by the MacCarthys; the Geraldines as a result confined to the northern half of modern Kerry.

1329   Maurice FitzThomas (Geraldine) created Earl of Desmond.

1348   The Bubonic Plague ("Black Death").

1366   Statutes of Kilkenny, a failed attempt to prevent intermarriage with the Irish, use of the Irish language, laws and customs.

1492   "Discovery" of America by Colombus, an Italian in the service of the King of Spain

1517   Martin Luther nails 95 Theses on the church door at Wittenberg, Germany. His action signals the division of western Christendom and the beginning of the Reformation.

1529   The Treaty of Dingle between the Earl of Desmond and Charles V. Later missions from the Desmonds will attempt to place Ireland under a Catholic monarch.

1536   The Irish Parliament recognizes Henry VIII as head of the church.

1545   The Council of Trent inaugurates the Counter-Reformation.

1558   Elizabeth ascends the throne of England. She soon sets about reducing Desmond, including Kerry.

1580   Massacre at Dún an Óir in West Kerry of Spanish invasion force

1583   Death of Gerald, the "Rebel" Earl of Desmond at Glenageenty, three miles east of Tralee.

1586   Munster Plantation.

1588   The Spanish Armada, aimed at the overthrow of Elizabeth, fails. Ships scattered on the western coast, including off Kerry.

1598   Ulster leaders Hugh O'Neill and Hugh O'Donnell take the Nine Years War to the South and find allies in the Súgan Earl of Desmond and Florence MacCarthy Reagh.

1601   Battle of Kinsale: defeat of the Irish and their allies the Spanish.

1603   Treaty of Mellifont: surrender of Hugh O'Neill ends the Nine Year War against; it signals the end also of the war in North Kerry in which FitzMaurice and the knights of Kerry and Glin took the rebel side.

1606   Creation of the county of Kerry. The name derives from Ciar-Rioghacht (after the leader Ciar) a tribal region in the northern part of Kerry.

1607 Louvain (Belgium) College of the Irish Franciscans founded by Florence Conroy (September). "Flight of the Earls" to Europe from the North of Ireland as Hugh O'Neill (Earl of Tyrone) and Ruairi O'Donnell (Earl of Tyrconnell) leave Ireland, making possible the Plantation of Ulster.

1612 Tralee receives its Charter from King James I.

1631 (20 June) Sack of Baltimore by Algerian corsairs, early morning.

1641 The Confederate Wars begin. An Ulster insurrection is again the catalyst. Tralee Castle is besieged by the Irish.

1645 Papal Nuncio Rinuccini lands near Kenmare: he will cause sharp division in Kerry.

1649 Charles I executed; arrival of Cromwell in Ireland.

1650 Martyrdom of Boetius MacEgan, Bishop of Ross (Skibbereen region) at the hands of Lord Broghill (Boyle) near Macroom

1652 The Fall of Kerry to the Cromwellians with the capture of Ross Castle by Ludlow

1653 Martyrdom of Thaddeus (Tadhg) Moriarty, Prior of Holy Cross, Tralee, at the hands of the Cromwellians at Keelaclohane Wood, near Castlemaine

1653 Execution of Piaras Ferriter, poet, leader of the rebels who attacked Tralee Castle

1659 Corpo Santo, a Dominican college in Lisbon, founded by Tralee native Dominic O'Daly (1595-1662), having founded its temporary house in that city in 1634.

1660 Restoration to the throne of the Stuarts in the person of Charles II). Dominic O'Daly helps arrange his marriage to Catherine of Braganza (Portugal).

1688 The "Glorious" Revolution sets William, Prince of Orange, on the throne of England

1689 (March) King James arrives at Kinsale, and convenes Parliament in Dublin for May

1689 The German Palatinate is attacked by King Louis XIV; an exodus of Palatines takes place in 1709; some settle in Kerry and Limerick

1690 (March) The first Irish brigade, under Mountcashel, departs Kinsale for France

1690 Irish Regiment of Viscount Clare (O'Brien), many Kerrymen included, departs for France.

1690 William establishes his monarchy with victory at the Boyne.

1691 Treaty of Limerick will inaugurate transfer of land in Kerry to new planters, and voluntary exile in Europe for Jacobites (those who took the side of James II).

1701 War of the Spanish Succession. Leading Kerry Jacobites are participants.

1704 "An Act to prevent the further growth of Popery" is the culmination of anti-Catholic Penal Code; it compels the subdivision of remaining Catholic estates

1726 Death of poet Aogán O Raghaille

1730 A Danish ship, bound for Tranquebar, Den Gyldne Løve (The Golden Lion) is wrecked at Ballyheigue in the early morning hours of 28 October; on the night of 4 June its cargo of gold, which has been stored in Ballyheigue Castle, is stolen; an international incident ensues as Captain Johan Heitman seeks the return of the gold

1745   Landing in Scotland of Charles Edward Stuart (the "Young Pretender", aka "Bonnie Prince Charlie").

1746   Defeat of the Bonnie Prince Charlie's army at Cullodden.

1760   Use of the term "Kingdom of Kerry" in the diary of Lord Chief Baron Edward Willes ("From Newcastle to Tralee in the Kingdom of Kerry, as the Irish affect to call it ..."); John Philpot Curran will use the term in Parliament in 1787

1773   Killing of Art Ó Laoghaire (Arthur O'Leary) at Carriganimma inspires the famous Caoineadh (lament) written by his wife, aunt of Daniel O'Connell

1776   American Declaration of Independence.

1782   William Petty, Earl of Shelburne, becomes PM of England. He owns a huge estate in the south of Kerry.

1786   The rural campaign of the Rightboys puts Kerry on the front pages of the Dublin press.

1787   Inauguration of the baronial police, the "Barnies" in four southern counties, including Kerry.

1792   December, the Irish Catholic Convention takes place in Dublin, with delegates from Kerry.

1793   Catholic Relief Act supported by Tralee's Robert Day MP.

1795   Maynooth College (the Royal College of St Patrick) founded by the British government for the formation and ordination of Irish priests.

1798   Rebellion (begins night of 23 May) foreshadows the achievement of independent nationhood in the twentieth century; little immediate action in Kerry.

1798   Battle of the Nile won by Nelson over the fleet of Napoleon clears the way for the conquest of India by Marquess Wellesley; many Kerry gentlemen encourage their sons to serve the new British Empire there.

1800   The Act of Union is officially supported in Kerry, a rival campaign suppressed.

1802-06 George Canning MP Tralee.

1803   (23 July) Robert Emmet Rebellion.

1806   The Denny Act of Parliament settles the succession to the Denny estate and provides for the satisfaction of creditors (George III 46, Cap. 142).

1810   Military barracks "to be erected at Ballymullin, near Tralee, on the estate of S. Morris, Esq." (Limerick Chronicle, 14 March 1810).

1811   The Kildare Place Society set up to distribute grants for elementary level education; Kerry recipients will include the Hibernian Bible Society.

1814   Robert Peel's Peace Preservation Force (the "Peelers").

1815   Battle of Waterloo: Napoleon defeated by the Duke of Wellington.

1817   Partial failure of potato crop, typhoid fever epidemic and widespread distress.

1819   Murder of Ellen Hanly in the Shannon off Glin; she will become The Colleen Bawn of literature and the subject of an Irish opera, The Lily of Killarney.

1821   Partial failure of potato crop

1828   Act of Parliament (9 Geo. IV, Cap.cxviii) for a canal at Tralee "and for otherwise improving the Harbour of Tralee" (15 July 1828).

1828   Daniel O'Connell elected MP for Co. Clare; the government will grant Catholic Emancipation and admit him to Parliament by waiving the Oath.

1829   Catholic Emancipation achieved: the first Catholic High Sheriff of Kerry is shortly appointed.

1831   Chief Secretary Stanley's Irish National School system; by degrees the pay schools ("hedge schools"), for which Kerry is famous, will cease to exist.

1832-3 Asiatic Cholera epidemic in Kerry.

1838   Tithe Act, commutation of tithe to a rent charge payable by the landlord; Irish Poor Law (authorises the building of the work houses); Fr Theobald Mathew (from Thomastown, Golden) launches his temperance Crusade; Dingle Protestant Crusade begins, with centres at Dingle, Ballyferriter, Ventry.

1839   "Night of the Big Wind" (6-7 January, widespread storm damage)

1840   Municipal Reform Act democratises town and city government.

1842   St Mary's Killarney Cathedral begins construction. The designer is Augustus Welby Northmore Pugin. Construction will cease 1848-53. It will be consecrated for use in August 1855 by Bishop Moriarty, receive its spire extension in 1908-12, and undergo a controversial renovation in 1972-3 during the episcopate of Bishop Casey.

1845   The Devon Commission reports the real state of Ireland.

1845-1852 the Great Famine.

1846   Tralee Ship Canal opened, construction provided for under a bill of 1829.

1848   The "Jeanie Johnston", owned by Tralee merchant John Donovan and Sons, sails for Quebec with 200 passengers from Blennerville; The Encumbered Estate Act facilitates the sale of estates by landlords;
Maurice Leyne arrested in Tipperary for participation in the Young Ireland Rebellion.

1860   Bishop David Moriarty re-establishes a Franciscan community in Killarney; building of the present Friary commences in 1864 with a stone from Muckross Abbey.

1861   Queen Victoria visits Killarney and stays at Muckross House.

1861   Bishop Moriarty re-establishes the Dominicans in Tralee; he will lay the foundation stone of the present church in 1866.

1869   The Disestablishment of the Anglican Church of Ireland.

1879   The Land League founded by Mayo man Michael Davitt after partial failure of the potato crop; 1879-82 the Irish Land War.

1884   Reform Act gives the vote to the poorer tenantry, including labourers, single men and non-householders; the Gaelic Athletic Association (GAA) founded in Thurles; its games, particularly football, will thrive in Kerry.

1885   Ashbourne Land Act commences the process of transferring land ownership to the land occupiers.

1889   Parnell is cited as co-respondent in divorce action taken by Captain O'Shea; Kerry opinion is divided.

1896   Great Southern Hotels Company acquires ownership of five hotels: Killarney, Caragh Lake, Kenmare, Parknasilla and Waterville.

1898　Establishment of the County Councils: the franchise for which is given to the head of every household, no matter how poor.

1901　(January) Tom Crean, aboard the Discovery with Robert Falcon Scott, anchors off Ross Island in the Antarctic; they will spend two years there.

Census, the first complete census of Ireland; it and the 1911 census will have added importance when many other records are destroyed in the burning of the Four Courts during the Irish Civil war in 1922.

1903　Wyndham Land Act completes land transfer to the Irish farmers.

1903　Kerry football team wins the county's first All Ireland competition – the game is played in 1905.

1905　Sinn Fein is inaugurated; many I.R.B. (Irish Republican Brotherhood) are among the membership and will later use the new movement to advance I.R.B. policy.

1907　First performance of John M. Synge's *The Playboy of the Western World*; the tale of a young Kerryman who kills his father and escapes to Mayo inspires a riot in the Abbey Theatre.

1910　Robin Flower, Yorkshire man and graduate of Pembroke College, Oxford, visits the Great Blasket Island; places himself under instruction of Tomás Ó Criomhthain .

1911　(January) Tom Crean returns to the Antarctic with Scott on the Terra Nova.

1912　Home Rule Bill passes the British House of Commons.

1914　The Great War (World War One) begins;

Tom Crean embarks again for the Antarctic, this time with Sir Ernest Shakleton, leaving South Georgia on the Endurance; in two years he returns to Chatham.

1916　Easter (Monday) Rising, Dublin; Roger Casement has arrived on at Banna Strand the previous Good Friday.

1917　Thomas Ashe (Lispole), dies on hunger strike.

1918　End of World War One is Armistice Day.

1919　(January) Outbreak of Ireland's War of Independence.

1920　(March) Tom Crean of Annascaul retires from the British Navy after three expeditions to the South Pole; Tom Crean dies 1938.

1921　(December) Signing of the Anglo-Irish Treaty ends the War of Independence.

1922　(7 January) Treaty ratified in Dail Eireann by a vote of 64 to 57.

1922　(28 June) Beginning of the Irish Civil War. Bombardment of the Four Courts (Dublin) by the forces of the Free State.

1922　Michael Collins shot dead in an ambush at Bealnablath (between Dunmanway and Macroom).

1923　(7 March) At Ballyseedy nine Republican prisoners are tied to stump of a tree with mine attached, and the mine detonated; all but one (Fuller, later a TD) are killed.

1923　(24 May) Republicans ordered to bury their weapons. The Civil War ends.

1932　De Valera at the head of Fianna Fail wins power in the general election.

1933　Fiche Blian ag Fas (Twenty Years A-Growing), by Muiris Ó Suilleabháin of the Great Blasket Island, appears; becomes an international best seller.

1937 Steve "Crusher" Casey (1909-1987) from Sneem becomes World Heavyweight Champion Wrestler, retaining the title to 1947.

1939 Second World War begins. Britain declares war on Germany after Poland is invaded by Germany under Adolf Hitler. Ireland remains neutral.

1944 Charles Kerins of Strand Road, Tralee, executed in Mountjoy Jail for shooting a police man (a GAA club and housing estate in Tralee will be called after him)

1945 End of World War 2 and the commencement of building reconstruction in Britain, in which many Kerry emigrants participate.

1953 Abandonment of the Blasket Islands; a pattern of emigration to Springfield, Mass., USA continues.

1959 Listowel Drama Group wins the All Ireland Drama competition (Esso Tophy) at Athlone with Sive by John B. Keane.

1960 Irish television service (Telifis Eireann).

1960s Small regional railway lines deemed economical, including many in Kerry, are taken up (the policy will be regretted during the boom of the 1990s).

1964 Free Secondary education is introduced by Minister Donough O'Malley (free University will follow in 1968).

1967 Founding of the Kerry Archaeological and Historical Society; the Cork Hist. and Arch. Society founded 1891 has carried much Kerry research.

1968 A Civil Rights march in Northern Ireland is attacked, leading to a revival of the I.R.A. campaign and thirty years of violence.

1968 (October) – 1970 (March) the filming of Ryan's Daughter by David Leen near Dunquin (extreme West of Kerry) transforms the economy of the district and inflates expectations of future prosperity.

The Pocket History of Kerry

Prologue: Pre-Christian and Early Christian Kerry

Before the advent of history *proper* – before the tyranny of facts and dates – Ireland is home to the *Tuatha De Dannann*, the people of the goddess Dana or Áine. The name survives in Europe in the river Danube. With the advent of Christianity she becomes the benevolent spirit inhabiting our holy mountains. The Paps of Anu, the aptly named hills to the right of the road from Killarney to Rathmore, is her dwelling place. So is Knockainy not far from Lough Gur in neighbouring County Limerick (from which point the *Paps* can be seen). There are cairns atop these holy mountains, the single-stone contributions of pilgrims. Pilgrims prayed the *Rounds* just as they did at the holy wells below near the villages; *Rounds* continue to be performed, and strips of cloth are still tied to the "lone thorn tree".

Áine becomes transmogrified into the weeping banshee (Irish fairy woman) sometimes seen at Lough Gur, though she may appear anywhere in the territory of the FitzGeralds, earls of Desmond, and not only at Lough Gur. Often she is a small old woman, an ancestral figure engaged in the peaceful activity of washing clothes, or she is the wailing voice heard in the aftermath of some catastrophe like the Battle of Aughrim. The female principle at the origin of life and the centre of the psyche appears also in the more malevolent figure of the *Caileach Beara* (Hag of Beare Island). She directs her anathemas at the first Christian missionaries, those representatives of the male order soon to overwhelm the world of mythology. More vague and mysterious is the presence atop the hill called Slievenamon ("The Woman's Mountain") in south Tipperary.

These mysterious but inoffensive Tuatha De Danann are overcome by the Milesians. *Mile Spaine* is the progenitor of the Milesians who come to Ireland, and Kerry is where the Milesians land, before they drive the Danaan Host underground to inhabit the faery forts. They reemerge as the Faeries to fill the imaginations of story tellers and children at bed time, until the advent of electric light when the stories peter out. In the Romantic Era of the nineteenth century Kerry public figures will claim Milesian, by which they mean native Irish, ancestry.

Early Middle Ages

The christianisation of Kerry is said to owe very little to any specific efforts on the part of Ireland's National Apostle, St Patrick, who is not thought to have set foot in Kerry. Some say he came as far as Knockpatrick (near Foynes, on the Shannon) from where he blessed our region with *Beanaím uaim Siar sibh* (I bless you all to the West).

The county's patron saint is Brendan, (b. 484, d.577). He is widely known in Europe where the *Navigatio Sancti*

Brendani Abbatis could be found in monasteries and schools. He is Brendan the Navigator for his nautical adventures, said to include a landing in North America long before the caravels of Columbus. He founded a monastery at Ardfert (which used to be the name of the Kerry diocese), also Clonfert (Co. Galway), and Annaghdown (on the east bank of Lough Corrib just north of Galway city), dying at Annaghdown in 577. Ardfert was the seat of the bishops of Kerry for many centuries; the Cathedral ruin still stands; then the bishops moved to Killarney, perhaps because the ancient deanery of Aghadoe was nearer the Gaelic part of Kerry. Brendan is in Mount Brandon, one of Kerry's holy mountains, also in the civil parish of O'Brennan (*Uaimh*, or cave, of Brendan), and the townland of Brandonwell near Ardfert.

Churches and crosses from the early Christian period proliferate. The cone-shaped rock off the south west coast, Skellig Mhichil, has individual hermit cells similar to bee-hive huts, of which there are some examples on the adjacent mainland. A pilgrimage known as "The Saint's Way" (in Irish, "Cosán na Naomh") began at Gallarus Oratory and continued to Mount Brandon via Kilmalkedar. St Michael is remembered also near Ballinaskelligs.

Cárthach (Carthage), patron saint of the diocese of Lismore, over in the East of Munster, is also known as Giolla Mochuda in his native Kerry, whence he departed to found monasteries in the Irish Midlands before arriving in Lismore in 635 – which is the date given in the visitor literature in the Cathedral named after him in Lismore. A branch of the great O'Sullivan clan, of the saint's native South Kerry, took Giolla Mochuda as a patronymic – MacGillycuddy.

Of the female saints we have Ita (Íde) in West Limerick, and Gobnait, a saint of Muskerry (Ballyvourney, Mallow) or belonging to wherever we find a place called Kilgobnet – the cell, or church of Gobnait; she is found in the Aran Islands and at Dunquin at the western tip of Kerry.

The Round Towers, like those of Rattoo and Scattery Island (the island of St Senan's in the mouth of the Shannon), belong to the tenth century, while the Hiberno-Romanesque doorways of Aghadoe and Inisfallen are typical of the twelfth.

The re-evangelisation of Europe after the Dark Ages (when western Europe suffered the Barbarian/Germanic/ Gothic invasions from east of the Rhine) is spearheaded by monks from Britain and Ireland. Outstanding examples are Saints Columbanus, Fergal and Killian, all of whom are well remembered in Europe today: statues of Killian, large and small, are to be seen in Würzburg, Germany, where he is the Apostle of Franconia.

Monasteries in Ireland, including that of Senan on Scattery Island, are looted by the Vikings for their religious treasures. Meanwhile the siege of Europe is halted and some of the invading hordes assimilated. The conversion of the Frankish king Clovis to Christianity is a turning point, before Christendom is triumphally established with the coronation of Charlemagne by the Pope in 800.

The eleventh and twelfth centuries witness a second surge of Irish missionary activity: the "Schottenkloster" (*Irish monasteries*) of southern Germany begin with a foundation at Regensburg, followed by Würzburg, Erfurt, Vienna and many more. In them are preserved Irish manuscripts containing histories, necrologies, saints lives - including Ita (Ide) of Killeedy (Newcastle West), Senan, Flannan (Killaloe) and others, many not yet edited for publication.

Late Middle Ages:

"To the turning of the Road with a MacCarthy,
To the end of the World with a Geraldine"

"Lean an Cárthach go casadh an Bhothair/Ach lean an Gearaltach go
deireadh an Domhain"
(collected c.1945 by Ruairí O hIcí from Minnie Quill in Newtowshandrom)

"Ard Ferta Brénainn was plundered by the Clann Chartaigh,
and they carried off all the livestock they found therein.
They put many good people to death inside its sanctuary and
graveyard ..."

MacCarthy attack on Ardfert 1180, from the *Annals of
Innisfallen*

The Anglo-Norman advance into Kerry

The Anglo-Normans are originally Vikings who settled in the Normandy region in northern France. They invade England in 1066 and win the Battle of Hastings. Ireland is next – a more peaceful arrival in 1169 at Wexford. The great Norman King, Henry II, justifies the invasion with the "enormous disorders and unchristian practices of that island". A compliant Englishman is on the throne of St Peter: this is Pope Adrian IV who praises Henry's intentions and issues the bull *Laudabiliter* as his authorisation. We must not forget the famous invitation to Henry from a Leinster kinglet, Dermot MacMurrogh: he wishes to square a quarrel with another kinglet, O'Rourke, who has abducted Dermot's wife. When Henry arrives in Ireland, a short time after the first wave of his invading knights, a queue of Gaelic lords is there to meet him. Little wonder that historian and Kerry native F.X. Martin disliked the expression "Norman invasion", preferring to speak of the Norman *arrival* in Ireland.

Among the first wave is Maurice FitzGerald. His descendants become the outstanding settler family in Munster and Leinster, the Munster branch becoming the principal Anglo-Norman family of Kerry. Historian and Dominican Dominic O'Daly (of Kilsarkan, near Castleisland) repeats the legend that the Geraldines are native to Florence (indeed originally Trojan), "From the banks of the Arno, and the shores of the blue Tyrrhene Sea", who, venturing to Ireland, "penetrated regions whither Roman legions never dared to venture" (the quote is from Thomas Moore, the "Bard of Erin" at the turn of the nineteenth century).

The Anglo-Normans infiltrate Kerry from the direction of Limerick. Geraldine castles at Adare, Croom and Rathkeale follow the construction of a castle in Limerick city in the time of King John, son of Henry II. ("King John's Castle" commands the Shannon and the O'Brien territory of Thomond, modern Clare.) The final pre-invasion step is the construction of Shanid near Askeaton, giving us *Shanid Aboo*, the motto of the Munster Geraldines. The bridgehead is in place; the conquest of Kerry can begin.

Kerry, granted originally to the childless Miler FitzHenry, is confirmed to the Geraldines by King John on Miler's death. FitzHenry's grant of Killorglin devolves on Geoffrey de Marisco, who brings the Augustinian canons to found Killagha. Among the knights who settle in West Kerry are Bowler, Hussey, Ferriter, Moore, Trant, Mayhew, Hoare, Landers; in north Kerry we have Browne, Cantillon and Geoffrey de Clahull (Barrow Castle).

A line of castles will mark the limit of the southern

advance of the Anglo-Normans: Castlemaine, Currans, Killorglin. The taking of Castlemaine will be an important prize for the English when the Geraldines are rebels at the time of Queen Elizabeth.

The Geraldines will be ennobled with the title Earl of Desmond in 1329: Kerry will become the earls' Palatinate, and a Liberty with its own jurisdiction. A great castle is built at what becomes known as Tra-lee (*shore* of the river Lee) where a town evolves with the long main street characteristic of Norman towns, and institutions such as corporation and Provost (mayor). Those entitled to participate in governance are burgesses. Tralee becomes the burial place of the earls of Desmond.

There are three Geraldine families of somewhat obscure origins but who may be cadet branches of the first of the Munster Geraldines: the White knights (FitzGibbon, settled around Kilmallock south to Fermoy), the knights of Glin (referred to in state documents as "Knight of the Valley", colour green), and the knights of Kerry (black) owning much territory on the Dingle Peninsula and castles such as Rahinane (near Ventry) and Gallarus.

The very important FitzMaurice family (barony of Clan *maurice*) is thought to descend from the original Geraldine who came to Ireland, Maurice. FitzMaurice castles include Listowel, Lixnaw and Beale. The family will become Barons Lixnaw and Earls of Kerry

Strictly speaking these conquistadores were Welsh- or Cambro-Normans. They are frequently referred to by historians as the "Old English". Ponyaunt gives his name to Ballybunion, while Ferriter gives his to Ferriter's Islands, now the Blaskets. East over the border in modern Cork we have Barry, who occupies territory centred on Buttevant (family motto *Boutez en Avant*), Roche (a Flemish family from west Wales) who take over the district of Fermoy and Glanworth; Condon and Prendergast.

Kerry does not receive a dense Norman settlement. By contrast, when we proceed east through Tipperary and Kilkenny we find many more monumental artefacts, including tomb effigies, than we do in Kerry. But Kerry will enjoy all the benefits of Norman settlement. Where Irish society under its native lords was strife-ridden and disunited, Norman society is feudal. In modern times "feudal" has become a pejorative term, but it really signifies the contract relationship between the English king and the baronage (the glorious outcome of this evolving relationship is Magna Charta – the great Charter – of King John and his barons in 1215), a mutual dependency of overlord and vassal down the line as far as the immediate lords of the soil. The Irish clans will witness a new and impressive concept of societal organisation. Ownership will be vested in the individual; primogeniture will decide succession. All of this will contrast with the interminable wrangling and instability characteristic of Gaelic society, the cornerstone of which is *tanistry*, or inheritance from within the limits of second cousins. In short, the Common Law – common throughout the king's realm – will supplant Brehon Law. It will be a slow process and in remote Kerry the government will continue to fear the power of bards and brehons.

New Monastic Foundations: Cistercians,
Franciscans and Dominicans

The new monastic foundations of Europe at this time will constitute perhaps the most visible and enduring legacy of the Normans in Kerry. The Cistercian order (in reality a reform of the Rule of St Benedict) actually becomes established in Ireland before the Normans. Its most famous member is St Bernard, a towering figure of the church and abbot of Clairvaux in Burgundy. He influences the decisions of popes and preaches the second Crusade against the Turks. He appeals to Rome against the philosopher Abelard with accusations of heresy, Bernard favouring mystical experience over the pursuit of knowledge as the route to holiness.

Malachy of Armagh visits Clairvaux en route to Rome in 1140. There he meets Bernard. On his return to Ireland Malachy establishes the first Cistercian foundation at Mellifont (Co. Louth) in 1142. The first abbot of Mellifont is Christian O'Conarchy who later becomes bishop of Lismore (Waterford). O'Conarchy retires to the Cistercian house at Abbeydorney, a few miles north of Tralee; the abbey there was founded by the FitzMaurices and named *Kyrie Eleison*, a play on the name Kerry; O'Conarchy dies and is buried there in 1186. It is surely no coincidence that his retirement has been spent in an abbey in Kerry – given that the patron of Lismore, Carthage, was a Kerry man.

With the coronation of Charlemagne in the year 800 the Papacy claims to have "translated" the imperial crown from Byzantium (the Greek, or Eastern church) to the leaders of Western Europe. Some remarkable medieval popes, including Gregory VII (1073-1085) and Innocent III (1198-1216), increase the power of the Papacy, but a split develops between East and West leaving the Greek orthodox church outside the jurisdiction of Rome.[1] Trade revives and towns appear; later

---

1   The split deepens with the Crusades, that great series of adventures by westerners behind their knights to free the Holy Land from Islam. The diversion of the Fourth Crusade from its proper putpose in order to attack Constantinople, capital of the church of the East, greatly deepend the division between East and West.

again, the universities grow up around the towns, and leading scholars argue the claims of the Pope to supersede kings and emperors.

New mendicant religious orders appear: the followers of St Francis of Assisi (Franciscans) and St Dominic (Dominicans). We will see how these become the vanguard of papal (Roman) power – directly answerable to Rome and scarcely avowing the jurisdiction of the local bishop. Their principal raison d'etre is to evangelise the new towns. The Normans introduce them to Ireland – where there are few towns.

The Anglo-Normans promote these new monastic orders in the North of Kerry where the Geraldines rule: the Cistercians at Abbeydorney (*Kyrie Eleison*), founded by the FitzMaurices shortly after the first Irish house of the order at Mellifont; Holy Cross, in Tralee, founded for the Dominicans in 1243 by John FitzThomas (who will lose his life with his son at Callan); Ardfert, founded for the Franciscans in 1253 by Thomas FitzMaurice, Lord Kerry.

Monastic foundations are slow to appear in the Gaelic South, the region defended by the MacCarthys since the battle of Callan. The *Annals of Innisfallen* record numerous attacks by the Irish on existing monasteries, on Innisfallen itself in the following example from 1180:

> "There was committed in this year a deed which greatly vexed the clergy of all Ireland, namely the plundering of Inis Faithlinn by Mael Duin, son of Domnall Ua Donnchada, and the carrying off by him of all the worldly wealth therein, which was under the protection of its saints, clerics, anc consecrated churches."

North of Kerry, across the Shannon in Clare, where the O'Briens hold sway over an area corresponding with the modern counties of Clare and Limerick, there emerges a great native church builder. Donal Mór O'Brien, King of Thomond founds the Cistercian house at Monasternenagh (Maigue Abbey, near Croom) in 1151. In 1188 it becomes the parent house of Abbeyfeale.

The "Conspiracy of Mellifont", Crusader Monks and Observant Franciscans

One of the diverting episodes of Irish twelfth-century history is the running dispute between Cistercians in the Irish and Anglo-Norman monasteries: the "Conspiracy of Mellifont". The great bone of contention is the introduction of reform. The monasteries affiliated to Mellifont implement the Roman reforms, meanwhile the Irish houses appear determined to resist change. When Stephen of Lexington comes to Manasteranenagh to investigate practices there, he is refused entry:

"Moreover, making the Abbey, including both the cloister and the church, a fortress against God, they placed thirty dead bullocks, seasoned with salt, under the dormitory ..."[2]

Kerry becomes connected with the work of certain orders of knightly monks, formed to protect the crusaders in their journey to the Middle East. This is the era of the Crusades, a great movement led by the kings and knights of Western Europe to free the holy places of the Middle East from Islam. The Knights Templar (originally the *Poor Fellow Soldiers of Christ and of the Temple of Solomon*) are formed in 1118 to protect Christian pilgrims against Muslim attack. St Bernard knows the founder and prepares a Rule, which receives papal approval in 1128. Even their habit is Cistercian, white, with a red cross sewn on. Killorglin has a house of the Templars. The Middle Temple in London derives its name from the Templars, and it will be the training gound for centuries for Kerry barristers, who will then pursue their careers in and around another Temple foundation, Kilmainham in Dublin, the vicinity of the Dublin court and the country's largest prison.

Another order of military monks is Knights Hospitallers of St John of Jerusalem. Like the Templars it will have houses in Western Europe and accumulate resources from the generous endowments of princes and magnates. The Knights establish a house or *hospital* in Tralee, *Teampal an tSolais,* where John's Lane is now, off the present Ashe Street (site of the present Church of Ireland). A reminder of its nursing duties is in the nearby Clounalour (lobhar, Ir. leper).[3]

The Observant Franciscans arrive in Ireland in the early fifteenth century, causing a "sudden increase in the Franciscan presence in Kerry".[4] And this time the Gaelic lords lend their support. The Observant reform coincides with a Gaelic resurgence against the Crown and the Norman settlement; and the welcome given to the new Observants places the native Irish at the cutting edge of church reform – quite a change from our resistance to the Cistercian reforms at the time of

2   Stephen of Lexington, "Letters from Ireland 1228-1229, translated with an introduction by Barry W. O'Dwyer" (Kalamazoo, 1982), in Roger Stally, *The Cistercians Monasteries of Ireland* (York, London, New Haven 1987), p.18.
3   The Crusade against Islam is also the context for the Teutonic Knights who settle in the north of present-day Poland. Their great endowments of land, in what used to be a great wilderness, is the tribute of Western kings to their crusader work in the Holy Land.
4   Katherine Walsh, "Franciscan Friaries in Pre-Reformation Kerry", in *Journal of the Kerry Archaeological and Historical Society*, no. 9, 1976, pp.16-31; p.27. Quin, not far from Bunratty Castle, is given as the first Observant foundation in Ireland, in Patrick Conlan O.F.M., "Franciscan Ennis" (1984), p.14.

the Conspiracy of Mellifont. The Observants will conflict with the older Franciscans (known as Conventuals) until the Pope separates them. Later, at the time of the Reformation in the sixteenth century, the Observants will lead a distinguished opposition in England and Ireland to Henry VIII and his plans to dissolve the abbeys.

Where are these new (Observant) Franciscan foundations situated? Blessed Trinity is at Muckross (otherwise Irrelagh), Killarney, founded around 1430 by Donal Mór MacCarthy, and Lislaughtin (Ballylongford, near the Shannon), founded in 1464 by the O'Connors. (Three aged priests will be killed here during the Desmond Rebellion in 1580, Daniel Hinrechan, Philip O'Shea and Maurice O'Scanlan.) In the Geraldine-controlled West Limerick the Conventual Franciscans are established at Askeaton by the earls of Desmond in 1420. They later transfer to the Observants. Adare is established for the Conventuals in 1467 by the Kildare Geraldines, owners of the nearby castle. It too will transfer to the Observants.

The Irish of all races are by now visiting the principal pilgrimage sites of Europe. Santiago de Compostella in North West Spain has an old association with the South West of Ireland, where Dingle is a principal point of embarkation for pilgrims and where the old church of Dingle bears the name of St James (Iago). Pilgrims have been going to Santiago for centuries to pray at St James's shrine, arriving at La Coruña before walking the final stage to complete their pilgrimage at the great Cathedral and the tomb of St James, before returning with the Shell, the symbol of Santiago. In 1472 Fineen O'Driscoll Mór, lord of Baltimore, dies after returning from Compostella; his son Tadhg also dies – after the same pilgrimage, within a month of his father. Commerce follows pilgrimage, and the great fairs of Compostella, which host merchants from all over Spain, enable Irish and foreign merchants to rub shoulders. Later, when an Irish College is founded in Santiago to provide Irish priests, it has for students "the two sons of Oliver Hussey of Kerry", as well as Thaddeus O'Driscoll, son of the Lord of Castlehaven, also Daniel O'Driscoll, son of Lord Baltimore, and Thomas Geraldine FitzGerald, son of the Knight of Glin.[5]

---

5   Richard Hayes, 'Ireland's Links with Compostella' in *Studies, An Irish Quarterly Review*, September 1948, pp.326-332, pp.328,330.

The Settlement Overthrown:
Resurgence of the Native Irish

The Geraldine progress into the south of Kerry is halted when John FitzThomas is defeated by the MacCarthys and killed with his son Maurice at the battle of Callan, near Kilgarvan. The year is 1261. What we now call Kerry becomes divided into two entities. Kerry – governed by the Geraldines – lies north of the River Maine; Desmond, under the MacCarthys, is to the south. The "Killorglin line" marks the boundary with castles at Killorglin, and on the River Maine at Castlemaine, Currans and Castleisland.

The MacCarthys are now the guardians of the South, a rugged mountain terrain with sea coast containing innumerable coves for pirates, smugglers and privateers. The South has very strong links with continental Europe, and the English give it a terrible, probably exaggerated, reputation for lawlessness.

The Geraldines are confined, after Callan, to the North of the county, where they look to Dublin and London, the centres of Norman influence and the Common Law. But the Norman influence becomes diluted. The folk dictum at the top of this chapter ("To the turning of the Road with a MacCarthy ...) makes sense when we remember that the Geraldines levy tribute on the MacCarthy Mór, and that when in the sixteenth century Geraldines rebel against the Crown, the MacCarthy Mór remains loyal, a situation which contributes to the destruction of the Geraldines and their rule over Kerry and most of Munster.

Thomas "an Appa" (from Ape), infant son of Maurice killed at Callan, is made a ward of court (his name derives from the legend that he was taken from his cradle by an ape and brought to the top of Tralee Castle or Abbey before being returned safely).

"An Appa" is father of Maurice, who becomes the first Earl of Desmond in 1329,[6] a time when the expansion of the Hiberno-Norman colony in Ireland is reaching its zenith. Maurice and other settlers seek to vindicate their rights as Englishmen in order to secure themselves against a resumption of estates under royal grant. The Geraldines are becoming more and more gaelicised (Irish school students learned *Hiberniores ipsis Hibernis*, Latin for "more Irish than the Irish themselves"), and the first Earl enters a number of alliances with the native Irish to challenge the Crown for regional dominance; on occasion he uses such alliances to make war against his fellow Anglo-Irish lords. The Geraldines adopt Gaelic dress and language, and–

6   The title Earl of Desmond is confusing as Desmond refers to southern half
     of the modern Kerry, the very region from which the Geraldines were driven
     out when defeated at Callan.

more ominously – the Irish custom of succession by tanistry in lieu of primogeniture. They also lapse into some of the oppressive governing customs of the Gaelic lords, including *coign and livery* for the maintenance of armed retainers.

Kerry will become Earl Maurice's Palatinate and the Castle of Tralee one of his principal castles; the Dominical Abbey of the town will become the earls' burial place. For most of the remainder of the fourteenth century we have the romantic and magical figure of Gerald, the third or fourth in line.[7] This "Gearoid Iarla" (1350-1398) is a figure of Irish mythology, seen riding across the waters of Lough Gur in Limerick until his horse's silver shoes wear down; he is also "the Poet Earl", a "witty and ingenious composer of Irish poetry", according to the Irish annals.

With England engaged in the Hundred Years War (1337-1453), the Anglo-Norman hold on Ireland is loosened. This era gives us the sixth earl, Thomas, "the Love Lost", and the story of his love for a poor girl from a cabin near the castle of Portrinard (Abbeyfeale). Distracted by his romantic pursuit from the task of governing, or perhaps temperamentally unsuited, he eventually suffers exile in Europe, and dies 1420. He is "the Discrowned Earl" about whom the poet Thomas Moore wrote Desmond's Song:

> "By the Feale's wave benighted, Not a star in the skies,
> To thy door by Love lighted, I first saw those eyes."

The end phase of England's Hundred Years War with France, and the beginning of the English civil wars (the "Wars of the Roses"), is dominated in Munster by the next earl, James, uncle of his predecessor Thomas and seventh Earl of Desmond. James reigns from Thomas's death in 1420 to 1463. He is given extraordinary latitude, not only because of the war with France but because of the need to counter the resurgent Irish. James accumulates great power with the result that he in turn is viewed as a threat to the government in Dublin. Here is an assessment of him from a Kerry historian of the nineteenth century – the years are 1445-9:

> "The ambitious James, Earl of Desmond … took the government of all Munster by Royal Patent, and the Kingdom of Cork he obtained possession of by covenant from Roger Cogan; a license of government, accommodation and value was granted to him to sequester himself from Parliament during his life. This extent of territory and compass of power render'd him

---

7   Gerald, the "Poet Earl" is generally listed as the third earl in recent
    scholarship.

altogether independent of the English government and enabled him to exercise in the recesses of Munster a sovereign authority beyond the control and observation of England. The next step was easy and short. He disclaimed all allegiance to the English crown, to maintain in rude grandeur a Court, becoming a native Prince. Ormonde took the field against him but found him so well prepared that a Truce was all the English could accomplish."[8]

A complicating factor in the tale of the earls is the rivalry between the Desmonds and the Butlers, earls of Ormonde. The Butler lordship covers the modern counties of Tipperary and Kilkenny. The Desmond lordship encroaches on Ormonde, and though the rivalry dates from the time of the first Earl it has mighty implications at the time of the "Wars of the Roses" which are well under way by 1461 when the Yorkists defeat the Lancastrians at Towton. This is the rivalry and these are the wars that bring disaster to the Desmonds.

There is no inkling of trouble ahead when Thomas, eighth Earl, is made Lord Deputy of Ireland in 1463 as a reward for the Desmonds taking the side of Edward IV and the Yorkists.[9] While occupying the office of Lord Deputy, Thomas is attainted and beheaded at Drogheda in 1468. If Thomas's execution, at the hands of Viceroy Tiptoft, is the case of a son being punished for the sins of the father (James), then the continued allegiance of the Desmonds to the Yorkist faction in the years ahead is a mystery. Perhaps King Edward IV had no part in Thomas's execution, and, as we shall see, Edward promotes the interests of Thomas's successor in an attempt to stave off the fury of the Geraldines. For now all is shock and grief. In the words of the *Annals of Ulster*:

> "A great deed was done in Drogheda this year; to wit, the Earl of Desmond … was beheaded. And the learned relate that there was not ever in Ireland a foreign youth that was better then he. And he was killed in treachery by a Saxon Earl …"

The Geraldines are not to be mollified. Following Thomas's execution they attack the Pale around Dublin with over 2000 horsemen and 20,000 gallowglass (Scottish mercenaries).[10] To quiet matters, the dead Earl's lands are returned to his son James, who demonstrates a matching enthusiasm for his king

8   R.I.A., Day ms.Sr24n2, Judge Robert Day, History of England.
9   Anthony M. McCormack, *The Earldom of Desmond 1463-1583* (Dublin 2005), p. 59.
10   McCormack, p. 60.

with certain diplomatic initiatives of his own in Europe. He (obit. 1487) and his son Maurice (10th earl, the "Lame", obit. 1520) "cultivated political and diplomatic contacts with the duchy of Burgundy and the kingdom of France through their trading links with Bruges and Bordeaux", according to a recent study.[11]

The Burgundy connection is the Countess of Burgundy, sister of Edward IV. By the time of the Lame Earl this relationship with the Burgundians is no longer wise as the Yorkists have been ousted from the throne by the Henry VII at the battle of Bosworth (1485). And the Tudors are enjoying the support of the Butlers, the earls of Ormonde. When the Yorkist pretender Perkin Warbeck lands in Munster in 1491 and 1494 Maurice supports him. Warbeck has previously obtained troops in Burgundy, and it is his potential as a troop provider for his struggle with the Butlers, rather than as a potential threat to Henry, that induces Maurice to consider doing business with him. King Henry obviates the danger by opening negotiations with Maurice: the problem can be parked for now.

With the Wars of the Roses over and Henry's successor (Henry VIII) reigning over a newly unified England, the circumstances change again. Henceforth the religious war that divides all of Europe will become the catalyst for the subjugation of Ireland by Henry VIII and his daughter Queen Elizabeth. Ireland will be in the front line of this conflict for her stubborn refusal to embrace the Protestant Reformation, and Kerry will become the principal Irish theatre of this war in the war's final phase, the earls of Desmond assisting in their own ruin when they dabble on the side of England's enemy Spain. We are entering the era of the son of Maurice, the Lame, James, 11th Earl.

Henry VIII divorces his Spanish queen, Catherine of Aragon. Spain controls the Pope through Catherine's nephew Charles V, who is both Emperor of Germany and King of Spain, so the Pope refuses to acknowledge the divorce. During the impasse, James, Earl of Desmond, sends a deputation to San Sebastian and on to Toledo to offer Desmond's allegiance to Charles V, and his earldom as part of Charles's dominion, in return for protection and aid against Henry VIII.[12] A representative of Charles arrives in Dingle in April 1529 and the Treaty of Dingle is signed on April 28 submitting Desmond to Charles V.[13]

This is the same James who has encountered a bitter

11 Declan Downey, "Irish-European Integration, The Legacy of Charles V", in Judith Devlin and Howard B. Clarke (eds.) *European Encounters, Essays in Memory of Albert Lovett* (Dublin 2002), pp. 97-117, p. 102.
12 Ibid., p. 103.
13 Ibid., p. 105.

defeat, some years previous to the Dingle Treaty, at the hands of the MacCarthys of Muskerry, when James's uncle Thomas ("the Bald") joined with Cormac Laidir MacCarthy to defeat his nephew at the battle of Mourne Abbey (south of Mallow).

With the fragmentation of the earldom an ever-present danger (the MacCarthys are uneasy tributary lords to the Earls) what happens next will not come as a complete surprise: The 14th Earl of Desmond, James FitzJohn, reverses policy and takes the earls back to a course of cooperation with the Tudor state. The Tudor adoption of Protestantism has won wide approval in England, not least because of the share-out of the spoils from the Dissolution of the Monasteries under Henry VIII; Henry's grip on power is further strengthened by the distribution of the estates of his Catholic opponents, who pay the price of their opposition by attainder and forfeiture. In the 1530s the 14th Earl recognizes the way the wind is blowing, begins to promote the English power in his earldom, and participates in the Dissolution in Ireland. He becomes very influential. He is Lord Treasurer of Ireland in 1547, as such the third most important person in government in Ireland and automatically a member of the King's Council. He fronts English expansion in Munster after the death by food poisoning of the Earl of Ormonde.

When James FitzJohn dies in 1558 his son Gerald, the future "Rebel" Earl, does not succeed to his dignities, and somewhere in this failure to command a stature commensurate with that of his father recommences the story of the demise of the earldom of Desmond, and Gerald's embarkation on the slippery slope to insurrection and eventual ruin. The sad fate of the "Rebel" Earl will be considered in a separate chapter.

Tudor Era: the Re-conquest of Kerry

The sixteenth century witnesses the successful re-conquest of Ireland and the arrival of the so-called "*New* English". The credit for this is owed to a new dynasty on the throne of England: the Tudor. Its founder is Henry VII who defeated Richard III on Bosworth Field in 1485. There is widespread relief at Henry's victory: Richard was the one who murdered the Little Princes in the Tower of London, making him one of the most reviled characters in English history and a great villain of Shakespeare's history plays. In England the Tudors will become a popular dynasty. Bosworth will be seen to have put an end to the civil wars known as the Wars of the Roses (red rose of Lancaster/white rose of York).

Among those displaced by the New English will be some of the "*Old* English", such as the earls of Desmond. A number of factors help explain the motivation behind the Tudor re-conquest of Ireland. One is the rival achievement of the enemy Spain in exploring the world and laying claim to vast territories in South America. The English wish to match, if not surpass the Spaniards, at the same time guarantee England's territorial security. Another factor is the embrace of the Protestant Reformation by the son of the man who won at Bosworth, Henry VIII: Spain's position as the leading Catholic power makes her an even greater threat to England as religious tensions increase. The Spanish fleet returning from the New World will be attacked by English privateers, and England will demonise Spain for her practice of crushing religious dissent, including Spain's cruel treatment of Protestants – the *legenda negra* that colours the English view of Spain is born.

Henry VIII is actually a reluctant Protestant. He is slow to break with Rome, and in fact he will die a Catholic. But he needs a child and the Pope refuses to give him a divorce. (His wife Catherine is a Spaniard and a devout Catholic.) So Henry takes the papal authority on himself, founds the Church of England and arranges his divorce and remarriage. As head of the church Henry now sets about dissolving the monasteries and settling their wealth on his leading supporters, among whom are the future dukes of Devonshire (Cavendish) and Bedford (Russell). They become enormously rich. As we have seen, the fourteenth Earl of Desmond promotes the dissolution of monasteries within his earldom.

The determination of Ireland to remain Catholic will affiliate Ireland with Spain. The coast of Kerry will be the first landing in the event of a Spanish invasion; and the position of the earls of Desmond is a precarious one no matter which side they take. The destruction of the Desmonds after a series of ruinous wars in West Munster will come during the reign of Elizabeth, Henry's daughter by Ann Boleyn; Elizabeth comes to the throne in 1558. Actually, Elizabeth is also a religious moderate, and she is a notorious temporiser when it comes to making decisions about the fate of any of the ancient Gaelic lordships. Naturally she is committed to advancing the Reformation, but she adheres to her father's moderate political course – that is until the Pope makes the fatal move of excommunicating her in 1570. Excommunication is a charter for the Irish and the Spanish to depose Elizabeth, opening the way for the Queen's fanatically Puritan servants to descend on Munster, people like Pelham, the poet Spenser, and the author of the massacre at Dún an Óir in West Kerry in 1580, Lord Grey de Wilton.

Cattle Raid. Woodcut from John Derrick's Images of Ireland

Elizabethan Kerry:
Downfall of the Earls of Desmond

"He that England would ruin,
Must with Ireland first begin"

"Out of every corner of the woods and glynnes they came
creeping forth upon their hands, for their legges could not
beare them; they looked like anatomies of death, they spake
like ghosts crying out of their graves; they did eate the dead
carrions, happy where they could finde them, yea, and one
another soone after, insomuch as the very carcasses they
spared not to scrape out of their graves; and, if they found a
plot of water-cresses or shamrocks, there they flocked as to a
feast for the time, yet not able long to continue therewithal;
that in short space there were none almost left, and a most
populous and plentifull countrey suddainely left voyde of man
and beast; yet sure in all that warre, there perished not many
by the sword, but all by the extremitie of famine, which they
themselves had wrought."

Edmund Spenser, *View of the State of Ireland*

The First Desmond Rebellion

We have seen how since the early fourteenth century the Geraldines have been raising revolt against the Crown. Now, in the reign of Elizabeth, the consequences of dabbling in European politics threaten to inundate and destroy what is essentially a vulnerable regional power completely out of its depth. The Earl is Gerald, the "Rebel" Earl, who – unfortunate for him – lives through the climax of the conflict between Protestant England and Counter-Reformation Spain.

Gerald's lordship is a scattered patchwork of territories extending from the West of Kerry to Waterford, in all parts of which he has subject clans bound to him by ties of tribute and intermarriage. Amid the rude grandeur of his castles and court are to be found his bards and brehons, the one trained in composing praise poems in honour of his family, in which they recite his genealogy, the other dispensing the traditional justice of the Gaelic legal system. Opposed to him is the encroaching power of the Tudor state, with its alien religion, its equally alien Common Law, and its utterly subversive innovation of primogeniture as the means of property succession. To try and prevent the clash of worlds a compromise has been tried elsewhere back in the time of Henry VIII: under the formula of *Surrender and Re-grant* chiefs freely submitted to the Crown in return for the return of their lands and agreement to dispense with succession by tanistry. The compromise has failed: the Queen's Puritan adventurers are insatiable, and the Tudor state has an implacable ally in the shape of the new science and the new philosophy – its high priests Bacon, Galileo and Descartes who teach the world to subject everything to the ruthless test of efficiency and demonstrable use.

First we witness a phase of skirmishing between Gerald and his traditional rivals to the east, the Butlers. Gerald is defeated by "Black Tom", tenth Earl of Ormonde, at the battle of Affane in 1565 in the border country between Tipperary and Waterford. Gerald is injured in the hip and will have difficulty in mounting a horse for the rest of his life.

"Black Tom" Butler, Earl of Ormond, was raised at court and assisted in the suppression of the Wyatt rebellion against Mary (Elizabeth's predecessor and half-sister). His relationship with Elizabeth, the future Queen, continues to intrigue historians. She referred to him as "my black husband", and we find her face in the plasterwork at his house in Carrick-on-Suir in Tipperary. (To complicate matters, "Black Tom" is actually the son of Gerald's first wife, Joan, dowager countess of Ormonde, who died in 1550.[14])

---

14   Anne Chambers, *Eleanor Countess of Desmond, A Heroine of Tudor Ireland*
      (Dublin 1986), p.39.

Dispirited and wounded in the hip at Affane, Gerald is incarcerated in the Tower of London. While still there in 1570, the Pope excommunicates Queen Elizabeth. Gerald's cousin-german and *Captain*, James FitzMaurice FitzGerald, now raises the first Desmond Rebellion. The sentence of excommunication names Elizabeth a heretic, a "bastard" (as the daughter of Ann Boleyn) and a usurper. It cites her for "stirring up to sedition and rebellion the subjects of other nations about her" (meaning Holland), and "procuring ... to bring in our potent and cruell enemy the Turke". Excommunication has authorised Catholics to overthrow her, so James FitzMaurice FitzGerald will now assist the Pope and the Spanish to introduce an alternative European sovereign power into Ireland. The conspiracy is only halted by a prudent release of Gerald and his return to Ireland in 1573. James FitzMaurice FitzGerald decamps for the Continent.

No sooner back in Ireland, Gerald inaugurates a pre-rebellion phase of his own and lays the foundation for his reputation as "Ingens Rebellibus Exemplar" in the State Papers. After a brief incarceration en route at Dublin he appears before his assembled followers at Lough Gur, in Limerick, where he makes a symbolic demonstration of his independence: he removes his English clothing, and "He and his wiefe put on Irishe raiment and made proclamation that no deputie nor constable nor sheriff should practise their office in his countrey".[15] Equally disturbing to the Queen's officials is his mental condition, "more fit to keep Bedlam than to rule a newly reformed country".[16] Whether as a consequence of personal instability, or sympathy with the aims of the Counter-Reformation or gross official provocation – or a mixture of all three – Gerald now embarks on the slippery slope to open rebellion. Askeaton Castle in the west of his country becomes his base, and (the fight at Affane and its sequel having ensured his removal west from the sphere of Ormonde) it is in this region of Limerick that the great Desmond Rebellion will take place.

In 1575 Lord Deputy Sydney appears in Cork city to take the submission of the Irish chieftains. He repeats the exercise at Limerick. It is all part of his project to create a presidency of Munster, to abolish Gerald's Palatinate jurisdiction of Kerry and to impose those deputies, constables and sheriffs, and other necessary accoutrements of English rule. To Gerald it constitutes a renewed exercise in English aggression. Sydney's successor, Drury, will be reported to have hanged 500 or more "malefactors" between 1577 and 1588.[17]

---

15 Justice Nicholas Walshe to Lord Deputy FitzWilliam, 24 November 1573, quoted in Anne Chambers, *Eleanor Countess of Desmond*, p.87.
16 Ibid. Perrot to the Queen.
17 Quoted in Thomas Morrissey S.J., *James Archer of Kilkenny* (Dublin 1979).

Where is FitzMaurice, the Lord of Kerry (referred to in the State Papers as "MacMorris") during this rebellion? Does he lie low at his seat of Lixnaw – safe in the wilds of Clanmaurice? Thomas, the current Lord (1502-1590), married a sister of the "Rebel" Earl – the second of three wives. But more significant is his family's pattern of intermarriage with the House of Thomond (O'Brien) across the Shannon at Bunratty. Thomas himself goes there for his third wife; and one of his own daughters marries the 3rd Earl of Thomond.[18] The importance of Thomond as the keystone of Tudor loyalism (and the Protestant faith) in West Munster would be difficult to overstate, and Thomas is very aware which way the wind is blowing. So, with Thomond there is amity, with brother-in-law Desmond a relationship "founded on mutual suspicion and distrust", according to a recent study.[19] How the English rub their hands at these divisions! The result is that Lixnaw keeps out of the first Desmond Rebellion. The cost is high: with Desmond (Gerald) in the Tower of London since 1565 after Affane, his representative James FitzMaurice FitzGerald makes a series of destructive raids into Clanmaurice until foiled and driven back by Thomas.

Let us go further back to visit an episode from Thomas's childhood and how he learned of his inheritance from his old nurse, Joan Harman:

> " ... Thomas (successor to the lordship) had long since sought his fortunes abroad and was at the time serving in Italy under the Duke of Milan. His remaining relatives showed no anxiety to find him, and one of them quickly possessed himself of the estate. But the heir had one faithful friend in the person of his old nurse, one Joan Harman. In spite of her years she did not hesitate to take ship from Dingle to France and to travel thence to Italy in order to tell her foster-son of his good fortune. She had hardly delivered her message when she died from her unwonted exertions. All went well with the 16th Lord after his return. In 1551 he was formally recognised by King Edward VI as 'Lord of Kerry and Captain of his Nation'. Two years later he received from Queen Mary a confirmation of his estates and sat in Parliament as 'Baron de Lacksnawy vulgariter vocatus Baron de Kerry'. He was 'the most beautiful man of that age', so strong that 'there were not three men in Kerry who could bend his bow' ..." [20]

---

18 *Burke's Peerage and Baronetage* 1999: Inchiquin; Lansdowne.
19 *The FitzMaurices Lords of Kerry and Barons of Lixnaw,* Lixnaw Heritage, 1993, pp.21-22.
20 Marquis of Lansdowne, *Glanerought and the Petty-FitzMaurices* (Oxford 1937), p.220

Preparing to Crush Munster – gaining experience in the Netherlands

We remain in Europe for a moment to visit the environment where some of those fanatical Puritans about to descend on Munster are gaining their spurs. We visit the Spanish Netherlands (modern Belgium) where the Spanish king, Philip II has embarked on a policy of repression calculated to retain the Spanish Netherlands and immunise them against the influence of their rich northern neighbour, the United Provinces (modern Holland). The United Provinces are eager adherents of the Protestant Reformation; moreover, their commercial energy threatens Spanish commerce overseas, for which twin reasons they are natural allies of England. The Spanish commanders in the Netherlands are Don John of Austria (fresh from the naval victory over the Turks at Lepanto in 1571) and the Duke of Parma. On the opposing side we have the great symbol of Dutch resistance, the House of Orange.

The great struggle of the Counter-Reformation has begun, to halt and roll back the Reformation in territories where it has succeeded in gaining a grip (England, Bohemia, Holland, northern Germany) and to consolidate Catholicism where Catholicism is perceived to be in danger (Spanish Netherlands, Ireland, Spain, Portugal and even Italy). The struggle is two-pronged: military conflict and re-evangelisation. The newly founded Society of Jesus (the Jesuit Order, founder Ignatius of Loyola) will send its priests to accompany the military on the actual battle campaign, typically hearing confessions and saying Mass on the eve of battle; and it will evangelise the public through its new schools and seminaries. There is also an artistic dimension: the glory of Baroque church architecture and some of the most edifying choral music ever written, from the likes of Palestrina (Giovanni Pierluigi Palestrina 1529-94).

These are the circumstances in which the new Irish Colleges are established on the Continent for the training and ordination of Catholic priests. Expect persecution and martyrdom when priests begin to filter back into Ireland to celebrate Mass and distribute the sacraments. Priest catchers will be ready to earn their reward. But the survival of Catholicism is ensured, and the Puritan Edmund Spenser – settled in North Cork – will concede the failure of the Reformation:

> "It is a great wonder to see the odds which is between the zeal of Popish priests and the ministers of the Gospell, for they spare not to come out of Spain, from Rome and from Remes by long toyle and dangerous travayling hither, where they know peril and death

awytheth them, and no reward or richesse is to be
found, only to draw the people into the Church of
Rome."
(Spenser, *State of Ireland*)

Ireland is to England what the Netherlands is to Spain,
so Munster will attract some of those in the vanguard of the
fight against Spain. Walter Raleigh is one. He has become a
favourite of the Queen who rewards him with the franchise to
import England's wine, the first of many signs of the Queen's
favour. Raleigh reciprocates in poems that cast the Queen as
Cynthia. His native region is Devon – home of many of the
leading Munster planters – where the coast appears to inspire
great ambition for foreign adventure. Raleigh's early military
experience is gained in the late 1560s fighting for the Huguenots
(French Protestants) in the French civil wars. Next he and his
half-brother Humphrey Gilbert fit out private expeditions to
attack the Spanish on the high seas. He is in the war in Kerry in
1579-80 (below), and then he returns to sea adventures using
his wealth to finance a number of expeditions to the coast of
Virginia to found colonies; the expeditions fail but they become
the forerunners of the successful establishment of Jamestown
in 1607.
   Edmund Spenser, like Raleigh, is a poet, though not
a West Country man (he was born and raised in London).
He arrives in Ireland as Secretary to Arthur Grey de Wilton,
the commander who will shortly preside at the extermination
of the Spanish-Italian force at Dun an Óir. When Spenser is
granted a seignory and a castle at Kilcolman (near Doneraile
in North Cork) his exile there inspires the writing of *The Faery
Queen*, where Elizabeth appears again as Cynthia. Spenser
invites Raleigh to Kilcolman in the autumn of 1589. They
journey together to London where Raleigh introduces Spenser
for the first time to the Queen; belated recognition will follow
for Spenser, and he will return to Kilcolman to write more of
the *Faery Queen*. It and another Kilcolman poem, *Colin Clouts
Come Home Again*, are filled with the topography of that corner
of of North Cork, the hills and rivers becoming dwelling places
for the spirits of Spenser's mythological creations.
   Edward Denny, Hertfordshire knight, who comes to
Ireland in time for Lord Grey's campaign in Kerry, is strongly
connected with the West Country, as well as with the court where
he is related to some of the leading figures of the time. He is son of
Anthony Denny (1500-1549), who as "king's remembrancer" and
"groom of the stole" (rest room attendant), became the Henry
VIII's "constant and familiar attendant in all his progresses,

and in his magnificent excursions to the continent".[21] Anthony accumulated a great estate in Hertfordshire and Essex in the Dissolution, including a grant in 1540 of parts of the valuable lands of Waltham Abbey, Essex.[22] Sometime after 1541 he became a member of the king's Privy Council.[23] On 30 September 1544 Henry knighted Anthony Denny at Boulogne-sur-Mer. At Henry's approaching demise Denny was entrusted with the task of advising him to prepare to meet his Maker, at which "the King desired him to send for Archbishop Cranmer".[24]

Edward Denny was probably born at his father's residence, Cheshunt, in 1547. His mother, Joan Campernowne, daughter of Sir Philip Champernowne, of Modbury, Devon, dies while he is still young. His first-cousin is Sir Francis Walsingham, son of his aunt Joice Denny. Walter Raleigh and his step-brother are his first-cousins on the Campernowne side – their mother Catherine, the sister of Joan Champernowne (Denny's portrait is said to bear a resemblance to both Walsingham and Raleigh).

Denny arrives in Ireland shortly before Lord Deputy Lord Grey de Wilton to participate in the Grey's campaign to crush the Earl of Desmond; Denny and Grey de Wilton are related by marriage, Grey's sister married to Denny's brother Henry. We now consider the Rebellion that preceded their campaign to crush the Earl.

The Second Desmond Rebellion; the Counter-Refromation comes to Ireland; the Killing of the Earl

James FitzMaurice FitzGerald returns to Ireland with four small vessels and a papal force of fifty or sixty Italian and Spanish troops. He lands in West Kerry in July 1579 and occupies a promontory overlooking Smerwick Harbour known as Dún an Óir (Fort of Gold). He is accompanied by the Jesuit Dr Nicholas Sanders. They come ashore chanting litanies and they unfurl the banner of the religious crusade.

The government sends two envoys to inspect Smerwick Fort: Henry Davells and the Provost Marshal of Munster, Arthur Carter. Both are killed on their return journey at an inn in Tralee by Sir John and Sir James of Desmond, brothers of the Earl. The Earl temporises. He has not assisted the government during the mission of Davells and Carter to Dingle, perhaps because worried that his army has been defecting to Sir John of

---

21 Edmund Lodge, *Portraits of Illustrious Personages of Great Britain, with Biographical and Historical Memoirs of their Lives and Actions*, 8 vols (London), vol.1, 156.
22 Ibid.
23 *DNB*.
24 Ibid., quoting Burnet's *History of the Reformation*.

Desmond;[25] There are fears that James FitzMaurice FitzGerald has aspirtions to supplant his cousin as Earl, fears which add to the pressure coming on the Earl to declare himself on the side of James FitzMaurice and his papal force. And although James FitzMaurice is killed in a skirmish near Limerick on 18 August, the pressure remains on the Earl when supporters of the crusade look to Sir John of Desmond as a more viable candidate for the earldom than the Earl himself in the present crisis.

Smerwick inaugurates the second and final insurrection of Desmond. Now the region centred on the castles of Newcastle and Askeaton (both in Limerick) eclipses the middle of Kerry as the centre of action. The Limerick countryside is attacked and a defeat is inflicted on the Desmonds at Monasteranenagh (near Croom) in October 1579 as the Earl looks on from Tory Hill. There follows the terrible destruction of the Friary of Askeaton which houses the bones of the Earl's ancestors and his first wife. Pelham, a fanatical Puritan, is appointed Lord Justice and he appoints the 10th Earl of Ormonde as Military Governor of Munster. Ormonde is "Black Tom" Butler, that childhood friend of Elizabeth already met, and perhaps her lover ("my Black Husband"). In him we find all the old enmity of the Butlers for the FitzGeralds when he brings terror to Kerry in the final hunt for Gerald. In early November 1579 Pelham proclaims Gerald a traitor following an unsatisfactory parley with Gerald's Countess, Eleanor, in which Gerald's complaints – including the destruction of his relatives' graves in Askeaton Friary – have been conveyed. At the end of the year the Countess is attempting (with no assistance from Pelham) to go to London to intervene personally with the Queen, to protest her husband's loyalty and the intolerable provocation of Pelham[26]; but the cause of the Earl is dealt a fatal blow when he and his forces attack the town of Youghal amid scenes of wanton cruelty and destruction. There is no turning back now: Gerald, walking with a limp and prey to pain in the hip since his injuries at Affane, has linked his fortunes irrevocably with the rebellion begun by his kinsman after the landing of his papal force at Smerwick.

In April 1580 Ormonde and Pelham join up at Rathkeale before dividing to sweep the country wast as far as Carrigafoyle, where they meet having taken Askeaton and Glin Castles on the way. Some short time later Ormonde raids from Tralee west into Corkaguiney, "and so marched to Dingle-a-Cush, and as they went they drove the whole countrie before them into

25 Sr Margaret MacCurtain, "The Fall of the House of Desmond", in *J.K.A.H.S.* no. 8, 1975.
26 Anne Chambers, *Eleanor Countess of Desmond,* pp. 150, 158-161.

the Ventrie ... and took alle the cattell in the countrie ... and
all such people as they met they did without mercie putte to the
sworde".[27] Pelham's separate expedition to Corkaguiney some
weeks later, in June, is preceded by a sweep into the wooded
Glen of Aherlow to parley with, and ensure his rear against
Roche, Barry, McDonough, O'Keeffe and O'Callaghan; then
via Duhallow he proceeds to Castleisland before camping at
Castlemaine in preparation for his descent on Corkaguiney. At
Dingle he finds the town in ruins after an attack by Sir John of
Desmond:

> "We find the chiefest merchants of the town's houses
> rased, which were very strong before and built
> castellwyse, done by Sir John of Desmond, and the
> Knight of Kerrie, as they say, cursing him and Doctor
> Saunders as the root of all their calamities. The
> Burgesses were taken into protection by Sir William
> Wynter before our coming, to helpe building the
> towne again ..."[28]

This, then, is the unpromising scenario awaiting a force
of 600 Spanish and Italian soldiers which lands at Dún an Óir in
late autumn or early winter of 1580. The new lord deputy, Lord
Grey de Wilton proceeds personally to Kerry, then out West
to appear at Dún an Óir and manage the siege. He takes the
surrender, and at dawn the garrison hands over all its weapons.
Grey then sends in his soldiers – and they massacre everybody
in the Fort. Edward Denny, founder of the Tralee Dennys, is
part of the massacre, though the presence of Sir Walter Raleigh
at Dún an Óir is disputed by some historians, including M.A.
Hickson and Valerie Bary. Grey later testifies that the foreign
force "made four sallies to have beaten our labourers from
work, and gave us their volleys very gallantlie, but were as
gallantlie set in again *by Ned Denny* and his companye, who had
this night the watch". Edward Denny is knighted at Dún an Óir
and is sent to London with the news of the events there. [29]

Reduced to a handful of followers and driven to stealing
cattle to stay alive, the Earl is run to ground at Glounageentha,
a few miles east of Tralee. The State Papers relate the final

---

27 *Hooker's Chronicle*, reproduced in "Dingle in the Sixteenth Century", in *The
    Kerry Archaeological Magazine* 1912-14, pp. 203-211, p. 204.
28 Sir William Pelhem to Lord Burghley, 22 July 1584, in "Dingle in the
    Sixteenth Century", *The Kerry Archaeological Magazine* 1912-1914, p. 208.
29 Rev. H.L.L. Denny, "Biography of Sir Edward Denny, Knight Banneret,
    of Bishop's Stortford, Herts., Gentleman of the Privy chamber to Queen
    Elizabeth, Governor of Kerry and Desmond" in the *Transactions of the East
    Herts. Archaeological Society*, vol. 2 part 3, pp. 247-260 (originally prepared for
    the *Hertfordshire Dictionary of Biography*), which appeared subsequently in the
    Kerry Evening Post of 22 and 26 September 1906.

desperate days and weeks, beginning with a letter in April from Ormonde to the Queen:

> "Desmond being long since fled over the mountaine into Kerye, is nowe gon to seke relief by suche spoiles as he can take from the Earle of Clamcartoe (his brother-in-law) ... and being nowe kept from cowes in the mountains of Desmond, famyn will destroy them, as daily it dothe. God send them all the plague, and blesse your Majesty wth a most happy raigne".

The end comes on 11 November. Soldiers from the fortress of Castlemaine led by a local man, O'Moriarty, storm the Earl's cabin near Glounageentha. "I am the Earl of Desmond", he pleads, "Save my life!" His captors try to take him to the castle at Castlemaine, but the Earl is injured and weak, and they fear that his supporters will catch up and rescue him. So O'Moriarty orders him executed. How is the deed done? Ormonde again, on 15 November, to the Privy Council:

> "Donill M'Imoriertaghe ... being accompanied with 25 kerne of his owne sept, and 6 of the ward of Castlemaigne, the 11th of this moneth at night, assaulted thEarle in his cabban, in a place called Glaneguicntye nere the river of the Maigne, and slew him, whose heade I have sent for, and appointed his boddy to be hanged up in chaines at Cork."

We leave for now the sad end of the Earl of Desmond to consider how the FitzMaurices of North Kerry have reacted to his destruction. The present Lord Kerry, Thomas, is at this time a very old man: we remember how during his youth his nurse, Joan Harman, made that journey to Europe to inform him of his inheritance, and how he later marries into the ultra-loyal House of Thomond, of Bunratty. In June of 1580 this old man comes in to parley with Pelham at Castlemaine as Pelham is preparing to move west into the peninsula of Corkaguiney. Later the old man remembers his blood relationship with the Rebel Earl, and he has no wish to be seen to profit from the events at Dún an Óir. In the mopping-up operations after Dún an Óir his two sons are taken hostage as part of the no-nonsense policy of Lord Deputy Pelham aimed at forcing spectators like their father to take the government side. But the sons escape, join the rebellion and attack the garrison at Ardfert. Thomas continues to temporise but he enters the rebellion in 1582 and orders his castles of Lixnaw, Beale and Ballybunion to be dismantled. The fighting goes east to Ormonde territory, but Ormonde, seeing the need to concentrate on the Rebel Earl, pardons a number of lords including Thomas. When Thomas dies in 1590 long after the rebellion is over the annals assess his long life thus:

> "He was the best purchaser of wine, horses and literary works of any of his wealth and patrimony, in the greater part of Leath-Mogha at that time; and Patrickin, his heir, was at this time in captivity in Dublin".[30]

Now the delayed process of church and monastery dissolution can be renewed, with the three Franciscan houses of Kerry on the take-over list: Lislaughtin (1580), Ardfert (1584) and Muckross (1589). Now also can begin the attainder of the Earl and the distribution of his earldom among the fanatical Puritan adventurers, Raleigh and Spenser included.

The Munster Plantation

> "There was not the lowing of a cow to be heard from Dunquin (Kerry) to The Confluence of the Three Waters (Waterford Harbour)"
> *Annals of the Four Masters*

Once the Desmond Survey has ascertained the extent of the escheated territories, the carve-up of the Earl of Desmond's territory can begin.

This may be the point at which to consider the Earl's leading tributary lord, and how he conducted himself in the recent rebellion. Donal MacCarthy Mór, described by Professor Butler as "a drunkard, a profligate, and a spendthrift … also a religious poet of no small merit",[31] lords it over a vast territory of Kerry and Cork from his seat near Killarney. His principal subject clans are O'Sullivan Mór (Dunkerron Castle, near Kenmare) and O'Donoghue – O'Donoghue Mór (Ross Castle), and the Black O'Donoghue of the Glens (east of Killarney around the Flesk river). During the Desmond rebellions MacCarthy Mór, though the Earl's brother-in-law, remained loyal to the government, who rewarded him with the title Earl of Clancar. However, some of his tributary chiefs, chafing under the weight of MacCarthy exactions, supported the Earl – the O'Donoghues and MacCarthy of Dunguile included.[32]

---

30 Bernadette Cunnngham, "The Historical Annals of Maolin Og MacBruaideadha, 1588-1603", quoted in *The Other Clare*, vol.13, March 1989, pp.21-24, p.24; his wife was Jane Roche, daughter of David Roche of Fermoy.

31 William F.T. Butler, *Gleanings from Irish History* (London 1925), p. 10. Butler's excellent survey of the MacCarthy lordship has stood the test of time.

32 The principal unit of Dunguile territory was just east of Killorglin on the north bank of the Laune river.

Given the extent of disunity among the Irish clans, the task of the land-hungry English opportunists arriving in Kerry is greatly simplified. The Spaniards are unlikely to threaten the coast again – at least for the time being – even if the English are nervous of just such an event: "The people in these parts are for the most part dangerously affected towards the Spaniards, but thanks be to God, that their power, by Her Majesty's good means, is shorter than it hath been, and that the Spaniards' forces are so much weakened as they are".[33]

Sir Thomas Norreys, of Mallow Castle, Plantation of Munster (statue in Westminster Abbey, image courtesy Westminster Abbey).

33 *Calendar of State Papers* (Ireland) 1588-92; Sept.10 1588, Attorney-General, Sir John Popham to Burghley.

The leading Kerry planter names are Sir Edward Denny, William Herbert, Valentine Browne and Jenkin Conway. Denny will inhabit the Earl's castle at Tralee as the centre of what the state papers call *The Seignory of Dennis* (sic) *Vale*. A near neighbour is Daniel Chute, whose father – the first Kerry Chute, a native of Kent, – also arrived during the Desmond Rebellion; Chute acquires the MacElligott land at Tullygarron (Chute Hall) with his marriage to the daughter of MacElligott.

Valentine Browne's seignory occupies the territory of one of the MacCarthy subordinate clans, Sliocht Eoghain Mhóir (MacCarthy), a considerable district south of the Maine and Brown Flesk rivers, whose chief took the side of of the Rebel Earl against his overlord MacCarthy Mór. Here Browne will occupy the castle of Molahiffe, ten or twelve miles south east of Tralee. The Brownes will move to Killarney to occupy their other principal territory, that of the rebel O'Donoghue Mór (Ross Castle). In time the family will convert to Catholicism and intermarry with the defeated Irish: Valentine's son, Sir Nicholas, will marry a daughter of O'Sullivan Beare, *and their son* will marry either a daughter of the "Rebel" Geraldine himself or one of the Kildare Geraldines – the pedigrees disagree.

Sir William Herbert, of St Julian's in Monmouth, will occupy the Earl's castle in Castleisland, what the Earl used to call "the sweetest Island of Kerry";[34] in time the estate will descend by marriage to the lords Herbert of Chirbury. The great Herbert houses we know today, Muckross and Cahernane, are the descendants of Thomas Herbert of Montgomery who comes to Ireland during the years of Cromwell to act as agent to the owners of Castleisland.

Jenkin Conway is granted Castle Conway (Killorglin), which will descend for centuries in the Killorglin branch of the Blennerhassett family (the Tralee Blennerhassetts are tenants of Denny). The name Spring may be included here: he is made Constable of Castlemaine castle in the immediate aftermath of the Earl's death, and given the attached lands of the Priory of Killagha, known as *Our Lady de Bello Loco*.

The O'Connor Kerry territory (the barony of Iraghticonnor near the Shannon, between the Norman Geraldines to the south and knights of Glin to the east) is granted in 1597 to Trinity College; the O'Connors have suffered defeat at the battle of Lixnaw in 1568 and been attainted.

In neighbouring Cork the great settler names are St Leger at Doneraile and the poet Edmund Spenser at nearby Kilcolman Castle. Sir Thomas Norreys inherits the Desmond's castle at Mallow (passed down to the Jephsons by marriage in the next generation); further east we have Phayne Beecher at Bandon, and Sir Walter Raleigh whose estate centres on

---

34   This is Herbert's "Seignory of the Island of Kerry, alias Mounteagle Loyall".

Lismore and Youghal. To the north, in Co. Limerick, Sir William Courtenay inherits the Desmond castle at Newcastle West, and elsewhere in Limerick we have Trenchard (Foynes), Fitton near Knockainy, and Bourchier (Lough Gur).

Disunity among Undertakers,
the Spanish Armada, 1588

Sir Edward Denny finds himself unable to pay the Queen's quit rents. These are assessed on the basis of the tributes paid to his predecessor, the Earl of Desmond. The trouble is that the tributes were paid in "beeves", which prove an unwieldy currency for the newcomer Denny. Besides, livestock is a very scarce commodity just now. So Denny defaults. Sir William Herbert, corresponding with the Queen's Secretary, makes rancorous allegations about Denny's shortcomings as a representative of the undertaker ideal: too quick to associate with the Irish, but forever boasting about his connections at Court. Yet Denny has received a seignory of only 6,000 acres, while Herbert receives 13,000 acres. Why the unequal distribution? Our Kerry historian Mary Agnes Hickson believed that the Tudors favoured fellow Welshmen, such as Herbert. Or is it that those who did the fighting to defeat the Earl were not always considered promising planter material? Either way, Denny's court connections seem to have counted for less than he might have expected.

Herbert is a punctilious individual and very committed to the advancement of the Reformation, to promote which he has the Prayer Book translated into Irish. He is also anxious to win over the Irish with an efficient working of the royal courts and other institutions of government. In this respect Denny is again proving an obstacle, and Herbert recommends that he be brought to account for his actions:

> "Whereas injuries and exactions throughout Mounster have been done by Sir Edwarde Denie's soldiers and others his lordship gave direction to, that the Vice-President and Council there see them severely punished and the parties satisfied, with caution that the like be not committed hereafter."[35]

It is against this backdrop of domestic bickering among the New English planters of the Tralee region that the Spanish Armada sets sail. King Philip II of Spain (incidentally, the husband of Elizabeth's predecessor and half-sister, Queen Mary) launches the Invincible Armada against England in

35   William Herbert, early 1589, (to the Lord Deputy of Ireland ?), W.J.Smith, *Herbert Correspondence* (University of Wales Press, 1963), 1968 edn., p.62.

early 1588. Inclement weather and a hostile naval reception on the south coast of England scatter the Armada up the North Sea and around the top of Scotland.

The remnants of the defeated Armada sail round the Orkney Islands and appear off the north-western coast of Ireland in the second week of August 1588. By September they are being buffetted by storms against the rocks of the Blasket Islands. One of the mariners on the *San Juan Beautista* keeps a record.[36] He observes the arrival of a second ship, the *San Juan*, commanded by Juan Martinez de Recalde:

> "On the 17th Juan Martinez (de Recalde) sent a large boat with 50 arquebussers to look out for a landing place on the coast, to collect information and to treat with the Irish for a supply of water, which was badly wanted, and of meat. They found nothing but steep cliffs on which the sea broke; and on the land some hundred arquebussers were waving a white flag with a red cross."[37]

Recalde, of the *San Juan*, is Admiral of the entire Armada (whose military commander is the Duke of Medina Sidonia), and Recalde knows the Kerry coast as he commanded the squadron that landed the ill-fated expedition at Dún an Óir in 1580. On this occasion his men are captured, or perish when they go ashore.

On 21 August the *Santa Maria de la Rosa* arrives at mid-day in a very bad way, with all her sails torn to ribbons and seeking help. She goes down with all her crew, "not a soul escaping – a most extraordinary and terrible occurrence".[38]

James Trant, Sovereign of Dingle, sends a report to Sir Edward Denny in Tralee of the arrival of the great ships resting now between "Ferriter's Great Island" (the Great Blasket) and the shore. It was probably Trant who captured the small group of men sent ashore by Recalde to obtain fresh water. (Did he have them executed?) Sir Edward is absent when Trant's report reaches Tralee, but Lady Denny is present, and it is she who has the Spaniards placed in captivity. When her husband returns he has twenty-four captives summarily executed, "because there was no safe keeping for them".[39] The Queen, who hates any unnecessary shedding of blood, is unhappy with

---

36 "Account of what happened to Marcos de Aramburu, Controller and Paymaster of the Galleons of Castille in the vice-flagship of those under his charge", in Rev. William Spotswood Green, L.B. M.S., "Armada Ships on the Kerry Coast" in *Proceedings of the Royal Irish Academy*, vol.27, 1908-9, 263-269.

37 Ibid., p. 265.

38 Ibid., p. 266.

39 *Calendar of State Papers (Ireland)* 1588-92, 9 September 1588, Vice-President of Munster Thomas Norreys to Walsyngham.

Denny's action, but it is Denny's confiscation of certain small treasure that provokes a letter to Sir Francis Walsingham from his neighbour, the pious William Herbert. Herbert writes from the *Castle of the Island* (Castleisland) on 27 December 1588:

> "I cannot omit what in Sir Edward Denny hath passingly displeased me, those rare things in trewth of goods value of the Duke of Medina Sidonias, cast in his hands, as I interpret by God's good providence, to the end they might be presented to her Majesty, he being her Highnesses sworn servante of her Privy Chamber, sworne counsellor of the province, sworne Sheriffe of this countie, he shewed certeyn friends of his at his house of Trally, and declared how he meant to dispose of every part of them, some to this nobleman, some to that." [40]

Today, more than four hundred years later, the wreck of the *Santa Maria de la Rosa* still lies on the bottom of the sea near the Blasket Islands. Elsewhere along the Irish coast lie other casualties, such as the *Anunciada* off Carrigaholt and the *San Marcos* off Spanish Point. The Sheriff of that county, Boetius Clancy, gave a brutal reception to landing Spaniards, more brutal than their reception on the western coast of Kerry.

Sir Walter Raleigh

---

40   Quoted in Rev. H.L.L. Denny, *Biography of Sir Edward Denny.*

The Nine Years War and the Road to Kinsale 1601

"Before the siege (of Glin Castle in July 1600) Sir George Carew, the Lord President of Munster, captured the Knight's six-year-old son and tying the child to the mouth of a cannon threatened to blow him to bits if the Knight did not surrender. The reply in Irish was blunt: 'the Knight was virile and his wife was strong and it would be easy to produce another son!'."

Guide book to Glin Castle

Prologue: A "Contemptuous Marriage" Confounds the Undertakers – and Queen Elizabeth

In the year of the Armada (1588) Florence, or Finín, heir to MacCarthy Reagh, described in the *Pacata Hibernia* as "like Saul higher by the head and shoulders than all his people", presents Queen Elizabeth and her chief minister with an unforeseen challenge: he contracts and goes through with a "contemptuous marriage". When marriage is proposed of one so great, the Queen expects prior notification. And Florence is very great indeed. The territory of MacCarthy Reagh is all of Beare and Bantry, otherwise Carbery, meaning the extensive area from the mountains north of Dunmanway, south to the sea and over to near Kinsale. To add insult to injury, Florence is nephew to the "arch-traitor" James FitzMaurice FitzGerald.

Marriage of Florence MacCarthy Reagh and Ellen MacCarthy
(drawing courtesy of Paddy McMonagle)

Who is the bride? Florence marries Ellen MacCarthy, daughter of MacCarthy Mór. The ceremony – held somewhere in Killarney at what is described as a "small church", possibly the Franciscan abbey at Muckross – unites the lordship of MacCarthy Mór around Killarney and most of South Kerry with Florence's Carbery. It is the ultimate in territorial amalgamation, in direct contravention of the Tudor policy aimed at "the dissipation of the great countries" and the introduction of lineal descent in lieu of the Gaelic practice of of succession by election, or tanistry. Some additional alarm bells ring: the bride's mother is a sister of the late "Rebel" Earl, and there are rumours that the groom, Florence, has been studying the Spanish language and holding pro-Spanish views; of him it is said, that "he is fervente in the olde religion".

Spreading accusations about the Spanish is David Barry, Viscount Buttevant, who took the side of the "Rebel" Earl in the recent war when Florence and his father served with the MacCarthy Mór and the English. Equally frightened of Florence, for different reasons, are two of the new English settlers, the undertakers Browne and Herbert, who occupy MacCarthy Mór territory. Young Nicholas Browne planned to marry Ellen and secure his seignory, however Florence married her that night at the old church. Florence is given a stretch in the Tower of London for his contemptuous marriage, but no advantage accrues to the Brownes or to Herbert: a half-brother of Ellen, known variously as "Donal the Bastard" and "the Munster Robin Hood" (MacCarthy Mór's illegitimate son), now enhances a reputation for lawlessness exceptional even by Kerry standards, by attacking the Brownes, killing English settlers and driving off their cattle ("playing the Robin Hood in taking meate, drink and spoil where he can get it, not without the consent of his wicked father"[41]), happy in the knowledge that the other planters are tied up with their own seignories and with mutual rivalries.

In a second and desperate attempt to retrieve the situation by a strategic marriage, Nicholas marries a niece of David Barry, Florence's enemy. In 1593 Florence is returned to Ireland by the Queen: the principal reason for his enlargement is to counter "the Robin Hood of Munster", Donal. Soon he is offering to do service against the rebels of the North, O'Neill Earl of Tyrone principally. But when his father-in-law MacCarthy Mór (her Majesty's Earl of Clancar) dies in 1596 the undertakers become nervous at the prospect of Florence's claim to succeed. From 1600 and the arrival of George Carew as President the pressure will become intolerable and Florence will be tempted to consider the advantages which a Spanish

41   Daniel MacCarthy Glas, *The Life and Letters of Florence MacCarthy Mor* (London 1867, reprint Cork 1975), p.73.

invasion might bring him. Great care will be needed to deflect suspicion: in the State Papers his temporising earns Florence the epithet "Ambidextrous".

The war of the Súgan Earl and Florence "Ambidextrous" McCarthy Mór

"About the 5th of this present moneth of October there came into the said province, by Arlough, and son into the com of Lymerick, about 3000 rebells, sent from the arch Traitr Tirone, under the leading of John Fitzthoms, second sonne to Sir Thoms of Desmond, Knight deceased, elder brother to the last attainted Earle of Desmond, and of one Tirrell, as is reported; and psently upon their coming into the said province, the said John was proclaimed Earle of Dessmond." (William Saxey, Chief Justice of Munster to Robert Cecil, 26 October 1598)[42]

The "Nine Years War" comes to Kerry in late 1598 after the northern chieftains, the Earl of Tyrone (Hugh O'Neill) and Hugh O'Donnell, defeat the forces of Elizabeth in the great battle of the Yellow Ford. They now bring the struggle south, via Aherlow in Tipperary, precipitating an insurrection of the dispossessed Irish in Munster. The rebellion scatters the Munster Plantation; Edmund Spenser is forced to flee his tower house at Kilcolman (near Doneraile), where, it is said, his child is killed. Ormonde writes to the Queen that "all the undertakers, three or four excepted ... had most shamefullye forsaken all their Castells and dwelling plases before anie rebel cam in sight of them, and left their Castells with their municons, stuff and cattell to the traytors, and no maner of resistance made..."[43]

Any remaining settlers are attacked again late in the following year, and yet again from January 1600 when Tyrone himself comes south. (Ormonde's own loyalty is on the knife edge: his Butler kinfolk are Catholic, and in the event of a Spanish conquest what matters to him is his great estate, centred on Kilkenny/Tipperary.)

Tyrone promotes two important allies in the south. One is the bastard son of MacCarthy Mór (Donal "the Bastard"), seen as likely to unhorse the Brownes at Molahiffe. (Greater wisdom will prevail when Florence MacCarthy Reagh, acclaimed by the Gaelic nation as *the* MacCarthy after his father-in-law Clancar dies, comes over to the side of Tyrone.) The other rebel promoted by Tyrone is the claimant to the Desmond earldom, the Súgan Earl (*sugan*, Irish for straw rope, suggesting an ineffectual individual).

42   *Life and Letters of Florence MacCarthy Mor*, p.178.
43   Ibid., p.177. Earl of Ormond to the Queen, 12 October 1598, p.177.

This Súgan Earl is James FitzThomas, eldest son of the late "Rebel" Earl's half-brother. He claims that the earldom is not extinct since the "Rebel" Earl usurped the rightful heir to the earldom: Súgan's father. Súgan does not lack for rebel pedigree: his grandfather was Roche, Lord Fermoy, a participant in the late Earl's fatal rebellion.

Sir George Carew arrives in April 1600 as Lord President of Munster to counter Tyrone. His war will engulf Kerry. The Killarney district has not suffered in the wars of the "Rebel" Earl, and now also a temporising policy on the part of Florence in Killarney will prevent the worst; besides, the guardian of the white rod of inauguration, O'Sullivan Mór, has resisted inaugurating "the Bastard", and Florence is amenable to an accommodation with Carew in return for the Queen's approval of his inheritance as MacCarthy Mór.

The northern baronies of Kerry are another matter, the region becoming one of the important theatres of this war, with Lord Kerry (FitzMaurice) and the Knight of Glin on the rebel side.

On 3 May, the writer of *Pacata Hibernia* informs us, Florence makes his submission to Carew at Shandon Castle in Cork, and names his terms. Satisfied with his day's work Carew proceeds north for Limerick hoping to pass that great rebel refuge of Kilmore Wood, a few miles south of Kilmallock, then sweep west through the Limerick country via Croom and Askeaton, to take the castles of Glin and Carrigafoyle, both on the Shannon. He knows the collaboration with men and supplies he will receive from the Earl of Thomond across the river at Bunratty.

Carew captures the Súgan Earl, but the confederates, including Patrick FitzMaurice, succeed in releasing him. To recover the upper hand Carew now lays siege to Glin Castle (July 1600) which the Knight of Glin defends defiantly: when Carew apprehends his six-year-old son and ties him to the mouth of the cannon, threatening to fire, the Knight replies that he and his wife are young and there are more sons to be born. Eventually the castle is yielded up, and no slaughter ensues.[44] O'Connor Kerry, nephew of Florence, now takes fright and surrenders Carrigafoyle. The way is open to the heart of Clanmaurice.

The latest Lord Kerry, Patrick FitzMaurice (1555-1600), despite an upbringing at the Elizabethan court, has been in rebellion since possibly as early as the overthrow of the Munster Plantation in 1598. His forces and those of his adversary Carew will turn North Kerry into a vicious new theatre of the war.[45]

---

44 Thomas Stafford, *Pacata Hibernia, or A History of the Wars in Ireland during the Reign of Queen Elizabeth* (Standish O'Grady ed.), 2 vols. 1896; vol.1, pp. 88-9.

45 The cutting down and sale of the woods of Clanmaurice is noticed in the press in the 1770s, just before the FitzMaurices finally sell out

A private interest is at work on the part of Carew: Carew has a near obsessive interest in browsing old pedigrees for ancestral claims to Irish estates; one of these pedigrees yields a Carew claim to the FitzMaurice estate at the first arrival of Carew's Anglo-Norman ancestor in Kerry.

A treacherous subordinate of the FitzMaurices, Maurice Stack ("a man of small stature, but of invincible courage"), secures Liscahane Castle for Carew. This invites the well-known siege of Liscahane by FitzMaurice and the use of what is described as a "sow", or covered siege vehicle, filled with FitzMaurice's men. But the defenders "made her cast her pigs and slew twenty-seven of them dead in that place".[46] To the rescue comes Florence MacCarthy who tries to negotiate the surrender of Liscahane; to no avail. The demoralisation of Patrick FitzMaurice is complete when Sir Charles Wilmot (sent by Carew and assisted by the Earl of Thomond who has sent men and supplies over from Kilrush and then up the Cashen river) takes Lixnaw. In order to destroy his own castle Patrick had it "sapped and underset with props of timber", however "the sudden coming of Sir Charles prevented his intention".[47] The shock of losing Lixnaw shortens Patrick's life, and he dies:

Donach O'Brien, "Great Earl" of Thomond (courtesy Shannon Heritage)

> "1600. MacMaurice of Kerry, i.e. Patrickin, the son of Thomas ... died in the prime of his life, after having joined the Earl of Desmond in the aforesaid war. It was a cause of lamentation that a man of his personal form, blood and hospitality should thus die in his youth. His son Thomas assumed his place."[48]

---

46 *Pacata Hibernia*, vol. 1, p. 91.
47 *Pacata Hibernia*, vol.1, p.101.
48 Cunningham, Annals of MacBruaideadha, *The Other Clare*, p.22.

Thomas, Lord Kerry (d. 1630), successor to his father Patrick, has also been brought up at court in London, which it is expected will make him loyal; and his marriage to Honora O'Brien, yet another cross-Shannon (Bunratty) alliance, argues loyalist sympathy, she being a sister of the reigning 4th Earl of Thomond. Strange to relate, this lady distinguishes herself by doing the rebels some service when she facilitates revenge against Maurice Stack for his work at Liscahane. Here is what happens: She invites Stack to dine with her at Beale Castle (on the Shannon), and during the evening she cries out in a manner suggesting maltreatment, whereupon her servants rush in and knife Stack to death. Later she feels remorse and takes refuge with her brother Thomond, who is said never to have spoken to his sister again on account of her treachery. Let the annals tell it: "Honora … wife of the MacMaurice … fled from the plundering and insurrection of her husband, and came to her native territory under the protection of the President and the Earl of Thomond, and afterwards died at Dangan-Mac-Mahon, and was buried in the monastery of Ennis."[49] She was young, in her twenties.

Her son is the centre of what happens next, one of the great historic episodes in FitzMaurice history. Wilmot captures Listowel in the early days of December 1600 after a siege of some weeks. Thomas FitzMaurice's son and heir, Patrick, a motherless child of five, has been spirited out of the castle with the women and children prior to the execution of those forced to remain inside. The boy is hidden in a cave five miles east of Listowel. A priest, Brody, is captured and bargains for the boy's life – successfully. With the boy a hostage in the hands of Carew, Thomas goes north with the Knight of Glin as summer approaches to offer his services to Tyrone and O'Donnell – in time for the Spanish landing at Kinsale a few months later.

All this time Florence "Ambidextrous" MacCarthy has been seeking the Queen's affirmation of his right to the dignity of MacCarthy Mór and MacCarthy Mór lands around Killarney and the southern half of Kerry, as well as the tribute of his subject lords. But his position is greatly prejudiced by Tyrone's injection of support (principally Irish mercenary soldiers, known as *bonies*, Ir. bonnaghts) for the Súgan Earl. With the tide apparently favouring the Súgan and his Kerry support, Florence protests the pressure he is under, all the time hoping "that my temporisinge with the rebels untyll I maye effecte my purpose may not be misconstrued".[50] Whatever about the Queen's affirmation, the acclaim of his Gaelic countrymen is essential to his acceptance as MacCarthy Mór. All changes

---

49   Cunningham, Annals of MacBruaideadha, p.24.
50   Florence MacCarthy to Sir G. Carewe, 14 May 1600, *The Life and Letters of Florence Macarthy Mor*, p.280.

with Carew's successes at Glin, Carrigafoyle and Liscahane, and with rumours everywhere of a Spanish landing Florence is tarnished by the recurring allegations of his pro-Spanish sympathies. In May of the following year, 1601, the Súgan is captured (having been betrayed) and, shortly after, Florence is arrested. They are shipped to London in August where the Súgan will be sentenced to death and Florence will begin his long imprisonment in the Tower.

The work of Spanish conspiracy finally bears fruit when Don Juan del Aguila at the head of a force of 4000 makes his ill-fated landing at Kinsale in 2 October 1601 and occupies the town. In early December a smaller squadron lands west along the coast at Dunboy, the castle of O'Sullivan Beare. Kinsale yields to Lord Deputy Mountjoy on Christmas Eve 1601. Wilmot mops up in Clanmaurice with another siege of Lixnaw, which is again taken, though without wholesale slaughter. After the capitulation of Kinsale Don Juan also surrenders Dunboy and some smaller castles, but Donal O'Sullivan, Prince of Bere, refuses to yield up Dunboy. Carew besieges Dunboy in the first days of January and takes it on the 17th; during the siege Carew attacks Dursey Island where his soldiers commit terrible atrocities. It is all recorded by Carew's secretary, Stafford, in *Pacata Hibernia.*

We might note a number of pathetic sequels to this war. One is the March of Donal O'Sullivan Beare at the head of a bedraggled remnant of his people from Glengarriff to Leitrim village (in O'Rourke's territory in the North West of Ireland). The episode has exercised the pens and imaginations of poets like Robert Dwyer Joyce and Thomas Davis. O'Sullivan sets out from Glengariff on 31 December 1602 leading four hundred fighting men and six hundred non-combatants. He reaches O'Rourke's castle with thirty-four followers, eighteen of whom are soldiers, eleven horse boys, and one a woman. In 1605 Dónal Cam O'Sullivan Beare makes his escape to Europe, where in 1618 he is killed on a street in Madrid by a John Bath.

A second sequel is the "Flight of the Earls" to Europe. First comes the departure of Red Hugh O'Donnell on one of the Spanish ships returning to Spain from the coast of West Cork. He will be pursued by James Blake, one of the Galway Blakes and an agent of Carew: it seems that Blake succeeds in poisoning Red Hugh O'Donnell at Simancas. O'Neill (Tyrone) capitulates formally to Mountjoy at Mellifont in March 1603 when he signs the Treaty of Mellifont with the English to end the Nine Year War: it grants continued security to him and the other northern chieftains in their ancestral territories. He learns too late that the Queen is dead. Thereafter he and the other chiefs experience the growing belief that their situation can never be secure, so they sail away from the North in 1607. Modern historians, including Micheline Kerney Walsh, believe they are making a tactical retreat. But they never return. They arrive on the coast of France and make their way to the newly founded Franciscan college at Louvain (in modern Belgium), before recommencing their journey to Rome.

From the Roll of Martyrs – Elizabethan

1579. Smerwick and Kilmallock. Bishop Patrick O'Healy and Fr Cornelius (Con) O'Rourke, son of the chief of Breifne, land at Smerwick. They are captured in Limerick while trying to make contact with the Earl of Desmond (some say the Earl's wife Eleanor betrays them). They are conveyed to Drury, tortured and executed at Kilmallock on or about 13 August 1579 after trial by martial law. The charges are Treason (as Papal agents and assistants to James FitzMaurice FitzGerald's rebellion), and refusal to take the Oath of Supremacy acknowledging the Queen as head of the Church.

1579, Tadhg O' Daly, O.S.F, priest at Askeaton Friary, dies after torture (multis variisque tormentis affectus). "Having undergone many varied (kinds of) torture, he was run through with a sword and his head cut off as he clearly uttered the verse: 'Pity me, O God, according to your great mercy'."[51]

1580, April. Three Franciscan priests of the Friary of Lislaughtin (Ballylongford), Daniel Hinrechan, Philip O'Shea and Maurice O'Scanlan, murdered before the high altar of Lislaughtin 6 April 1580.

1580, November. Smerwick. Father Laurence Moore, Oliver Plunkett and William Walsh (the latter two Anglo-Irish laymen): their arms and legs smashed on an anvil, the priests' fingers chopped off, they are hanged on the ramparts of the fort at Smerwick "and made targets for the arrows and bullets of the soldiers". They die at Smerwick 11 November 1580.[52]

1584, Dermot O'Hurley, Archbishop of Cashel, executed in Dublin in 1584; Richard Creagh, Archbishop of Armagh, dies in the Tower of London 1585.

51 *Analecta Hibernica* VI (1934), p. 174 has the St Isadore (Rome) record of the martyrdoms of Bishop O'Healy, Fr Con O'Rourke and Fr Tadhg Daly, from the collection of Fr Francis Matthews (Franciscan provincial 1626-29) in his *Brevis Synopsis Provinciae*, Rev. Denis Murphy, S.J., *Our Martyrs: A Record of those who Suffered For the Catholic Faith under the Penal Laws in Ireland* (Dublin 1896), p. vi., 106.

52 Information pamphlet of the Annual C.T.S. Conference and Eucharistic Congress, Killarney, 25-27 June 1937.

Perfecutiones aduerfus Catholicos à Proteftan-
tibus Caluiniftis excitatæ in Hibernia.

Spumanti diuifa freto glacialis Hibernæ
Diſtat, & abſciſsis interluit æſtus arenis,
Vt regione tamen, ſic & feritate Britannis
Proxima, pernicies eadem confinia fecit.
In ſanctos pietate viros graſſatur eodem
Impietas odio, rabiemꝗ exercet eandem.

L

Martyrdom of Archbishop Dermot O'Hurley of Cashel 1584,
from Richard Verstegen, Theatrum crudelitatum haereticorum huius temporis,
2nd Edition, Antwerpen, Hadrianus Huberti, 1604
(courtesy University of Leuven)

The Early Stuarts

"Stephen Rice, Esquire, lies here,
Late Knight of Parliament,
A Happie Life for Four Score Yare
Full Virtuously He Spente,
His loyal Wife, Helena Trante,
Who died Five Years Before
Lies Here also –
Lord Jesus Grant
Them Life for Evermore
MDCXXII"

Tombstone in Dingle churchyard
of Stephen Rice, MP Kerry 1613,
recorded by
historian Mary Frances Cusack
(the "Nun of Kenmare")

The Defeated regroup: the Reign of James I (1603-25)

King James is the first of the Stuart kings. His mother was the unfortunate Catholic Mary Queen of Scots, prisoner of Elizabeth, whose execution was the final straw that prompted Spain to send their Armada to invade England; Mary was a child of the French family of Guise, hence the "Auld Alliance" between Scotland and France, particularly in the Scottish highlands, which will continue to play a part in our story. For now, all is optimism and as soon as James is enthroned the Catholic chapels in the South of Ireland reopen in anticipation of religious liberty.

To the year 1606 belongs the creation of Kerry as the county we know today: the former county of Desmond (region south of the Maine River though not including Beare and Bantry) is united with the "Countie Paleyntine of Kerrie lately escheated".

In the aftermath of Kinsale and the Flight of the Northern Earls to Europe in 1607, hundreds of Kerrymen and women and their children begin to settle in France and Spain, taking their lead from the cavalcade of the Northern Earls which trundled along the roads of the Netherlands to Louvain, and from there south to begin their exiles in Rome. The majority of the Irish head for Spain. Some of the Irish soldiers in the Spanish military will gain entry into the military orders set up centuries before as part of the *Reconquista* to drive the Muslims out of Spain and back to North Africa: the orders of Alcantara, Calatrava and Santiago. The two sons of Donal O'Sullivan Beare (obit.1618) are admitted knights of the Order of Santiago.

Philip II and arch-rival Queen Elizabeth are now dead. Philip III (son) is on the Spanish throne, surrounded like his father by Irish exiles pushing for another descent on Ireland. But times have changed. Any attempt will encounter an England where the Reformation has become consolidated, and with it English nationalism. The great plays of Shakespeare, now being staged, will only stiffen the English populace with a sense of their country's historic struggle against the powers of Europe. And for long periods of the reigns of Philip and James it suits Spain and England to be at peace.

In this new set of circumstances Spanish-Irish cooperation will be in the field of education and the training of priests: it is now we see the expansion of the Irish Continental college movement of Spain, the Spanish Netherlands and France. Thomas White, a native of Clonmel, is the founder of one of the earliest Iberian colleges, *El Real Colegio de Nobles Yrlandeses* in Salamanca in 1592, the majority of whose seminarians will be from Munster. A policy of Munster intake is also implemented in the colleges of Santiago and Seville, while to the north, in France, the college at Bordeaux (founded in 1603 by Corkman Diarmuid MacCarthy, one of the Muskerry MacCarthys) "is from its beginnings in 1603 an enclave of Cork, Cloyne, Kerry and Waterford."[53] Liking none of this, Fr Florence Conry, host to the Earls when they arrived in the Netherlands, and founder of the Franciscan college at Louvain, campaigns for years to overturn the Munster monopoly in Salamanca, because he believes that the Munster men are not nearly as patriotic as the Ulster men and those of his own native Connaught.

The Franciscan Conry is a separatist, and indeed he is one of those who give Irish nationalism its very Catholic character at this period, a period to which the early disagreements on how to liberate Ireland can be traced. There are those, like Conry, who are prepared to see Ireland a subordinate kingdom under a European Catholic monarchy, and others who counsel taking an oath of allegiance to the James I. (In truth, James FitzMaurice FitzGerald, landing at Smerwick with the banner of the Counter-Reformation and the religious crusade, belongs to the first group; and perhaps his cousin, the ill-fated Rebel Earl, who was never in Europe, belongs to the second.) We will see more of this in the troubled century now beginning.[54]

At home in Ireland the defeated Catholic families of Kerry begin to regroup. Valentine Browne, son and heir to Sir Nicholas, is raised a Catholic by his mother, the daughter of O'Sullivan Beare. The long and fraught association of the Brownes with the Old Irish has begun – and with their Catholic faith. This Valentine marries twice, first the daughter of the Rebel Earl, secondly the daughter of Charles MacCarthy, first Viscount Muskerry; in a later generation the descendants will marry each other – the main branch at Killarney, the other at Hospital, Co. Limerick. (We will see shortly how Muskerry's son becomes the leader of the rebel Irish forces in Munster when the great Rebellion of 1641 spreads to Kerry from the North.) The next Browne – also Valentine – marries again one of the Muskerry MacCarthys, and *his* son – a third successive Valentine – is ennobled by James II with the title Viscount Kenmare.[55] (The name Kenmare comes from a townland of

53 T.J.Walsh, *The Irish Continental College Movement* (Dublin and Cork 1973), pp. 45, 49.
54 The case of James FitzMaurice FitzGerald makes it clear that the separatists and advocates of the religious crusade are by no means always Old Irish; indeed many of the Old Irish of Kerry (names like MacCarthy and MacGillycuddy) will prefer an arrangement with the English crown.
55 During the reign of James II's successor, the Protestant William of Orange, no official paper ever concedes the Brownes their title – they are always referred to as the "titular" earls of Kenmare.

that name near Hospital in Co. Limerick – not from the town bearing that name in the very south of Co. Kerry.)

It would be too easy, and wrong, to overstate the effect of settlement and inter-racial marriage: what we tend to see is a compromise on both sides founded on a desire for peaceful coexistence. Let us look at the Irish neighbours of the Brownes, the great Irish family of MacGillycuddy of the Reeks. Donagh (Geraltach/Geraldine) MacGillycuddy, killed in the Rebel Earl's rebellion sometime in the years 1590-95, forfeited his lands. In 1615 his son Conor marries Joan Crosbie, daughter of Bishop Crosbie, which marriage is presumed responsible for the rescue of the MacGillycuddy estate; at the same time it secures the practice of the Catholic religion to the MacGillycuddys, the bride's mother (the Bishop's wife), herself Catholic, having raised her daughters as Catholics.[56]

In Lixnaw we find that Thomas FitzMaurice, having adhered to the recent family pattern of rebellion, now turns a protracted semi-circle to loyalism and the Protestant faith. Despite a career in rebellion, he surrenders when O'Neill surrenders and in October 1603 is regranted all of his lands. His son – the child smuggled out of Listowel Castle – is handed to his brother-in-law Thomond (O'Brien, Bunratty) to be raised a Protestant, and the FitzMaurices are given the wardship of his wife's nephew, the future "Murrough the Burner" O'Brien, hammer of the Irish for most of the civil wars of the 1640s.[57] Thomas marries secondly in 1615, to Julia Power of the Curraghmore family (Waterford); it is the sons of this marriage who become leading rebels in the coming civil war of the 1640s; at the same time the boy spirited out of the Castle at Listowel tries with difficulty to remain a royalist.

One family of Elizabethan settlers never wavers in its allegiance to the English: the Blennerhassetts. Over in Killorglin in 1622, Elizabeth Coway, daughter of Elizabethan planter Jenkin Conway, marries Robert Blennerhassett of Ballycarty; a grandson Blennerhassett will make a second Conway marriage and inherit Killorglin, which will remain in the hands of the Blennerhassetts to the end of the eighteenth century.

If co-existence is becoming more and more a feature of life in Kerry, the case is distinctly otherwise elsewhere in Ireland and in England – and these outside tensions are bound to impact Kerry. From the beginning of his reign King James

56 W. Maziere Brady, D.D., *The MacGillycuddy papers, A Selection from the family archives of 'The MacGillycuddy of the Reeks' with an introductory memoir, being a contribution to the history of the county of Kerry* (London 1867), introduction xvii; see M.A. Hickson in *Kerry Evening Post*, 17 and 24 May 1893. The mother of the Bishop's wife was Lalor of Co. Laois.
57 Ivar O'Brien, *Murrough the Burner, Sixth Baron and First Earl Inchiquin 1614-74* (Ballinakella Press 1991), p.4.

finds himself at the mercy of his Parliament, and though we are entering a long period of peace with the enemy Spain, the Puritan leadership affords him few supplies while at the same time demanding a right to have a say in taxation and foreign policy. James responds by using prerogative courts like the Star Chamber to try his opponents. He lacks the advantage of his Tudor predecessors who had the wealth of the monasteries at their disposal to distribute among their supporters. Also, the Tudors were better politicians, or perhaps it would be more true to say that the radical Puritan faction was more easily held in check, even at the cost of channelling its energies in military adventures against the Spaniards.

James must tolerate (we assume he knows) the activities of the new Munster president, Brounckner (1604-7), who we are told "launched a virulent attack on the recusants of Munster".[58] This and the "Gunpowder Plot" (1605), an alleged attempt in London to blow up the Houses of Parliament and overthrow the state, may provide the background to the crackdown on prominent Catholics like Sir John Burke of Brittas Castle, near Cappamore (Co. Limerick), executed in 1606 or 7. Sir John has made no secret of his friendship for the Dominicans in Limerick city, and his adherence to the Mass, which is celebrated in his castle; when some of his neighbours betray him to Brounckner, Sir John is offered the Oath of Supremacy; he refuses to take it, and (though father of a large family) is tried and executed at Gallows Green in the city.

James wishes to continue the roll out of state institutions, including the courts, a process renewed by his predecessors Elizabeth and her father and grandfather; this programme is now helped by the departure in 1607 of the northern Earls from Ulster in the aftermath of Kinsale, following on the defeat of the Desmonds in Munster. Official policy tries to engage with the populace, and the royal courts begin to win slow acceptance. When judges arrive in Kerry 1606 - the first sessions in eight years – the number of cases before them leaves them in no doubt about the popularity of the royal courts.[59] Catholicism is as yet no bar to office, and many in Kerry attend the inns of court in London and are appointed justices of the peace and sheriff.

Parliament is still open to Catholics. But when James creates new parliamentary boroughs for the long-awaited Irish Parliament of 1613 his intention is to promote the Protestant faith, at the same time strengthen his position against the

---

58 Liam Irwin, "Politics, Religion and Economics: Cork in the Seventeenth Century" in *Journal of the Cork Historical and Archaeological Society* Jan.-Dec. 1980, pp.7-25; p.20.
59 David Dickson, *Old World Colony, Cork and South Munster 1630-1830* (Cork 2005), p.15.

forces arrayed against him in the Parliament in London. (One of the new boroughs is Tralee.) Of the 226 members 125 are Protestants. Stephen Rice of Dingle and Daniel O'Sullivan of Dunloe (Killarney), Catholics, are the county MPs returned for Kerry.[60] A representative Catholic group travels to London to present James with an offer of loyalty in return for toleration of their religion. The group is met with a royal rebuff: he calls them "half-subjects", from a country in league with Spain.[61]

The "Seven Septs of Laois" arrive in North Kerry at this time to occupy a tract of land around Tarbert consisting of twelve and a half carucates, or plow lands granted to Patrick Crosbie, originally the grant to an undertaker by the name of Hollis as part of the Munster Plantation:

> "a parcel of land in Munster called Tarbert, lying upon the mountain of Slewlougher in Kerry, between O'Connor's country and the Knight of the Valley's (Glin), which heretofore was surveyed at £70 per annum and passed to Sir John Hollis, who was soon weary of it, so that hitherto it hath yielded no benefits to the Crown."

Patrick Crosbie's grant is confirmed in 1607. The Seven Septs are: Moore, Kelly, Lalor, Deevy (Clan Melaughlin), McEvoy, Doran, Dowling, the exodus from Laois amounting approximately to three hundred people. The cause of the exodus is one of the earlier plantations when English planters settled the Irish South Midlands during the reign of Mary (Elizabeth's half-sister and predecessor). The region was shired as Queen's County, after Mary, its principal town Maryborough (we know them as County Laois and the town of Portlaoise). An Irish insurrection against the settlement lasted many years but ended with the death of its influential leader Owny Mac Rory Oge O'More. Thereafter it was decided to move seven septs out of the region and settle them in North Kerry.[62]

What of the Irish church? Few Catholic bishops will dare appear in their sees until the 1620s. On the other hand, we learn that the future bishop of Kerry, Rickard O'Connell "who guided the affairs of the diocese of Kerry from his

---

60 Robertus Blenerhassett and Humphridus Dethicke are returned for Tralee, Thomas Trant FitzRichard, Michael Hussey for Dingle.
61 Richard Bagwell, *Ireland Under the Stuarts*, 5 vols. London 19-9-16, vol. 1, p. 130-136.
62 Patrick Crosbie is not the ancestor of the Crosbies of Ardfert Abbey, (barons Branden, later earls of Glandore), nor of the Ballyheigue Crosbies, their cousins. The ancestor of these families is the brother of Patrick Crosbie, the Rev. John Crosbie, alias Mac Crossan, Bishop of Ardfert and Aghadoe 1600-21.

appointment as vicar about 1611 ... regularly attended fairs and public gatherings in all the towns of his diocese, especially Killarney, Castlemaine, Tralee and Ardfert, to make himself generally available to people, and also to try to curb drinking and fighting".[63]

The exodus of seminarians began under Elizabeth, but it now reaches a flood after Kinsale and the Flight of the Earls. Spain and the Spanish Netherlands (modern Belgium) provide the principal destinations, not only for seminarians, but for scholars, soldiers and ordinary emigrants. The preparation of seminarians follows the reforms of the Counter-Reformation as laid down by the Council of Trent, with this exception: Irish priests do not need the assent of their bishops to enrol in the Irish colleges – they need only declare for the Irish mission. (When Irish bishops succeed in occupying their dioceses in the eighteenth century, they will set about recovering control.) We will continue to have these continental-trained priests in the diocese of Kerry right up to the second half of the twentieth century. Daniel O'Connell has shed light on other features of the time, including prior ordination in Ireland, and burses – scholarships – for subsequent seminary training:

> "Those (priests) whom I remember as old men had all been educated abroad, and had naturally a tinge of jacobitism connected with them. ... (their training) began at a much later period of life. In general they could not go to the burses, as they were called in France and foreign parts, until they had been actually priested, for the burses were not in themselves sufficient for their entire support, they must have the advantage of the payments they raised for saying masses. They could not say mass without being priests; they could not be priested until the age of twenty-three and some months."[64]

It is in these seminaries that the manuscripts and history of Gaelic civilisation are saved, the new Franciscan college at Louvain, founded in 1607, leading the way. Louvain sponsors the work of the "Four Masters", a group of Donegal Franciscans led by Michael O'Cleary. In 1621 at Lisbon appears the *Historiae Catholicae Iberniae Compendium* of Philip O'Sullivan Beare, and Dominic O'Daly's history of the Geraldines is written in Portugal some decades later. O'Sullivan's *Historiae* sets the context for Ireland's liberty: Ireland a single nation under the Roman Catholic religion. Linked with it is the Irish language,

63 *Commentarius Rinucc.*, v, 151-7, quoted in Partick J.Corish, *The Catholic Community in the Seventeenth and Eighteenth Centuries*, p.31.
64 *Report of the Select Committee of the House of Lords, Disturbances in Ireland, 1825*; Daniel O'Connell 123-171, p.155

to conserve which the Louvain fathers eagerly embrace the new technology, the printing press, which has served so well to propagate the teachings of Luther and the Protestant faith. It is from the continental colleges that the catechisms as well as the Irish grammars will be brought back to Ireland for distribution among our countrymen.

The Munster Plantation meanwhile has settled down at the second attempt following the utter destruction wrought by the wars of the Súgan Earl and Florence MacCarthy. So too has the Reformation, particularly in the urban centres that now bridle the Catholic heartlands: Bandon and Mallow to the east, and the Denny and Herbert settlements in Tralee and Castleisland in the heart of Kerry. Markets begin to proliferate, under permits for the purpose issued by the government to Kerry as elsewhere. Roads and bridges are constructed to traverse the province and ford the rivers and streams. The thousands of new tenantry begin to inhabit slated houses rather than tower houses, with stone chimneys appearing "like mushrooms after rain".[65] Where defense continues a priority, existing castles are reconstructed and refortified. There are orchards, such as that of Sir Philip Perceval at Liscarroll, and ponds filled with carp.

How has the undertaker Denny been faring? Back in 1587, shortly after arrival in Kerry, and "before the late wars" of the Súgán Earl, "there was a fair house built in the Abbey of Tralee by Sir Edward Denny, and fifty other houses built by tenants, all destroyed in the time of the rebellion".[66] The planters are finding it difficult to attract English tenants, making it necessary for them to settle native Irish or Old English, a situation with predictable consequences in 1598-9 and again in 1601.

Arthur Denny succeeds his father at seventeen years of age when Sir Edward dies in 1599. He marries Elizabeth Forest and begins the task of rebuilding the settlement. Since the wars of the Súgan Earl and Florence he has constructed "one dwelling place for the chief Undertaker at Carrignesily (and) 79 houses and tenements, of which 32 are in the town of Tralee" (the others elsewhere in the seignory).[67] The chief undertaker (Arthur's) house is probably the long forgotten Elizabethan Mansion House of the Dennys situated close to the location of the Earl of Desmond's violent death, a few miles east of Tralee in the parish of Ballymacelligott.

Funds are scarce, and in 1607 Arthur petitions the King, "craving the remittal of certain arrears". The father, Sir Edward, having "lost his life and his cattle, goods, and benefit of

65 Michael McCarthy Morrogh, "The English Presence in Early Seventeenth Century Munster" in Brady and Gillespie (eds.) *The Makings of Irish Colonial Society 1534-1641, Natives and Newcomers* (Dublin 1986); p.183.

66 Robert Dunlop, "An Unpublished Survey of the Plantation of Munster in 1622" in *Journal of the Royal Society of Antiquaries of Ireland*, vol. 54, 1924, part 2, pp.128-146, p.136.

67 Ibid.

his lands which he had",[68] Arthur seeks remission of "the relief due upon his father's death and the arrears of rent since the beginning of the late wars until next Michaelmas following", asking also "that he might have the arrears and present growing rent due to the late Earl of Desmond from the burgesses of Tralee, amounting to the sum of eighteen marks half face by the year". The charges are waived: "The arrears are greater than by any likelihood can be paid in many years out of Mr. Denny's seignory, the same lying much waste, and charged with the yearly rent of 127*l.* 15s. 6¼."[69]

Arthur dies young at the Mansion House on 4 July 1619, leaving a son and heir, Edward, aged fourteen. Elizabeth Forest is married again by the time of the wars of the 1640s when Kerry is in the grip of another Irish rebellion.

A key figure in this transformation of South Munster is Richard Boyle (1566-1643), future Earl of Cork. He arrives penniless in Ireland in 1588, then departs again, returning in time to assist Carew at the siege of Carrigafoyle.

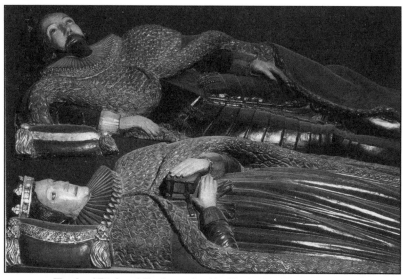

Tomb of Richard Boyle and wife, Katherine Fenton
(courtesy St Patrick's Cathedral, Dublin)

Boyle first marries the heiress Joan Apsley (1595) whose father William Apsley acquired the Knights Hospitallers property of Awney in East Limerick at the Dissolution of the monasteries. Though Joan dies without giving him an heir,

---

68 *Calendar of State Papers Ireland, James I, 1606-1608*, p.256, year 1607: Sir Arthur Chichester, Lord Deputy of Ireland, dated 26 August 1607, forwarded to the Chief Justice and Chief Baron.
69 Ibid., p.257.

Boyle acknowledges Awney as the foundation of his great wealth, "it being the beginning and foundation of my fortune". After Boyle's second marriage, to Katherine, daughter of Sir Geoffrey Fenton, Carew encourages him to take over the indebted and inefficient Raleigh seignory centred on Lismore, which includes Bandon and Clonakilty. He purchases the Raleigh land in 1602. (Raleigh is in no position to run his Irish estate and is placed on trial for treason the following year, found guilty and sent to the Tower of London, where he spends the next dozen years.) Within a few years Boyle notes that "every half-year God by his great mercy and bounty hath and doth enable me either by purchase, mortgage or leases, to increase my livelihood".[70] In 1611 he receives the transfer of the entire barony of Corcaguiney (the West Kerry peninsula) from the first Elizabethan planters.[71] He is raised in the peerage as Viscount Dungarvan and Earl of Cork in 1620, and we find this entry in his diary for 14 Feb. 1626: "I leased my moietie of the lands of the Blaskes in Kerry, reserving my Hauks, wrecks of the sea & all royalties ..."[72]

Some years later Boyle's lawyers begin to activate certain dormant claims in Tralee. One of these is *Teampal an tSolais* (the present St John's, Ashe Street) a daughter house of Awney, Boyle's Apsley inheritance. The district of Awney in Co. Limerick was acquired about 1200 by Geoffrey de Marisco who established there a church as a commandery of the Knights (of St John); the name derives from the goddess Aine[73] (pagan *Danu*) and survives in the name of Knockainy, as it does in a mountain range near the road from Killarney to Rathmore known as the *Paps of Aine*. (On a fine day the one can be seen from the other.) By Boyle's time *Teampal an tSolais* controls considerable property in Tralee town.[74]

Lady Denny now contests Boyle's Tralee claim, though Boyle (Lord Cork) has now a foot in the Denny family as the guardian of Lady Denny's son since the death of Lady Denny's

---

70 Quoted in John A. Murphy, "The Politics of the Munster Protestants 1641-49", in *Journal of the Cork Historical and Archaeological Society*, 1971, pp.1-20; p.7.
71 M.A. Hickson, "Old Kerry Records" in *KEP*, 30 March 1910; Paul MacCotter refers to "the possession of the bulk of Dunurlin parish by Richard Boyle, first Earl of Cork, in 1641 ... in one movement from the Ferriters to either Boyle or one of his predecessors as seignior of Corkaguiney", in "The Ferriters of Kerry", *J.K.A.H.S.* 2002, pp.55-82, p.65.
72 Grosart Rev. Alexander B., D.D., L.C.D. FSA. (Scot), *The Lismore Papers: Selections from the Private or Public (or State) Correspondence of Sir Richard Boyle never before printed*, 1886, 5 vols; vol. 2 p. 208.
73 Mainchin Seoighe, *Portrait of Limerick* (London 1982), which has much on Aine in his chapter "The Land Sacred to Aine".
74 Geoffrey de Marisco makes another link with the Crusades with the church he founds in Adare for the Trinitarian monks, whose job it is to obtain the release of Christinan prisoners taken by the Muslims; the same Geoffrey de Marisco establishes the Augustinians at Killagha, near Milltown.

husband Sir Arthur. Cork makes a diary entry of November 1623 recording a communication from his agent in Tralee, Thomas Joye, that one Roger O'Connyn, "did acknowledge my right to a tenement and garden and one acre of land in Traly, in Countie Kerry, called St John's L(an)e' as "belonging to the Commandery of Aneye" (Awney). Joye has found "another parcel of lands and a goode one adjacent to the same called Cloynaloure (Clounalour)" which also belonged to Awney, and therefore, now, to his master, Lord Cork.[75]

Whether credit should be given to Lady Denny or to Boyle is unclear, but the transfer of the church of the Knights Hospitallers in Tralee (the present St John's Church of Ireland) to the community of the Reformation may be dated to this first half of the seventeenth century.

The Earl of Cork attaches as much importance to his children's marriage arrangements as he did to his own. Two of his daughters marry into the leading Protestant families of the Pale around Dublin: Loftus and Jones. We will see how a Barry grand-daughter becomes Lady Denny at Tralee Castle at the end of the Cromwell wars. By the middle of the eighteenth century descendants in the male line of Richard Boyle (Earl of Cork) will have intermarried with the ducal family of Devonshire and Spencer (one of the former becoming a viceroy of Ireland). This web of connection will mean that the Denny descendants of Lord Cork will be a very wide connection indeed. Boyle's propertied presence in Kerry will endure as far as the turn of the twentieth century when Lord Cork is still the absentee owner of the Blasket Islands.

Charles I and Cromwell:
the Gathering Clouds of Civil War

Charles I succeeds his father in 1625. He inherits his father's arguments with Parliament over supplies (taxation/the royal budget) and he adheres adamantly to the Divine Right of Kings, now a more and more untenable doctrine in the face of Parliament's assertion of its right to participate in government. Compounding his difficulties, he has a French, Catholic wife, Henrietta Maria - actually a sister of King Louis. Charles's *ancien regime* view of monarchy is more in tune with the French model than the compromise formula more and more elaborated by the English since the barons negotiated Magna Charta with King John many centuries previously. The barons and their successors, the leaders of Parliament, will demonstrate a distinct unwillingness to transfer any concessions to the poorer

---

75 M.A. Hickson, quoting MSS from Mallow Castle in the possession of Sir Denham Norreys, in *Kerry Evening Post* 26 March 1910.

sort of people; unfortunately, the Irish (including many from Kerry) will invest their lives and estates in the doomed model of regal government operated by Charles and his cousins the Bourbon kings of France, particularly during the reign of the next French monarch, Louis XIV.

In England matters deteriorate for the Puritans when Charles appoints Bishop Laud as primate in 1628. Laud's and the King's policy of reinvigorating the rule of bishops, to impose the Trinitarian version of Protestantism, makes things very uncomfortable for Puritan divines and their congregations. These Puritans now depart the country in droves; their destination is the Bay colony at Massachusetts which traces its origins to the arrival of the Pilgrim Fathers at Plymouth Rock in 1620. In this Wilderness Zion it is hoped they will relieve England of an immediate problem. But their separatist tendencies will store mighty problems for their mother country in the next century – and the same Puritan colony, when it becomes the state of Massachusetts, will operate a policy   of No Irish Need Apply when our droves of Kerry immigrants begin to arrive at Boston in the nineteenth century.

Ireland again becomes the chess board in a wider conflict, that between Charles and the English Parliament. In return for military levies voted by the Irish Parliament, Charles agrees the "Graces", by which is meant certain concessions to the practice of the Catholic faith. In his heart he is pro-Catholic but as his hands are tied by Parliament and its Puritan element, the "Graces" will be reneged upon and Penal Laws will remain in force. The Franciscans are forced out of Muckross briefly in 1629, the same year as Lislaughtin is reoccupied by a Fr Valentine Browne for the Franciscans.

In Spain during the reign of Philip IV (as Velasquez is painting his many famous portraits of the royal family) Tralee priest, academic and founder of Irish colleges, Fr Dominic O'Daly, becomes chaplain to the Spanish viceroy to Portugal. Portuguese independence is not many years away.[76] O'Daly grows to love Lisbon and founds two convents for the Irish Dominicans in the city, Corpo Santo for male religious and Bom Successo for female (the latter continues part of the Irish Dominican province at the time of writing). In Portugal O'Daly also begins to write his history of the Desmond earls, *Initium, Incrementum et Exitus Familiae Geraldinorum* (Lisbon 1655).[77]

In Tralee the Dennys are very alert to the gathering clouds of civil war in England, and their allegiance to the King has been sealed by their connections with court. Lady Denny –

---

76   Back in 1580 Philip II annexed Portugal, a situation which remained until the restoration of the Portuguese monarchy sixty years later in 1640.
77   *The Rise, Increase, and Exit of the Geraldines, Earls of Desmond, and Persecution After Their Fall.*

Elizabeth Forest – now married to Sir Thomas Harris, is herself yet another former lady-in-waiting to Queen Elizabeth. When her son Sir Edward Denny (1605-1646) marries Ruth Roper in 1625, the daughter of Viscount Baltinglass, he faces the task of reconstructing the Great Castle of the Dennys which is still in ruins after the rebellion of the Súgan Earl. Sir Edward marks the completion of the work with an entry in the Denny Bible: "I finished this Great Castle of Tralee and came with my mother to live in it upon the 22 of December 1627." Ruth Roper moves in two years later: "The 20th of November 1629, my wife and I began house-keeping in this greate castle." In 1633 an ominous entry records the arrival of a new Irish viceroy, a figure hated by the English parliamentarians: Thomas Wentworth. "The 23 of July 1633 ye Lord Viscount Wentworth arrived in Ireland to govern ye Kingdome as Deputy. Many men feare."

Wentworth sets about raising cash for the King. In doing so he succeeds in alienating the two leading Irish communities: the recent settlers and the Catholics (comprising the Irish and Old English). Where the Catholics are concerned, when he convenes Parliament in Dublin in 1634 he reneges on the promises contained in the Graces. Wentworth compels recent settlers, such as Denny and many others, to take out new patents for their estates at great cost. He also restricts the possession of gunpowder, a move very detrimental to the defense of the Great Castle of Tralee in the rebellion to come. But the great personal vendetta of Wentworth's time in Ireland is his pursuit of Boyle, Lord Cork for what Wentworth alleges is Cork's alienation of church lands.

At the outbreak of the Rebellion of the Irish in 1641 Sir Edward Denny will depart Kerry to fight for the King's forces. By then he and his wife Ruth Roper are the parents of a large family, and can we blame the parents if they make the safety of their family their great priority? Ruth Roper and the children take refuge in England at Bishop's Stortford for the war's duration, leaving the defense of Tralee and the Great Castle in the hands of her mother-in-law Lady Harris and husband Sir Thomas.

We might note the arrival in Kerry by this time of the important family of Hickson. Rev. Christopher Hickson, the first to settle in Kerry, is appointed Rector of Stradbally and Kilgobbin in 1621, according to the Regal Visitation of 1633.[78] He is a direct ancestor of historian Mary Agnes Hickson, who is acutely aware of her mixed ancestry in settler and native Irish stock. Soon Hicksons intermarry with Husseys and later with the knights of Kerry.

---

78 According to the Ms. diary of the first Earl of Cork (Boyle), Christopher Hickson resigned Stradbally 23 November 1635. He was succeeded at Kilgobbin circa 1639 by Rev Devereux Spratt, tutor to the children of Sir Edward Denny (*Kerr Evening Post*, 27 April 1910).

The Rebellion of 1641 –
the Confederate Wars – Cromwell

"In the mean time I was not wanting in my endeavours to reduce the enemy in Ireland; and to that end marched with about 4,000 foot and 2,000 horse towards Ross, in Kerry, where the Lord Muskerry made his principal rendezvous, and which was the only place of strength the Irish had left ..."

Siege of Ross Castle, Killarney, from the Diary of Edmund Ludlow, Lieutenant-General of the Horse in the army of Oliver Cromwell

"The Great Rebellion" of 1641 and the
Confederate War in Kerry

In October 1641 the Ulster Plantation is thrown into turmoil by an insurrection of those dispossessed in Ulster to make room for the new settlers after the Flight of the Earls. Historians have argued over Planter casualties, with figures varying from 40,000 to three times that number. The insurrection spreads to Kerry (the Seven Septs of Laois to the fore) igniting a war between Old Irish and New English and between the opposing factions of Ireland and their adherents in Scotland and England. Never before or since will the fortunes of the two islands be so dominated by events in Ireland and by dominant Irish personalities.

Charles's Irish deputy James Butler, 12th Earl of Ormonde will work for a moderate solution. A great-grandnephew of the Ormonde who helped reduce Kerry in Elizabethan times, he is synonymous with the Butler patrimony in Killkenny-Tipperary (including castles such as Cahir, Carrick-on-Suir and Kilkenny), where many of his Butler kinsmen continue Catholic. But there are intransigents on both sides. In the North of Ireland the leadership of the insurrection will devolve on Eoghan Ruadh O'Neill. He is a nephew of Tyrone, has a background of military service in Europe, and sees the struggle as part of the Counter-Reformation. He will enjoy a significant level of support in Kerry.

The settlers again flee Kerry as they did in the previous overthrow of the English. Yet during the 1640s Kerry does not suffer on the same scale as elsewhere. The great battles of this war are in north Co. Cork; yet, if leaders across the cultural divide are at heart royalist, they are propelled into conflict by the bitter course of events. One such is the Confederate commander, Donogh MacCarthy, 2nd Viscount Muskerry, somebody we might expect to be royalist being married to Ormonde's sister and coming from a family staunchly loyal to the Crown in Elizabethan times.[79] Why the change? Muskerry explains to Lord Barrymore that, "though I were resolved not to stir nor join with the country as I have done, I have (seen) such burning and killing of men and women and children, without regard of age or quality, that I expected no safety for myself, having observed as innocent men and well deservers as myself so used".[80] Even after murder and massacre Muskerry continues favourable to a moderate resolution

---

79 "It was the menace from the Geraldines, joined to the wish to shake off all allegiance to MacCarthy Mór, that made the lords of Muskerry such consistent supporters of the English government during the sixteenth century" (Butler, *Gleanings From Irish History*, p. 113).

80 Muskerry to Barrymore, 1642, quoted in David Dickson, *Old World Colony*, p.31.

to the war, along lines decided by Ormonde in negotiation with the Catholic leadership (Irish and Old English) assembled at the Confederation of Kilkenny. But the Counter-Reformation, energised by the papal nuncio, will oppose the Confederation's efforts at compromise.

Ormonde

More recent settlers like Denny and Blennerhassett are from the beginning sympathetic to a moderate King-and-Parliament resolution to the conflict; their principal concern is the protection of their frontier settlements in the overwhelmingly native South West, rather than a desire to ally with either side in the English conflict.

The Blennerhassetts are besieged at their seat, Ballycarty Castle, on the eastern approach to Tralee, by Florence MacCarthy, son and namesake of Florence MacCarthy of the previous wars; and Richard Exham is besieged by Walter Hussey at Ballybeggan Castle, which commands the northern approach. (Both of these lesser castles will remain in the hands of the insurgents until relieved when Kerry is overrun by the Cromwellians at the end of the war.) It is late January 1641. Denny has been called away by Munster President St Leger to help quell the rebellion in Cork, and he sends his wife and children to England, where they settle at Bishop's Stortford. In his absence his Castle, the Great Castle of Tralee, is besieged. Rev. Devereux Spratt, tutor to Sir Edward's Denny's sons, keeps a record:

> "In February 1641, it reached us, the whole country being up in rebellion, and the two companies besieging us in two castles, when I saw the miserable destruction of 120 men, women, and children, by sword and famine and many diseases, among whom fell my mother Elizabeth and my youngest brother Joseph, both of whom lie entered there."[81]

Leading the siege of the Great Castle is Piaras Ferriter, poet and soldier from the far West of the Dingle peninsula, a legendary figure with a predilection to piracy on the seas adjacent to his native place. Wishing not to be present for the siege is Capt. Patrick FitzMaurice, Governor of Kerry – the boy smuggled out of Listowel Castle at the time of the Carew wars – who chooses to depart to England as the siege begins, there to sit out the war and guarantee the family estates against forfeiture. Patrick's wife tries her best but fails to persuade Ferriter to remain loyal. Ferriter is the captain of one of those companies authorised and funded by the King, which Ferriter has now brought over to the side of the insurgents:[82]

"To my very loving friend, Mr. Pierse Ferriter, at Ferriter's Towne in Kerry,
> Theese-
> Honest Pierse, (And I hope I shall never have reason to call you otherwise), this very daie is one coming out of Kerry unto me, that by chance fell into the companie of Florence MacFineen, and the rest of that rebellious crue, ye very daie yt they robbed Haly, who tells me yt you promised (as he heard Florence say) to be with them the week following, and to bring a piece of ordnance with you from the Dingell, and join with them to take the Castell of Tralee; but, and I hope in God it is far from your thoughts for you that had ever been observed to stand upon reputation on smaller

81 Rev. H.L.L. Denny, "Extract form the MS. autobiography of the Rev. Devereux Spratt", in *Journal of the Association for the Preservation of the Memorials of the Dead in Ireland*, vol.7, Dublin 1910. p.372.
82 John Caball, M.A., "The Siege of Tralee", in *The Irish Sword* 1954-6, pp. 315-7. Caball uses Elkanagh Knight's account of the siege; Knight was appointed overseer by Denny when Denny left Tralee.

matters, I trust will not now be tainted with so foule and offensive a crime to God and Man – nor give your adversaries yt just cause of rejoicing, and just way for them to avenge themselves on you, nor us that are your friends, that just cause of discontent that would make us curse the daie that ever we saw you. But I cannot believe any such thing of you, knowing that you want not wit nor understanding enough to conceive and apprehend ye danger and punishment justlie due to such offenders: and therefore doubt not of God's mercies, in giving you grace to avoid them, which none can more earnestly wish and praie for than your loving friend,
Honor Kerry.
Corke, ye last of June, 1641."[83]

The efforts of the FitzMaurices to adhere to the Crown of England are compromised from another quarter: the MacGillycuddys. Col. Donogh MacGillycuddy will deny any part in the insurrection of 1641, but in that very year he marries a first-cousin of Patrick FitzMaurice, Mary, the daughter of O'Sullivan Mór. Witnesses will report MacGillycuddy, his brother-in-law Owen O'Sullivan Mór and O'Donoghue of the Glens participating in the siege of Tralee Castle. Donogh MacGillycuddy and his brother-in-law will depart Ireland with Charles Stuart when the war is over, and MacGillycuddy will have great difficulty in recovering the MacGillycuddy estates at the Stuart Restoration.

Inside the Great Castle in charge of the garrison is Sir Thomas Harris, husband of Denny's mother; they preside over a water shortage and a diet consisting of bran, tallow and "raw hides that did stink".[84] When the Irish divert the Gabhail river, Harris and his men dig thirteen wells inside the Castle. The end comes in August after the death of Harris when quarter is given to the survivors.

David Crosbie meanwhile has retreated to Ballingarry Castle on the Atlantic above Causeway where he gives shelter to leading settler families. As winter approaches he also receives the remnants of those who have withstood the siege of Tralee's Great Castle.

The Old Irish are defeated at Liscarroll in late 1642 by O'Brien, Lord Inchiquin, after which they look for a deal with the Old English - both are Catholic; they meet in the Confederation of Kilkenny. The Old English dilute the proceedings of the Confederation and smooth the path to a truce with the King. Meanwhile Ballingarry fort has been

83   M.F. Cusack, A History of the Kingdom of Kerry (London/Dublin/Boston 1871), p. 246.
84   Caball, p. 317.

treacherously entered by the Irish, but its principal occupant, David Crosbie, is saved through the influence among the Irish of his nephew Donogh MacGillycuddy.[85]

> "When Ballingarry was at last taken by the Irish, through the treachery of the two warders appointed to guard the drawbridge connecting the precipitous shores of the island with the cliffs on the mainland, Col. David Crosbie's life was saved only through the influence of his nephews and his niece Katherine MacGillycuddy who was with him in the castle or fort. He managed with their help to escape into Cork ..." [86]

Ballingarry Castle
(photograph Marjorie Long)

The King's representative, Ormonde, agrees a cessation in September 1643 by which the Confederation advances money to the King for his fight against the Parliamentarian army in England. By the terms of the Ormonde cessation Crosbie should get his lands back, but this is a slow process: the Confederation only slowly overturns the will of the Irish in Kerry, and in 1645 Crosbie is still appealing to be reinstated in his lands.

---

85 M.A. Hickson's *Old Kerry Records* and Charles Smith's *Antient and Present State of the County of Kerry* (1756) are in substantial agreement on these events.

86 Mary Hickson, *The Irish Massacres of 1641-2, their Cause and Results* (London 1884), p. 121; "and returning to Kerry in 1649 (David Crosbie) was made governor of the county by Cromwell, which enabled him to save not a few of his friends and relatives from transportation".

The Ormonde cessation with the Cofederation drives the Protestant New English of the hinterland, settlers like Will Jephson of Mallow and Philip Perceval of Liscarroll, into the arms of the Parliamentarians. They fear for their estates and they mourn the loss of Richard Boyle's son, Kinelmeaky, killed at the battle of Liscarroll. Many are sickened by the transfer – under the terms of the cessation – of Irish Catholic soldiers to England to aid the King in his struggle with Parliament.

Whatever about the leanings of hinterland settlers like Jephson and Perceval, the Dennys remember their ties with the Court. The historian of the Denny family, Rev. H.L.L. Denny, believed the family was "probably quite prepared to espouse the cause of the house of Stuart (King Charles), for which their fathers had fought" - except for the pressure placed on them by the Irish. The conflict calculus now alters irretrievably in England when the King is defeated at Marston Moor and Naseby, 1644 and 1645 respectively. However, "Murrough the Burner" (O'Brien Lord Inchiquin) is uneasy with taking orders from the King's enemy, Parliament, which is suspicious of Inchiquin's native Irish race, being an O'Brien. Inchiquin dislikes the rise of a radical wing in the army under Fairfax, known as the Independents, who march on Parliament and London in 1647 to impose their radical solution: the capture and execution of the King. But Inchiquin has a rival in Roger Boyle, Lord Broghill, another son of Lord Cork. Broghill takes some regiments to England and begins to ingratiate himself with the Independents. Oliver Cromwell is trying to control this new radical turn of events, and when he shortly succeeds he will come to Ireland to mete out a final solution to Irish insurrection.

By this time the Pope's Nuncio has stepped ashore at Kenmare. He is Jean Baptiste Rinuccini, Archbishop of Fermo. He will greatly stiffen native Irish resistance in the South and West, at the same time oppose the compromise-orientated Confederates when they conclude another treaty with Ormonde in March 1646. The Treaty makes some concessions to the practice of the Catholic faith in return for a supply of more troops for the King. Rinuccini condemns the treaty and espouses the campaign of Eoghan Rúa O' Neill. Eoghan Rúa, as nephew to Tyrone, is heir to an all-Ireland and separatist heritage under the auspices of a Catholic European monarchy, to which end he has become a standard bearer of the Counter-Reformation. When he wins a great victory over a Parliamentary force at Benburb in June 1646, the Confederate Treaty with Ormonde is placed in jeopardy and Rinuccini threatens to interdict any town which ratifies the Treaty. The Nuncio's adviser is Fr Boetius MacEgan O.F.M. The future bishop of Ross (Skibbereen, the western division of Carbery), McEgan has been chaplain to the army of Eoghan Ruadh, and it was MacEgan who welcomed the Nuncio in Duhallow after his arrival near Kenmare. (About the same time, Rickard O'Connell, Bishop of Ardfert, met Rinuccini at Macroom and accompanied him to Kilkenny, the seat of the Confederation.)

Bishop O'Connell excommunicates John, Knight of Kerry, for not taking the side of the native Irish in Kerry, and remaining neutral.[87] Here we might consider the Knight's dilemma, and also that of his brother-in-law Patrick FitzMaurice who fled Kerry at the outbreak of the insurrection. Much was at stake for the great Old Irish and Norman families, and great was the temptation in the early stages to flock to the Old Irish banner. In *Old Kerry Records* Miss Hickson tells us that John FitzGerald, "although he was a Roman Catholic", suffered excommunication by the (Rinuccini-ite) Bishop of Kerry for his neutrality, and that the Irish plundered his land for having succoured the "distressed English", for which crime the Confederation of Kilkenny decreed his forfeiture. Little honour there. Later, the Cromwellians give the justice which the Confederation has denied: John, "marked down for forfeiture and transplantation to Connaught under the Commonwealth", is "dispensed" – deemed to have taken no part in the rebellion. And he retains his estates when the King returns at the Restoration.[88]

This John, Knight of Kerry, appears the quintessential meat-in-the-sandwich figure of history. His wife is Catherine FitzMaurice, daughter of FitzMaurice Lord Kerry. Her two brothers, Edmund and Garrett, are in rebellion, but not their half-brother Capt. Patrick FitzMaurice, Governor of Kerry, whose mother was sister of that ultra-loyalist fourth Earl of Thomond. It seems fair at this remove to assume an Ormandite loyalism on the part of John and the Governor of Kerry, and we note that Colonel Edmund FitzMaurice "forfeited Tubrid and Cloghir ... and Ayle and Dromartin ..." in the barony of Clanmaurice as the price of his rebellion.[89]

The intransigence of the native Irish under the influence of the Nuncio is used to justify the brutal campaign in 1647 of that great renegade from his own race, Parliamentary leader, O'Brien, Lord Inchiquin, "Murrough the Burner". Inchiquin has experienced the brutality of the on-going Thirty Years War in Europe, and he turns now to clean up Munster in a campaign that reaches a barbaric high with the notorious

87 M. A. Hickson , *Old Kerry Records*, vol.2, p.226.
88 *Old Kerry Records*, vol. 2, p.226.
89 "Of Forfeited lands from the Book of distribution", *Old Kerry Records*, 2ⁿᵈ Series, p. 42.

attack on Cashel in September where he kills thousands of soldiers and hundreds of civilians. More than ever in the ascendant, Inchiquin overcomes a Confederate army under Lord Taaffe at Knocknanuss (near Buttevant) in November 1647; some say that up to 4,000 are killed. (Taaffe wrote his opponent a letter the day before the battle in which he stated "Our quarrel is to preservee the King's interests".[90]) David Crosbie follows Inchiquin's orders in Kerry, one of which is to facilitate the settlers who wish to take refuge in Cork, and he orders Crosbie to take over the command of Kinsale. In January 1648 Inchiquin attacks Kerry:

> "I hastened with what speed I could into the county of Kerry, where, & in part of the county of Limerick, I have spent this last month, forcing some parts to composition & destroying others that were refractory, & by that means raised supportation for that part of the army which would have otherwise overburthened our garrisons ... I have brought home about 1000 pounds & taken hostages for some further small proportions of money to follow, being necessitated to retire for some time of refreshment into our garrisons; the country everywhere being so harassed & impoverished by our march & quartering amongst them as they were no longer able to produce anything that might continue against the soldiers, many of themselves being very likely ere the spring to perish of famine."[91]

Inchiquin has heard that the Catholic assembly has meanwhile "dispatched away several emissaries to Spain, France & Rome &c. to invite over the Prince, to implore assistance and advice".[92] But he has a greater fear, that the Independent republican faction will take over in Parliament, and it is this that makes him declare for the King in May 1648. The Confederates sign a truce with him. There are two effects. One is that it widens the Catholic split: the county of Kerry, Rinuccini and McEgan (now Bishop of Ross) resist the deal (which hands the diocese of Ross to a Protestant bishop). Second, the South Munster harbour towns now abandon Inchiquin (whose O'Brien ancestry they have always suspected).

The Protestant towns of Munster open their gates and their ports to Broghill and ease the Cromwellian conquest of Munster. Broghill takes the surrender of Kinsale from Col. David Crosbie in November 1649, and Crosbie marches away

---

90 Taaffe to Inchiquin, 12 Nov. 1647, quoted in "The Battle of Knocknanuss" in the *Journal of the Cork Historical and Archaeological Society*, 1899, pp.109-122, p.114.
91 *HMC* Ormonde, vol.2, p.68, Lord Inchiquin to Michael Jones, Commander-in-Chief in Leinster, 28 January 1647
92 Ibid.

having been appointed Cromwell's Governor of Kerry. Denny dies before the arrival of Broghill and the Cromwellians. King Charles is executed at the beginning of 1649.

Cromwell: his generals Ludlow and
Waller reduce Kerry

To now Kerry has been spared the worst effects of war, despite the episode of "Murrough of the Burnings". This is about to change: Cromwell arrives in Ireland, landing at Ringsend (Dublin), on 15 August 1649.

Cromwell's military campaign to defeat Charles's army in England has been severely hampered by Ormonde's deals with the Irish, which have included the raising of troops for the King. And Cromwell is haunted by the massacre of his co-religionists in the north of Ireland. The success of the New Model army under Cromwell and Fairfax has owed much to participation of Puritan sectaries, those "God fearing" men discriminated against by Parliament but eager to fight in the New Model, and to tactics which discard the strict formations used by the gentlemen officers of the royalists. After Marston Moor and Naseby, Cromwell prevented the junction of Parliament and King at the head of an army of (Presbyterian) Scots. The King's escape from imprisonment by the army was a final statement of his unwillingness to accept the new order, and Cromwell's power was underlined by the defeat of the invading Scots.

Cromwell's reduction of Drogheda is a warning of what is in store for other towns if they resist his offer to surrender. After Drogheda ("Tredah") he reports:

> "When they submitted, their officers were knocked on the head; and every tenth man of the soldiers killed; and the rest shipped for the Barbadoes; ... I am persuaded that this is a righteous judgment of God upon these barbarous wretches, who have imbrued their hands in so much innocent blood; and that it will tend to prevent the effusion of blood for the future."[93]

The pattern exhibited at Drogheda is repeated at Wexford, after which New Ross and Carrick-on-Suir agree to negotiate. It has been a campaign compared to which the previous hostilities were, in the words of Elizabeth Bowen, a kind of "Baron's war". Before New Ross is taken in November, the great Irish champion, Eoghan Rua, dies suddenly. As Cromwell prepares

---

93 Oliver Cromwell, Dublin, to William Lenthall, Speaker of Parliament, 17 Sept. 1649, in Thomas Carlyle, *Oliver Cromwell's Letters and Speeches* (London 1849) p.53.

to invest Clonmel, he considers the situation to the west.

Muskerry faces a formidable adversary as he prepares to defend Kerry: Roger Boyle, Lord Broghill. Broghill, founder of the town of Charleville, is the principal Cromwellian commander in the reduction of the South Munster towns and the town of Macroom on the approach to Kerry.[94] Like many on the Cromwell side, he is at heart a courtier. He visited Geneva as a boy, but preferred the less demanding regime of the Church of England to Geneva's strict Calvinism. He and his brother Kinelmeaky fought for Charles in the Bishop's War against the Scots in 1639,[95] some years before Kinalmeaky's death at Liscarroll. He is also a rising dramatist, inspired and encouraged in turn by one of the important poet-playwrights of this time, Suckling.

As Broghill assumes control of the Cromwellian campaign in Munster the southern port towns signify early their eagerness to submit.[96] David Roche of Fermoy raises a great force of about 2,000 men in Kerry and Cork in early 1650 and brings it east to relieve Clonmel. In April, Broghill arrives at Clonmel to assist Cromwell, from where he forces Roche back towards Kerry. He is before Macroom in May where Roche occupies the castle. Broghill takes the castle (10 May), ordering his soldiers to kill all survivors.[97] The Bishop of Ross, MacEgan is captured in the confusion. Broghill now uses the bishop to force the submission of the nearby castle of Carrigadrohid, sending Major Nelson with the message that the bishop will hang unless submission is made. Those inside hold tough; the bishop is hanged – and then they submit. The bishop is brought to a nearby tree, in full view of the garrison, and hanged with the reins of his horse.[98] Conflicting accounts embellish the event. In one, the bishop urges those inside the castle to defy the threat; in another, his body is later quartered and beheaded.

In late October 1651 after a siege of six months Limerick city is surrendered to Ireton, and the Bishop of Emly, Terence Albert O'Brien, is executed. Ireton has expended much energy in the conquest of Clare, but Ludlow and the regicide Sir Hardress Waller can now be released for the

---

94 His title comes from the estate in Somerset, Marston Bigot, which his father Lord Cork purchased for him at his marriage, at age nineteen, to one of the Howards of Suffolk.
95 Kathleen M. Lynch, *Roger Boyle, First Earl of Orrory* (Tennessee 1965), p. 32, 15, 22
96 The following is said to have been written by him on the gate of Bandon: "Jew, Infidel, or Atheist/May enter here, but not a Papist", which a passing scribed improved with "Who wrote these words composed them well,/The same are written on the Gates of Hell".
97 Fr Canice Mooney OFM, *Boetius MacEgan of Ross* (Killiney 1950), p. 46.
98 Mooney, *Boetius MacEgan*, p. 53-5.

conquest of Kerry. Carrigaholt (fortress of the O'Briens, future viscounts Clare) is taken in November. In the Shannon estuary Admiral Penn has exerted complete control and assisted the siege of Bunratty Castle. (Pen's son, also William, is the Quaker founder of Pennsylvania.)

Ludlow, Lieutenant-General of Horse, Broghill, Lieutenant General of Ordnance, and Waller advance into Kerry to invest Ross Castle, the last stand of the Munster Irish. Ross Castle is in the hands of the Confederate leader, Lord Muskerry; Muskerry's estate, including his rents and his castle at Blarney, is in the hands of Broughill – Cromwell gave their custody to Broghill after Cromwell's arrival in Ireland two years previously. Lord Muskerry is joined at Ross by O'Connor Kerry. They have 4,000 foot and 200 horse. David Roche is back again in Kerry after his defeat in Muskerry territory and the events at Macroom and Carrigadrohid. He has written to Ormonde: "I ame nowe rallyeinge the men aboute this place, and with them and the forces of some baronyes of this county, whoe appeared not hitherto, doe expect veary suddenly to advance into the enemye's quarters in a better condicion than formerly." He asks Ormonde, to "hasten the forces of the county of Clare especially horse to come to our assistance, and dispose of them on this side of the river of Shenon, which may much distracte and deter the enemy, and (if it seeme convenient) to the end we may bee incorporated and joine in one body …)".[99]

The historian Charles Smith tells us: "The Irish had a kind of prophecy among them, that Ross Castle could not be taken until a ship should swim upon the lake; and the appearance of this vessel contributed not a little to intimidate the garrison, and to hasten the capitulation." At the end of April 1652 Ross Castle is invested by Ludlow, and the prediction of the ship on the lake is fulfilled. Ludlow's Memoirs[100] relate the scene:

> "In the mean time I was not wanting in my endeavours to reduce the enemy in Ireland; and to that end marched with about 4,000 foot and 2,000 horse towards Ross, in Kerry, where the Lord Muskerry made his principal rendezvous, and which was the only place of strength the Irish had left, except the woods, bogs, and mountains; being a kind of island encompassed on every part by water except on one side, upon which there is a bog not passable but by a causeway which the enemy

99   David Roche to Ormonde, Killarney, 14 May 1650, quoted in Mooney, Boetius Egan, p. 66-7.
100 *The Memoirs of Edmund Ludlow, Lieutenant-General of the Horse in the Army of the Commonwealth of England 1625-1692*, by C. H. Firth, M.A., 2 vols, Oxford 1894, vol. 2, 320-21.

had fortified. In this expedition I was accompanied by the Lords Broghill and Sir Hardress Waller, major-general of the foot ... When we had received our boats, each of which was capable of containing one hundred and twenty men, I ordered one of them to be rowed about the water, in order to find out the most convenient place for landing upon the enemy; which they perceiving, thought fit, by a timely submission, to prevent the danger that threatened them; and having expressed their desires to that purpose, commissioners were appointed on both sides to treat."

Ross Castle, Killarney

After a fortnight debating terms, Ross Castle capitulates on 22 June 1652. Ludlow's diary:

> "Lord Muskerry and myself confirmed it; his son with Sir Daniel Obryan were delivered to me as hostages for the performance of the articles, in consequence of which about 5000 horse and foot laid down their arms and surrendered their horses."

Permitted to leave Kerry and serve any foreign state not at war with England, Muskerry, transports himself and five thousand men into Spain.[101] In July 1652 one or two vessels from France arrive in the Kenmare River with relief for Muskerry. But it is too late and Muskerry completes his surrender on 5 July.

By this time the Bishop of Kerry, Rickard O'Connell, is "very old and suffering from ailing bones and gout". He tells Rinuccini that his church buildings are falling into ruin. Bishop O'Connell is captured by a force under Nelson, the Cromwellian commander in Kerry; he dies and is buried at Muckross.[102]

The devastation left in the wake of the war appears in the following commentary from 1653. We learn of "the unruliness of the Tories ... fourteen captains & other officers being lately taken in Kerry and hanged; others of them have offered themselves prisoners till they be sent to Spain, & all very desirous to come in".[103] That fellow traveller of the war, the bubonic plague, is contained in something written by the agent of the Herbert estate at Castleisland: "Yet such has been the destruction of man and beast by sword and pestilence that famine has ensued there (especially towards Beer and Bantry) and elsewhere. Lord Herbert will need to send a new colony."[104]

---

101 Muskerry is created Earl of Clancarty by Charles II in 1658 and restored to his estates at the Restoration.
102 Rev. Kieran O'Shea, "Rickard O'Connell (1572-1653)" in *J.K.A.H.S.*, 1978, pp. 5-14, pp.13-14.
103 *Historic Manuscripts Commission*, Egmont Mss. Vol. 2, London 1905, John Percival to Lord Kerry, 25 June 1653.
104 *Herbert Correspondence*, p.139 Col. Thomas Herbert to Lady Herbert at Mountgomery Castle, 9 July 1653.

From the Roll of Martyrs – Cromwellian

Patrick J. Corish has written of the persecution of Catholicism under Cromwell:

> "All the sources agree in describing the ministry of the Catholic clergy as intermittent and extremely furtive. They could not turn to the laity for shelter and support, for this would have exposed their hosts to too much risk. They lived in huts in the bogs, in the woods, or on the mountains. They were probably safest in the towns, where some are known to have carried on a rather daring ministry under one disguise or another. However, as a general rule the priests moved about by night, saying Mass in some guarded retreat at or before daybreak. It was certainly in this decade that the tradition of the Mass-rock stamped itself on the Irish experience."[105]

In May 1650 Boetius MacEgan, Bishop of Ross is martyred at the hands of Lord Broghill by the castle of Carrigadrohid, near Macroom, shortly after the taking of Macroom Castle by Broghill. He is said to have been hanged with the reins of his horse. From Leland's *History of Ireland* (1773) the following: "Broghill ... promised to spare his life on condition that he should use his spiritual authority with the garrison of a fort adjacent to the field of battle, and prevail on them to surrender ... but the gallant captive, unshaken by the fear of death, exhorted the garrison to maintain their post resolutely against the enemies of their religion and their country, and instantly resigned himself to execution."

On 31 October 1651 the Bishop of Emly, Terence Albert O'Brien, is executed after Limerick falls to Cromwell's son-in-law, Ireton. The Bishop was a native of Cappamore, Co. Limerick, a village under the Slievefelim hills. Asked if he had anything to say, "he only desired time to confess his sins and prepare himself for death", after which he was led to execution. According to Clarendon's History, "The Bishop of Emly had from the beginning opposed the King's authority with the greatest passion, and obstinately adhered to the Nuncio".[106]

"Under Cromwellian rule", writes Ignatius Murphy, historian of the diocese of Killaloe, "the Catholic Church in Ireland suffered persecution of greater intensity than at any time before or after. There was no place for it under the

---

105 Patrick J. Corish, *The Catholic Community in the Seventeenth and Eighteenth Century* (Dublin 1981), p.49.

106 Quoted in J.J. McGregor and Rev. P. FitzGerald, *History of Limerick*, 2 vols. 1826, 1827, vol.2, pp.298, 300.

new regime, and the decision to ban 'popery' involved the total elimination of the Catholic clergy". Murphy records the hanging of two priests of Killaloe diocese by Cromwellian soldiers on 12 October 1652.[107]

In 1653 Thaddeus (Tadhg) Moriarty, Prior of Holy Cross, is arrested at Keelaclohane Wood, near Castlemaine. He is imprisoned in Ross Castle, tortured and hanged at Market Hill, Killarney. Thaddeus was a native of Castledrum and educated in Spain and Portugal, before returning to teach theology in Bishop Rickard O'Connell's Seminary in Tralee, afterwards becoming Prior of Holy Cross in 1643.

"To Hell or to Connaught"
1655: making room for Sir William Petty (1623-1687)

Cromwell's Act of Settlement of 1652 (given legal effect in the Act of Satisfaction 1653) authorises a huge land confiscation, for the payment of Cromwellian soldiers and to reimburse Adventurers (investors) in the Cromwellian conquest of Ireland. To obtain the necessary land there will be a mass transportation to Connaught and Clare of all classes of Irishmen above landless labourers. The deadline for transportation is fixed at 1 May 1654, later extended to December 1654, then to March 1655.

In order to assess the lands due for confiscation a proper land survey of Ireland will be necessary. William Petty, the physician-general to Cromwell's forces in Ireland, offers to prepare one. Petty is native to Romsey in Hampshire, his background natural philosophy and a career at Oxford University as professor of anatomy. Petty's marriage to Elizabeth, daughter of Sir Hardress Waller (c.1604-c.1666), will be the foundation of the Shelburne-Lansdowne dynasty, the titles and property of which will descend from a marriage of Petty's daughter Ann to Thomas FitzMaurice, 21st Lord Kerry and first Earl of Kerry.[108] (Waller was one of the judges of Charles I, and signed the death warrant; at the Restoration of Charles Stuart he will escape to France, return, surrender and be jailed for life.)

Let us introduce some of the lesser Cromwellian settlers. They include Godfrey, Bateman and Hewson, and Taylor at Dunkerron Castle in the South, and Frederick William Mullins, a Cromwellian officer, who settles in the far West.[109] The Godfrey

---

107 Ignatius Murphy, "Denis Harty – Vicar Apostolic of Killaloe 1657-1667", in *Tipperary Historical Journal* 1989, pp. 100-104, p.101.

108 Sir Hardress Waller was probably invited to Ireland by Richard Boyle. Waller's wife was Elizabeth Dowdall of Kilfinny, Co. Limerick, through whom he acquired the estate at Castletown in that county.

109 Frederick Mullins married Jane Eveleigh, daughter of Dean Eveleigh … "having purchased the large grants made to Robert Reading and his wife the Countess of Mountrath" (M.A. Hickson in *Kerry Evening Post*, 15 July 1914).

is "John Godfrey of Romney, County Kent, Lieutenant Colonel in Ludlow's Regiment of Cuirassiers", while Hewson is a London farrier (the "military cobbler" in references elsewhere). Ponsonby and Madgett are Cromwellian names, as are Sandes, Wren, Eager, Marshall and Markham. William Collis was an officer in Cromwell's army, "a Captain in Colonel Hierome Sankey's regiment of horse", according to all the pedigrees. The first of the Carriques settled on a Cromwellian land grant in the district of Camp, West Kerry, on territory forfeited by the FitzGeralds, knights of Kerry. William Carrique will succeed his uncle Ponsonby of Crotto in 1762 when he agrees to change his name to Carrique Ponsonby.

Sir William Petty (1623-1687), author of the Down Survey.
("We will set it down on paper.") Under Petty's direction the Survey is undertaken in the 1650s by Cromwellian soldiers; the results will not be superseded until the Ordnance Survey of 1825-40.

These new names are sometimes referred to as the "upstart gentry", though intermarriage will dilute distinctions over time. Slightly to the north, in Limerick, the first De Veres (descended from the earls of Oxford) receive a grant of land at Curragh Chase about 1657, according to family records.[110] A few years previously (1650) the ancestor of the novelist Elizabeth Bowen, Colonel Bowen, is campaigning in Munster with Lord Broghill when he sets eyes on "the light-shifted colours and contours of Garrett Cushin the papist's Farahy lands" (near Mitchelstown). The Colonel will become the first Bowen of Bowen's Court, and the family crest, from Gower, will be the hawk.[111]

110 Joan Wynne Jones, *The Abiding Enchantment of Curragh Chase – A Big House Remembered* (Cork 1983) p. 7. Curragh Chase house will burn down in 1941.
111 Elizabeth Bowen, *Bowen's Court* (London/New York/Toronto, 1942), pp. 49, 49.

Petty begins his survey work in December 1654. In the course of it he accumulates a vast estate in South Kerry. Much of this is the Kerry estate of Mac Finin Dubh O'Sullivan, lying around Kilmackillogue and Ardgroom; the rest is property in mountainous and coastal terrain considered useless by the Crowellian soldiers and which Petty purchases from these soldiers for a song. In 1657 Petty obtains grants of some 3,500 acres in Kenmare and Tousist, adding 2000 acres by purchase of soldiers' debentures, eventually amassing some 270,000 acres throughout South Kerry. [112] No less than the earlier Richard Boyle, Earl of Cork, his lawyers are adept at suing out defective titles, which is why he turns his attention to the MacGillycuddy estate above Beaufort, about which more will be said in the next chapter.

In order to keep Cromwell informed of the progress being made in transplanting people to Connaught, Sir Hardress Waller, Charles Coote, Robert King, John Hewson, William Jephson and Hierome Sankey write "To His Highness the Lord Protector (Cromwell), his Council for the Affairs of Ireland" of the designated regions in Connaught chosen for Kerry transplantees. Under a list of "Baronies in the Province of Connaught and the County of Clare appointed to receive the Inhabitants of certain Counties"[113] appears;

> "… The Inhabitants of the County of Kerry to be transported into Inchiquin and Burren baronys in the County of Clare, and into the territories of Artagh in the Barony of Boyle, County of Roscommon".

There will be a positive dimension to the Cromwellian settlement of Ireland. Erasmus Smith, described as "an Alderman of London" acquires certain estates in Ireland under the Cromwellian Act of Settlement which he then uses to endow five grammar schools. Their purpose is to educate students for entry to university, at the same time propagate the Protestant faith. The first of these grant-assisted schools is founded in the seventeenth century, and when the investment allows for more schools Robert FitzGerald, MP Dingle, succeeds in having one established on Valentia Island in the 1770s.

---

112 Gerard J. Lyne, "Land Tenure in Kenmare and Tousist, 1696-c.1716" in *J.K.A.H.S.* no.10 1977, pp.19-54; p.21.

113 Martin Blake, "An Old Kerry Record", in *J.C.H.A. Society*, vol. 8, April-June 1902, p.112: taken from Blake family papers and dated Dublin 12 February 1655; John P. Prendergast, *The Cromwellian Settlement of Ireland* (London 1865), 1996 edn. p. 192-3.

Dominic "of the Rosary" O'Daly

To conclude this chapter we go abroad again to follow the career of one of Kerry's most distinguished exiles, Dominican Fr Dominic O'Daly, founder of Irish convents in the Portuguese capital, Lisbon. The diplomatic career of O'Daly (Frei Domingos do Rosario, or Fr Dominic of the Rosary) has been recovered by Sr Benvenuta MacCurtain, who describes her subject as "an agile and subtle diplomat".[114] In the early 1650s O'Daly is sent to Paris by his patron, King John of Portugal, to win recognition for Portuguese independence and the restored Braganza dynasty. Portugal shook off the Spanish connection in 1640 (a reminder that during all the years of Ireland's involvement with Spain, Spain has been suppressing the independence of a neighbouring small nation, Portugal). O'Daly hopes to treat directly with Rome through Paris to persuade the Pope to deprive Spain of the practice of nominating candidates to the Portuguese hierarchy, a practice Spain has continued to exercise since Portuguese independence. But O'Daly finds himself in an anomalous position: France is at present in alliance with Cromwell's England and Protestant Sweden to curb the continuing Spanish hegemony in Europe. Spain has an unswerving ally in the Pope, and when eventually Spain accedes to the Pope's request not to appoint any more Portuguese bishops, King Louis proves no longer available to O'Daly on the question of Portuguese independence. All of this work for Portugal has enabled O'Daly to pursue quietly, in Rome and elsewhere, another objective: diplomatic efforts to ease the restoration of Charles Stuart to the throne of England. When Charles is finally restored in 1660 O'Daly's misgivings about an English alliance with Portugal can be safely put to rest; the alliance will be sealed by a marriage, which O'Daly helps to arrange, between the daughter of the Portuguese King, Catherine of Braganza, and Charles Stuart himself.

In the course of Dominic of the Rosary O'Daly's diplomatic travels in Europe he has probably been made aware of an important and significant movement of Irish military exiles. The movement in question – symbolic of the emerging importance of France in the next half century and longer – is the transfer of a cohort of Irish (including Kerry) swordsmen from the service of Spain to France. Here is what happens. Bordeaux, location of one of the Irish colleges, becomes a focal point of the French rebellion against the Crown of 1649-53 known as the Fronde. In 1653 a formidable force under the rebel leader Condé crosses the Pyrenees from Spain. Among the Spanish are Irish regiments drawn largely from veterans

114 Sr Benvenuta MacCurtain, "An Irish Agent of the Counter-Reformation, Dominic O'Daly", in *Irish Historical Studies*, Sept. 1967, pp. 391-406.

of the Confederate wars in Ireland, including, very probably, many of those shipped to Spain in 1652 after the fall of Ross Castle. Arrived at Bordeaux the Irish transfer en bloc to the French service; we know the identity of one of them, a Kerryman named O'Scanlon whose brother is Dr Cornelius O'Scanlon, contemporary superior of the Irish College at Bordeaux.

King Charles II. Fr Dominic O'Daly, of Kilsarkan, helped arrange his marriage to Catherine of Braganza.

The Later Stuarts: Restoration of Charles Stuart (1660-1685)

"Here are agents and solicitors from all the counties of Ireland to promote the Irish interest, and four or five crafty companions out of Kerry to solicit for the Irish proprietors."

Herbert Correspondence, J. Blennerhassett, London, to Lord Herbert, 28 January 1664/5.

Supporters of Charles try to recover their
Kerry estates

The Stuarts are restored in 1660 in the person of Charles II
– to whom is attributed the remark that he has no desire to
embark on his travels again. His cousin Louis XIV takes over
complete control of France in 1661 when he declines further
rule through a prime minister. Charles and Louis see eye to eye
on the Divine Right of Kings, but only Louis enjoys unfettered
powers to give this belief practical effect and to promote the
Counter-Reformation. In a less powerful position, Charles is
now inundated with claims for restoration from the dispossessed
Irish landowners, including those of Kerry; the new planters
recognise the volatile situation in which they find themselves
and they look to Broghill to protect their grants.

Vengeance is the air. General Edmund Ludlow and
another of the regicides, John Lisle, are pursued on Charles's
orders to their hideout in Vevay in Switzerland, where they are said
to be plotting the revival of the "Fanatick Party" and the overthrow
of the restored monarchy of England. On 11 August 1664 Lisle
is shot dead on his way to the Church of St Francis in Lausanne.
Sir James Cotter (we will meet him later on at the Denny Castle
in Tralee), if he does not actually fire the shot, is generally agreed
to be the head of the gang of assassins.[115] Ludlow, who took Ross
Castle, will die of old age in 1692 despite a price of £300 on his
head from Charles. The poet Dáithí (David) Ó Bruadair makes
Lisle's killing the subject of a poem, with Cotter the hero for
his pursuit and killing of Lisle: Cotter "adroitly from the world
removed the Bull (Lisle) that led their herd".[116] O'Bruadair
(1624-1698) hails from Springfield Castle near Drumcollogher,
home to a cadet branch of the FitzGeralds; his life spans the time
of Charles I, the Restoration and the Williamite war.

Kerry royalists, including those who have been in exile
with Charles, expect the Cromwellian confiscations will be
overturned. Here is what happens. A new Act of Settlement
(1662) appoints a Court of Claims. No estates will be restored
to those in rebellion against the monarchy during the 1640s,
but the court will restore "innocents" and the "49 officers",
i.e. those with Ormond to 1649. The task of the Court proves
impossible, so a second Act is necessary: the Act of Explanation.
It proposes to reduce the Adventurers' land entitlement by one
third, and the claims of the dispossessed likewise. As the process
fades away into oblivion there is little redress and widespread
disgruntlement among the Irish who have championed
Charles's Restoration.

115 Brian Ó Cuiv, "James Cotter, a Seventeenth-Century Agent of the Crown", in
    Journal of the Royal Society of Antiquaries of Ireland, vol.89, 1959, p.138-9.
116 Ó Cuiv, *James Cotter,* p.138.

We should record some reversals of confiscation. One is Cahernane:

> "By a Decree of the Court of Claims made the 28th July 1663 the 15th of Chas: II, the sevl. lands of Pallas, Muckruss, Cahernane, Castle Lough and sevl. other denominations of land &c. were restored to Dame Sarah MacCarthy ... widow of the *then* late Danl. MacCarthy-more, the eldest son of Florence MacCarthy and the Lady Ellen MacCarthy, the Earl of Clancare's only daughter and heiress, and to the eldest son of the sd. Dame Sarah and Daniel, viz: to Florence MacCarthy More, the sd. Sarah, Daniel and their son Florence being decreed by the Court to have been innocent Papists ..."[117]

Part of the estate of MacGillycuddy of the Reeks is recovered. Donogh MacGillycuddy burnt his castle and departed Ireland with his brother-in-law O'Sullivan Mór to further the cause of Charles Stuart, his estate passing into the possession of Cromwell's Ironsides and subsequently by purchase to Sir William Petty. Back in Ireland on Charles's Restoration he petitions in 1661 for the return of the estate, protesting that he had no part in the rebellion until 1648 (though one witness testified that he was at the siege of Tralee Castle). This has been the second confiscation suffered by the family: the MacGillycuddy estates were confiscated after two of Donogh MacGillycuddy's direct ancestors were executed for joining the "Rebel" Earl of Desmond; the estate's return in the next generation is atttributed to the marriage (1615 or 1618) of Conor (Donough's father) to the daughter of Bishop Crosbie of Ardfert.[118] On his Restoration Charles returns the MacGillycuddy estate to Donough, though there follows some litigation between Donough and Petty, litigation unsettled at the time of Petty's death.

Less fortunate is the case of O'Sullivan Beare, whose lands have become part of the Petty estate. Having suffered voluntary exile on the Continent he returns and in 1663 petitions Charles to restore his property, reminding him of his family's services to the Stuarts. Charles is sympathetic and tries to serve him. The trouble is that Charles has extended Petty's estate with new grants. In 1699 Beare's successor is residing "in a cabin at the foot of the hill".[119] Sir William Petty is taken

---

117 Egerton Ms. 116, quoted in *Life and Letters of MacCarthy Mor*, pp. 448-9.
118 Brady, *The MacGillycuddy papers;* intro. p. xvi.
119 Lyne, "Land Tenure", pp.21-22; quotation taken from Bishop Downes's *Visitation.*

away from Ireland during the 1660s by his various scientific interests. (He is one of the founder members of the Royal Society in 1662.) When he returns to Ireland his vast estate in South Kerry has come under the microscope of the tax farmers, whose attentions he is fending off in the same way as Richard Boyle had to fend off the attentions of Wentworth some decades before; the trouble Petty endures from the tax farmers appears a fair retribution for the distress endured by the MacGillycuddy and O'Sullivan Beare at the hands of Petty's legal agents.

The son of Piaras Ferriter, Dominic, has been in exile with Charles. He is granted the return of his ancestral lands; but restoration never materialises, and instead they are confirmed to the Countess of Mountrath, before passing into the possession of Mullins.[120]

To the Restoration we date the realignment through intermarriage of two of the leading Jacobite families of our region. The Knight of Kerry, John FitzGerald, son and namesake of the astute John who suffered excommunication as the price for remaining aloof during the Confederate wars and thus avoiding transplantation to Connaught, marries Dame Honora O'Brien of the family of the viscounts Clare from across the mouth of the Shannon at Carrigaholt. To this marriage alliance is owed the redirection of the family away again from FitzMaurice/Thomond loyalism to its distinguished leadership in the Catholic cause in the next century. How could it not, when we consider the record of the groom's family? Three of these O'Brien's – father, son and grand-son – assisted Charles Stuart in his exile following the ending of the Cromwellian campaign in Kerry at Ross Castle, on foot of the fall of their own fortress of Carrigaholt when the Cromwellians mopped up Co. Clare. At the Restoration these O'Briens are rewarded when old man Daniel O'Brien is created Viscount Clare in 1662; he dies the following year, and his son dies about 1670. The sister of the third Viscount is the Dame Honora O'Brien who marries John FitzGerald, the new Knight of Kerry, son of the excommunicated John of the Confederate and Cromwellian wars. But the Viscount Clare marriage brings an even stronger rebel heritage than fidelity to the Stuart: the wife of old man Daniel raised to the viscountcy by Charles – Honora's grand-mother – was daughter of no less a figure than the "Rebel" Earl of Desmond. Honora's brother, the 3rd Viscount Clare, founder of Clare's Irish Regiment, will lose all in the cause of the last of the Stuarts. He will be in James's army at the Battle of the Boyne, and at his side will be the young son and heir of his sister Honora and John FitzGerald.

---

120 Paul MacCotter, "The Ferriters of Kerry", *J.K.A.H.S.*2002, pp.55-82, pp. 70-71.

Ormonde competes for the heart of Kerry

Charles's Restoration has brought back the moderate and Catholic-connected Ormonde as Lord Lieutenant of Ireland. The Clarendon Code of English Chancellor Clarendon is more directed at the Protestant sects than at Catholics; however, the President of Munster, Broghill, is a more extreme figure, who sees as his priority the defense of Munster and its planter settlement. Broghill will be frequently at odds with Ormonde for requesting extra military resources against the Catholics of the South; and Broghill spends much of his time in London having his plays staged – he is a leading Restoration dramatist – while simultaneously attempting to undermine Ormonde. Many of his plays have Restoration themes, such as *The Indian Queen*, all about a rightful sovereign's restoration.[121] The only reason Broghill took a command under Cromwell was that Cromwell offered him a stretch in the Tower of London if he declined; after Cromwell's death Broghill persuaded himself – and others – that Charles should be brought back, for which Charles rewarded him with the title Earl of Orrery and the presidency of Munster. Recently he has been constructing a mansion on land he has acquired in North Cork. A town has begun to take shape. It will have the name Charleville, and be a borough with the right to return two members to the Irish Parliament.

While Orrery urges the need to protect the Protestant settlement in Munster, the moderate Ormonde (no less) is having problems from the native Irish and Rome. The Restoration sees a revival of the Old Irish/Old English division of the time of the Confederation of Kilkenny, with the result that once again a settlement which Ormonde attempts to engineer earns for him the anathemas of the Old Irish and the Vatican. (We can assume Valentine Browne on the Old English and Ormonde side in this quarrel: Browne marries Jane Plunkett of the Pale family, near Dublin, daughter of the man who chaired the Kilkenny General Assembly.) Ormonde's ally in the present negotiation is the Franciscan Fr Peter Walsh, in London in January 1661 as agent of the Irish Catholics (or some of them) and attempting to promote a formula of loyalty which, in the words of a modern Franciscan historian, "contains a statement of grievances, a petition for protection, and a protestation of allegiance (later known as the Remonstrance)". However, Rome rules it out and Fr Peter is excommunicated in 1670 for his trouble.[122]

---

121 Lynch, *Orrery*, p.172.
122 Patrick Conlan OFM, *Franciscan Ireland* (Cork 1978), p. 35.

As Rome and members of the Irish diaspora in Europe conspire to bring down Ormonde's compromise diplomacy, London is recovering from the Plague (1665), and the Great Fire of the following year. (Fire can be a good thing in the aftermath of plague and disease, and it proves equally good for the architect Wren who sets about erecting a number of beautiful churches which continue to adorn the city today.)

Meanwhile, the policies of King Louis of France have begun to menace the rest of Europe, and because his cousin Charles of England is in his pay, the enforcement of the Acts of Settlement in Munster can only be at best half-hearted. These are worrying times for the Cromwellian settlement, yet there is no overthrow of the new plantation, and therefore none of the martial law conditions that become such a feature of the next reign when Sir William Petty's colony around Kenmare is attacked.[123] A survey of the South of Kerry in 1673 reveals the continued presence of the old proprietors during the reign of Charles:

> "The Irish of this countrie are all branches of a few families, and chiefly of the Sullivans and Carties ... the three chiefs of the Sullivans themselves, namely O'Sullivan More, O'Sullivan Beare and Gillycuddy – although neither of them were adjudged innocent nor have any benefect of the late Act of Settlement, do nevertheless, *viis et modis,* enjoy considerable parts of their late estate, and that without paying quit-rent to his Majesty for the same, as even innocents are obliged to do, whereby they are able to engage great numbers of their name and families to assist them in such their progresses and intrusions."[124]

For a little background here, we recall the ideal of a unified Catholic Europe behind the actions of Louis, the *Sun King,* an ideal often ignored by historians writing in the glare of the scientific revolution and talk of man's progress from Faith to rationality. We remember those swordsmen who left Ireland after the fall of Ross Castle and who transferred their services from Spain to France shortly after. Their enemy is the coalition organised to fight Louis (England and Holland mainly), all the time seeing Louis as the man most likely to assist the liberation of Ireland.

Louis XIV came of age politically in 1661 when he

---

123 See, for example, M.A. Hickson, *Old Kerry Records,* vol.2, p.23-24: King James's warrant, dated "3 July, 5th year of our reigne"..

124 Lord Herbert to the Lord Lieutenant: "Report on the State of Kerry A.d. 1673", May 27th , in M. F. Cusack, *A History of the Kingdom of Kerry* (London, Boston, Dublin 1871, edn. 1995), p.285.

dispensed with a prime minister. He invaded the southern Netherlands in 1667 and made a secret money agreement with his cousin Charles of England. Charles's brother James, heir to the throne, has been practising the old faith openly and earning the enmity of the extreme Whigs under Shaftesbury. Shaftesbury's time will come, but not just yet. Charles made another secret treaty with the French in 1670, and in 1672 Louis embarked on an all out war against the Dutch by invading the Netherlands and sacking Amsterdam. This is the occasion on which the Dutch breached their dykes and flooded the country. Now enters the figure of Danby as Charles's principal minister: he reverses foreign policy to give the Whigs what they want, the overthrow of Charles's friendship strategy and a war against France. The Dutch leader is the young William, Prince of Orange. Danby arranges William's marriage to one of James's daughters, Mary (m 1677). Unfortunately international tension, instead of falling, rises. In 1676 Charles has made yet another secret arrangement with Louis; in London Orrery scents war and invasion in the air: "I never saw ye people in such Feares as they are inn. They keepe Guards in all Places as in Time of Warr."[125]

Louis achieves a number of naval successes against the Dutch, and in 1678 signs the Treaty of Nymegen to end the war. Shaftesbury replaces Danby at the summit of power, and the Duke of York, against whom moves have begun to exclude him from the succession, is advised to go into exile.

Orrery secures Kerry against French invasion

By now Orrery has acquired a new marriage connection in Kerry, one likely to rekindle memories of the great days when his father Richard Boyle was creating his Kerry property portfolio. In 1651 one of Orrery's nieces, Ellen Barry, daughter of his sister Alice Boyle, married the Denny heir, Arthur (1629-73), the little boy spared the siege of Tralee Castle when his parents Sir Edward Denny and Ruth Roper sent him and his brothers and sisters to Bishop's Stortford. His Barry marriage brought an important Cromwellian prejudice to balance the courtier in the Dennys; some years later, "at or about the Restoration", Arthur's sister Elizabeth Denny married her neighbour John Blennerhassett of Ballyseedy. Are we seeing a widening gulf between the settler and the native, and a circling of the wagons on the part of the settler families? The approaching wars will tell much. In 1673 the son and heir of Sir Arthur Denny and Ellen Barry, Edward, married Mary Maynard from Curryglass, a place in the Boyle country between Fermoy and Lismore; this is the couple who will preside at Tralee during the Jacobite

125 Lynch, *Roger Boyle, First Earl of Orrery*, p.215.

wars, and this is the Edward Denny to whom Orrery writes in 1678 in order to share his apprehension of a Kerry landing:

> "I doubt not but you know the probability there is of His Majesty's having a war with France, and I am sure you cannot but believe if that should happen that the discontented natives will be forward to disturb the peace of His Majesty's kingdom and all his subjects in it. We are preparing the best we can to weather such a storm should God permit it to fall on us, but in regard timely intelligence is essentially requisite, and that the County of Kerry is one of the most suspected parts, and also that I know you to be zealous for His Majesty's service, and very active and vigilant, I write this express to you and send it to Sir Boyle Maynard with a flying seal to convey it safely and speedily to you, and to desire you earnestly and diligently to lay out for the early discovery of any designs against His Majesty's Government which may be brewing in that County ...".[126]

The Popish Plot (1678-81), an alleged attempt to blow up the Houses of Parliament, is a direct consequence of Louis's victories against the Dutch. The perjurers concerned are a group of worthless renegades who wish to whip up hysteria against the King's brother and successor to the throne, James, the Duke of York. Invasion and the overthrow of the church establishment are the twin aspects of the hysteria, the whole thing orchestrated by Shaftesbury and his supporters. The Popish Plot is most associated in the public mind with that reprehensible character Titus Oates, an ex-Jesuit student from the English College at Valladolid, Spain. Its greatest martyr is the Irishman, Archbishop of Armagh Oliver Plunkett, scion of the noble Old English family of Plunkett in the Pale, who suffers torture and execution in 1681 following conviction for planning to introduce the French into Ireland and kill all the Protestants. The North is said to be the landing place, but at his trial Plunkett protests vehemently that the northern coast would make a most unsuitable landing place for an invasion of Ireland.

Orrery now reverts to the persona of Protestant frontiersman confronted by Catholic insurrection in Munster. And it is Orrery rather than the moderate Lord Lieutenant Ormonde who institutes fresh searches for Catholic bishops and regular clergy, with a view to their expulsion. Ormonde

---

126 *Hist. Mss. Commission* 1906, Calendar of Mss. of the Marquess of Ormond preserved at Kilkenny Castle. Earl of Orrery, Castlemartyr, to Edward Denny, 28 January 1678.

is compelled to go along by arranging for a new militia, which Orrery suggests might include "Sir Philip Perceval, Lord Kingston, Edward Denny, etc."; its task, says Orrery, will be "to detect Titulars and Regulars who will not quit the kingdom, and those who have arms concealed after the day limited to bring them in".[127]

We have heard much of Sir William Petty. A look at the family of his land agent, Orpen, reveals an interesting connection with the court of Charles II. Charles earned the title the "Merrie Monarch" for the dissolute character of his court. One of his own mistresses, Barbara Palmer, was the wife of Roger Palmer, Earl of Castlemaine; his brother is very probably the Rev. Palmer whose daughter married the first Orpen, ancestor of the historian Goddard Orpen of Ardtully, Kenmare. Remaining in South Kerry, and anticipating events by a century or more, the famous actress Mrs Jordan of the turn of the nineteenth century is of the family of Bland, of Derryquin (Sneem). The first of the Blands, a clergyman, settles in Kerry when he is presented to Killarney 1692, having arrived in Ireland as chaplain to the Lord Lieutenant and selected Killarney for its proximity to the estates of his father-in-law, Sir Francis Brewster. Mrs Jordan will become the mistress of the Duke of Clarence, later King William IV, with whom she will have many children, all bearing the surname FitzClarence.

---

127 Ibid. Orrery, Castlemartyr, to Ormond, 19 November 1678.

Kerry and the Jacobite Wars

"This is indeed a country worth fighting for!"
King William of Orange

"For on far foreign fields from Berlin to Belgrade
Lie the soldiers and chiefs of the Irish Brigade"

Thomas Davis, *The Battle Eve of the Brigade*

James II ascends the throne: Tyrconnell's Policies impact
Petty's plantation in Kerry

If Charles's Restoration proved a mixed bag for Kerrymen,
particularly for those who fought and died and suffered
confiscation for his father, worse is to come when Charles's
brother James succeeds to the throne. Almost immediately
there are heaves against him, and they culminate in the arrival
of his successor William of Orange at Torbay in 1688. The civil
war that follows engulfs Ireland.

The wider European context must be kept in view. The
war that accompanies James's accession is the War of the League
of Augsburg.[128] The League in question is formed in 1686 to
curb the imperial designs of Louis XIV. Those designs, and
the hopes of the Irish, are dashed when the forces of Louis's
enemy, William of Orange, are triumphant at Derry, the Boyne,
Aughrim and Limerick. The war ends formally in 1697, but the
major exodus of our Wild Geese to the Continent is already
under way. There will be a short lull for a few years, then it is
back to war again over Louis' plans to place his grandson on
the throne of Spain.

Let us recover the course of events. James II comes to
the throne in 1685 having survived an attempt to exclude him
in the hysteria that followed the Popish Plot. In one of the great
mysteries of English history he appears to set out deliberately to
alienate the English people. While still the heir to his brother
he has taken as his second wife Mary of Modena, the marriage
that produces the Catholic claimant to the throne (known
later as the *Pretender*) and disappoints the succession hopes
of his adult daughters Mary and Anne. Installed as king, he
adheres to the alliance with France, the country of his mother
Henrietta Maria. The Duke of Monmouth (illegitimate son
of the late king, Charles) leads an insurrection in England's
West Country which is defeated at the Battle of Sedgemoor and
ruthlessly suppressed. James shows no mercy, despite the pleas
of his own supporters. The "Bloody Assizes" after Sedgemoor
create an enduring horror in the minds of Englishmen and
deepen disillusion with the rule of James. Monmouth is turned
off on Tower Green, and even his execution is botched by the
axe man.

James's Irish policy proves a disaster for the Cromwellian
settlement and the follow-up settlement of Charles. He appoints
Catholic Richard Talbot as head of the Irish army. This is
"Fighting Dick" Talbot (to his enemies, "Lying Dick Talbot"),
later the Earl of Tyrconnell. He is the supreme Irish Jacobite,
overshadowing Limerick's Sarsfield in our story. Tyrconnell
used to be a member of the Stuart entourage in exile during

128 The *War of Two Kings*, has also been used, and the *War of Three Kings*.

Cromwell's rule, all the time hatching plots against the life of
Cromwell. The Irish Protestants hated him even then as a secret
agent working against the landed settlement (and they knew
his reputation as a philanderer among the ladies of the exiled
court). He gained the ear of Charles to the detriment of the
moderate Ormonde, with two principal effects after Charles's
Restoration: Tyrconnell becomes the leading advocate of the
restoration of estates to the Irish, and of the restoration of
Catholicism as official policy.[129]

Richard Talbot, Duke of Tyrconnell, after Rigaud
(courtesy National Gallery of Ireland)

129 Tyrconnell's family, the Talbots of Malahide, have a branch in the Talbots of
Mount Talbot, Co. Roscommon. In the Restoration period they intermarry
with the very Jacobite family of Dillon, of Costello-Gallen, who are present
with King James at the Boyne and found the regiment of Dillon, part of the
Irish Brigade. The marriage in 1775 of William John Talbot of Mount Talbot
to Lady Anne Crosbie of Ardfert will bring the Talbots to Ardfert when their
son Rev. John Talbot inherits Ardfert from his uncle Lord Glandore in 1815
and changes his name to Talbot-Crosbie.

Under James, Tyrconnell is appointed commander of the army in Ireland, and he embarks immediately on a purge of Protestants from the officer ranks. In late 1686 James withdraws the lord deputy, Clarendon, and puts Tyrconnell in his place. Tyrconnell begins to remove Protestant judges, replacing them with the likes of Sir Stephen Rice who is made Chief Baron of the Exchequer. Sir Stephen Rice becomes one of the leading figures in the promotion of James's Irish policies. One of the Dingle Rices, his grand-father (also Stephen, m Helen Trant) represented Kerry in King James's Irish Parliament of 1613. The well-known Bishop King describes Sir Stephen, as "most signal for his inveteracy against the Protestant interest and settlement of Ireland, having been often heard to say, before becoming a judge, that he would 'drive a coach and six horses through the act of settlement', upon which both depended".[130] Rice, with Nugent and Nagle make a famous visit to London in 1688 to obtain the King's permission to overturn the landed settlement – without success. They make a singular impression on the London populace who chant "Make way for the Irish ambassadors".

Tyrconnell's policies have begun to have a catastrophic impact on Sir William Petty's plantation at Kenmare, of which the most memorable incident is the attack at the White House of Killowen. Petty planted a colony at Kenmare about 1670 where he invested much time and resources in iron works and the fishing of herring, pilchard, mackerel and salmon. His agent is the Rev. Thomas Palmer, ably assisted by Palmer's son-in-law Richard Orpen. A "general calamity" descends on the colony in 1685,[131] after which the colonists find themselves "in condition of the persecuted Huguenots of France". They crowd into the agent's house at Killowen (the about-to-be infamous "White House of Killowen") and commence to build a "clod wall four foot in height" all around. Appeals for relief are sent to Tyrconnell's President of Munster, Justin MacCarthy, and to Valentine Browne, the Governor of Kerry, and they settle down to wait for their saviour King William to land in the south of Ireland. The stand-off continues as the crisis mounts to the day in February 1689 when the disarming of the Protestants of Ireland is decreed. The Kenmare settlers manage to escape by ship, but even then they encounter some more bad luck: their sails are taken and they have to pay a ransom of £5000 to get them back. They sail to Bristol.

130 Timothy P. O'Neill, "The Rices of Mountrice: solicitors' records of an epigonal family", in *Journal of the Kildare Archaeological Society*, vol. 18, part 3, 1996-7, pp.351-366, p.352.

131 J.F. Fuller, F.S.A. "An Exact Relation of the Persecution, Robberies and Losses sustained by the Protestants of Killmare in Ireland, 1689", in the *Journal of the Cork Historical and Archaeological Society*, July-September 1903, 175-189, p.176.

"Dutch William" arrives in England; Kerry MPs prepare for the Jacobite Parliament of 1689

William is invited to assume the throne and rescue England and Ireland from James (a case of Where Monmouth has failed the Dutchman will succeed). William arrives at Torbay (Devon) in 1688. Even now many Englishmen favour a resolution under which William can be designated Regent, to succeed James. But James flees to France to organise resistance, and so is deemed to have resigned the throne. Some months later, in March 1689, he lands at Kinsale from Brest to fight for his throne in Ireland. He is accompanied by the Kerrymen Sir Stephen Rice and Roger MacElligott. James makes Lord Clare (O'Brien) a viscount, and Talbot, Earl of Tyrconnel since 1685, takes another step in the peerage when James makes him Duke of Tyrconnell.

The temporary ascendancy of Kerry's Jacobites is clear from the MPs elected to King James' Jacobite (Patriot) Parliament held in May 1689, summoned after James's arrival at Kinsale. Three cousins of Kerry are prominent in both Parliament and the military. One is Sir Thomas Crosbie (son of Col. David who guarded Ballingarry, and created a baronet by Ormonde); the other two, Roger MacElligott and Cornelius MacGillycuddy, are returned for Crosbie's borough of Ardfert.[132] Sir Thomas himself and Nicholas Browne are MPs for the county, a Hussey represents Tralee and a Rice Dingle.[133] Roger MacElligott has strengthened the Jacobite alliance by his marriage to a daughter of the Knight of Kerry and Dame Honora O'Brien.

While James still held the throne in England, MacElligott commanded one of the Irish battalions brought over from Ireland to shore up James's power. The adventure did MacElligott's reputation no favours: soldiers under MacElligott's command wrecked the town of Portsmouth, robbing and drinking and beating up the inhabitants and causing a riot when one of them fired a shot into a Protestant church.[134] Now MacElligott prepares to take his seat in James's Patriot Parliament.

---

132 Burke's *Irish Families* (London 1976), Crosbie; Maurice G. McElligott, "Some Kerry Wild Geese" in *The Irish Genealogist*, vol.2, no.8, Oct. 1950, pp. 250-255.

133 All record of the Jacobite Parliament of James II is excised from the *Journals of the Irish House of Commons.* However, the attendance is preserved in William King, *The State of the Protestants of Ireland under the Late King James's Government* (London 1691).

134 J.G. Simms, *Jacobite Ireland* (Dublin 1969, reprint 2000), p. 46; MacElligott is later commended for the good order of his men's departure after the defeat at the Boyne.

The Jacobite Parliament reverses the Act of Settlement, then passes an Act of Attainder containing a list of named individuals who have fled the country and are deemed to have assisted the "most horrid invasion ... made by your unnatural enemy the Prince of Orange ... being persons who have notoriously joined in the said rebellion and invasion ...".[135] On the list are the great Kerry names of the Cromwellian plantation, together with the unrepentant family of Blennerhassett from the Munster plantation of Elizabeth's time: Robert Blennerhassett and his son John "of Killorglin, alias Castle Conway"; John's first-cousin and namesake John Blennerhassett of Ballyseedy, is there, together with Morris of Ballybeggan, Gun of Rathoe, Orpens, Taylor, Ponsonby, Collis, Palmer, Raymond of Ballyloghrane, Barry Denny of Barrow, Pierce Crosbie and his son Patrick, Staughton, and Wilson, "all late of the county of Kerry".[136]

Some historians have argued great malice behind the enactments of the Patriot Parliament. But William Lecky reminds us that not a single name of those listed for attainder and forfeiture is ever executed; and of course the arrival of William in Ireland and his subsequent Irish victories overturn everything decided by the Patriots.

To conserve Jacobite control of Kerry, Valentine Browne (Viscount Kenmare), is designated "Lieutenant of our County of Kerry" and Sir Thomas Crosbie, Stephen Rice and Richard Cantillon are made commissioners of array for a county militia, with the task "immediately to array and enlist the number of 50 horsemen and 300 foot soldiers, well appointed and fitted for the safetie of this our Kingdom, and for the resisting, opposing and destroying our enemies and rebels ...".[137]

Those families which suffer outlawry at the hands of the Patriot Parliament will live out the Williamite triumph for a century or more to come. So we do well to get to know some of them here. One is John Blennerhassett of Killorglin, the famous "Black Jack", who spends his later years writing the Blennerhassett genealogy. He is son of Robert (also on the list of outlaws) and his wife Avice Conway from the family of the original owners of the Killorglin seignory. Black Jack is "one of eight Kerry gentlemen who supported King William III ... (and was) captured in March 1688 while trying to join Lord Kingston at Sligo with 200 others and imprisoned for fourteen months at Galway and then at Dublin under sentence of death". Jack was on his way to welcome Schomberg and King William, both of whom separately landed in the North East. He is released

---

135 King, *State of the Protestants of Ireland*, Appendix p. 241.
136 *State of the Protestants of Ireland*, Appendix p. 251.
137 M.A. Hickson, *Old Kerry Records*, series 2, p.24-5. King James's warrant, dated 27 July 1689.

from his prison in 1690.[138]

Over in Tralee, in the spring of 1689, another John Blennerhassett entrusts "east and west Ballyseedy" to the care of MacCarthy Mór. This cousin of his namesake "Black Jack" appears to have an understanding with his enemy Charles MacCarthy, nephew of the Florence who took the surrender of the Blennerhassett castle of Ballycarty from his grandfather back in 1641; Blennerhassett can quietly leave Ballyseedy and return later when the victory of the Williamites is assured. He lives to 1709.[139] The facilitating of John Blennerhassett by Charles MacCarthy Mór shows how one family with Williamite sympathies can understand the opposing sympathies of its Jacobite neighbours, a foretaste of the amicable relations characteristic of both sides after the civil war in the new century. Charles MacCarthy Mór also departs Kerry: when Schomberg arrives at Carrickfergus he is confronted by MacCarthy Mór as one of the commanders of James's garrison in the castle there.

William wins the Battle of the Boyne on 1 July 1690, but his army is foiled at the siege of Limerick (whose walls are said to be so dilapidated that they could be destroyed with roasted apples) when a siege train is intercepted and blown up. In September Roger MacElligott is compelled to surrender Cork to Lord Marlborough (John Churchill), after which MacElligott is brought to the Tower of London, where he remains until the end of the war (after release he goes to the Irish Brigade in Europe). From Cork the Irish fall back to Limerick which is invested by William. The *Journal* of John Stevens[140] informs us that on Saturday 4 October 1690 Brigadier Col. Denis MacGillycuddy and Lord Kenmare's Regiment of Foot "marched out of Limerick towards the county of Kerry". Near the end of that year King William orders attacks on the Irish positions in Kerry in order to pressure the leadership at Limerick to negotiate a settlement. The result is an attack on Kerry in January 1691 by the Danes under the leadership of Major General Tettau who pursues the Irish to Ross Castle which, without the support of heavy guns, he fails to take.

William will ensure victory in Ireland at the Battle of Aughrim (near Ballinasloe, Galway, July 1691), and the second siege of Limerick. What appears a second attack on Kerry is launched in August under commander (Brigadier?) Levison who enters again from the north at the head of seven hundred

138 *Burke's Irish Family Records*, 1976.
139 Russell McMorran, "Ballyseedy Wood", in *The Kerry Magazine*, 1991;
    McMorran and Maurice O'Keeffe, *A Pictorial History of Tralee* (Tralee 2005),
    p. 49.
140 *Journal of John Stevens containing a Brief account of the War in Ireland 1689-91*
    (ed. The Rev. Robert H. Murray, Litt.D. Oxford Clarendon Press 1912,
    p.187).

horse. He is quickly joined by David Crosbie and opposed by, among others, Sir James Cotter at the head of a troop of dragoons.[141] Cotter has been appointed brigadier in command of the Jacobite forces in Kerry on 9 April.

Sir James Cotter enters our story again. We have seen how after the previous war Cotter helped run down some of the regicides in Switzerland and assassinate one of them. As the present war approaches its end, with Limerick again under siege and the tide now clearly favouring the Williamites, Sir Edward Denny departs Tralee; and his lady, Mary Maynard, is left to answer to Cotter and the Jacobites. They regard her husband as a turncoat, and despite giving an undertaking not to do harm, they proceed to torch the town. The deed is recorded in the Denny Bible:

> "The second of September 1691 the Mansion House, the Castell of Tralee, the seat of that worthy and loyal gentleman Edward Denny, Esq., was burnd by Coll. Ruth, by order of Sir James Cotter, Knight, who was the Governor of this county Kerry, after he had received a good sum from Madam Denny to save it, and engaged his hand and faith to the performance, butt not like a gentleman broke his engagement."

But Limerick has fallen by now, so Cotter receives orders from Tesse, the French commander in Limerick, to observe a cessation of hostilities: the negotiations for a Treaty at Limerick are about to get under way. Kerry is yielded up to the Williamites, and a militia is immediately arrayed to secure the county against a Jacobite insurrection. Lady Denny intercedes to save the lives of those apprehended for the burning of the town, and the Bill for the reconstruction of Tralee Castle is paid by the Irish Parliament.

At the side of James at the Boyne are the leading Kerry Jacobite families: Browne (Lord Kenmare), Maurice FitzGerald (Knight of Kerry), Roger McElligott, as well as Daniel O'Brien, 3rd Viscount Clare, brother-in-law of the Knight of Kerry. The forfeiture of the Kenmare estate does not extend beyond the life of King James's Viscount, Valentine, whose heir, Nicholas, obtains the reversion in 1700. Viscount Clare hails from across the mouth of the Shannon at Carrigaholt, but he has extensive landed interests in the north of Kerry around Tarbert. Under the Treaty of Limerick he is outlawed and forfeits all of his estates, those of Tarbert passing to the Williamite family of Leslie.[142] He departs for Europe to lead the Regiment of Clare as part of the famous Irish Brigade. Better fortune smiles on Clare's nephew, the Knight of Kerry: this Maurice FitzGerald

141 *The Kerry Magazine*, 1 October 1854, p.146.
142 Denis and Josephine Holly, *Tarbert on the Shannon* (Ballyshannon 1981), p. 28.

is a very young soldier of the army of James at the Boyne, and the family tradition has it that when he is brought before his captors they take his youth into consideration. The family estates are returned to him, and in 1703 he converts to the Protestant faith when he marries Elizabeth Crosbie of Ardfert. Their son is the Robert FitzGerald, barrister and MP Dingle, who from the 1750s is active in early efforts to dismantle the Penal Laws imposed on Irish Catholics after the Boyne.

Roger MacElligott forfeits likewise, but a career in Europe awaits him at the head of one of the Irish regiments, to continue the war and attempt to restore James to the throne. His two cousins are spared forfeiture: their estates are returned to Sir Thomas Crosbie and Capt. Cornelius MacGillycuddy under the articles of the Treaty of Limerick.

This has been a civil war on a huge scale on the two islands, equalling the great civil wars of the 1640s and presenting the same difficult dilemmas to our leading families. The feeling is inescapable that the leading Gaelic and Old English – MacGillycuddy, Browne (Kenmare), the Knight of Kerry (FitzGerald) and MacCarthy Mór – were forced by events on to the side of James, that their preference was the Ormandite compromise arrangements, rather than the politics of Tyrconnell so similar to the Rinuccini extremism of the 1640s. On the other hand, it is doubtful if the likes of O'Sullivan Mór in South Kerry or the O'Briens of Carrigaholt were amenable to compromise. Even Marlborough, who took the surrender of Cork from Roger MacElligott, wavered for years, and only his splendid victories in the next European war guarantee the Williamite succession against the son of James (the Pretender) supported by Louis. Our leading Kerry families chose the losing side, the side of a monarch sponsored by his cousin Louis who has similar dictatorial tendencies and who presides over a court so promiscuous and profligate that he helps sow the seeds of the French Revolution.

We end with a look at what happens to Orrery's mansion in Charleville. When the Jacobite commander, the Duke of Berwick, one of James's illegitimate sons (child of his liaison with Marlborough's sister Arabella Churchill), arrives in the South, he dines at Orrery's mansion. Then he has it burnt to the ground. It is October 1690.

Strengthening the Penal Code as Kerry's
"Wild Geese" depart

The Treaty of Limerick follows the fall of that city to the army of William. It marks the end of the Williamite/Jacobite wars in Ireland. King James has escaped from the Boyne before reaching Duncannon Fort in South Wexford where a ship, captained by Sir Patrick Trant of Dingle, takes him into exile in France, the guest of Louis.

The Penal Code against Catholics is now strengthened. The first of the laws is the Act of 1691 (3 William and Mary c. 2, passed by the English Parliament), under the terms of which Catholics are excluded from Parliament, civic office and the legal profession, and commissions in the army and navy; the instrument of exclusion is the Oath against Transubstantiation and the Pope's power to depose monarchs. This is the Oath taken by the burgess men of Tralee on election to the Denny corporation.[143] Now to the Irish Parliament. The first of its Penal Laws (1695) forbids Catholic education at home or abroad, the carrying of arms or owning a horse worth £5. The Banishment of Religious Act of 1697, a direct attack on ecclesiastics and regular clergy, comes into force in May 1698. Franciscans take the decision to obey the Act in principle, taking goods into safe keeping and sending novices to the continent, while seeking permission for the old and infirm friars to remain in Ireland.[144]

The foundation of the Irish Brigade in France is laid by the three Irish regiments who go to France in the spring of 1690 *before* the Boyne and Limerick: O'Brien's (known later as Clare's), Dillon's (Viscount Dillon. from Mayo) and Lord Mountcashel's (Justin, son of Donough, Lord Muskerry, who defended Kerry and Ross Caslte). When he arrives in France, Mountcashel is appointed overall commander of what will become known as the Irish Brigade. The Regiment of Lord Clare includes a high Kerry representation – not surprising in view of Clare's (O'Brien) marriage link with the knights of Kerry and Clare's landholding in the Tarbert district.

The Brigade is augmented ammediately from October 1691, after the Treaty of Limerick, by a huge exodus of approximately 19,000 Irish soldiers transported down the Shannon by the fleet of Chateaurenaud. The colonelcy of the individual regiments will remain with the founding families, each successive generation supplying the colonel proprietor.

Our departing Irish fulfil their desire to serve in

---

143 Reproduced in *Kerry Evening Post* of 20 June 1888; see transcription of 3 William and Mary c. 2 in Maureen Wall, "The Age of the Penal Laws" in T.W. Moody and F.X. Martin, *The Course of Irish History* (Cork 1967), p. 219.
144 Patrick Conlan OFM, *Franciscan Ireland*, p.39.

the armies of Louis, in the era when France excels in the profession of arms before all of Europe. Yet, they offer their services to Louis at a time of great division among Christian powers, indeed a time when the might of Louis is invariably opposed to those monarchies contending with the advance of Islam. Louis was absent when the Poles saved Europe from the Turks advancing from the Balkans. In Poland, Bernard Connor from North Kerry has become physician to Poland's king, Ian Sobieski. Ian Sobieski relieved Vienna of the Turkish siege in 1683, enabling the Emperor of Austria to reconquer the plains of Hungary. "In the same year that O'Connor wrote his *History of Poland*, Sobieski's death (1696) opened the grave of her glory", wrote Thomas D'Arcy Magee (of Young Ireland, below).[145] The undermining of Poland's campaign, and the consequent exposure of Europe to the Muslim threat from the Balkans, owes much to the policies of King Louis, against whom England helped form the League of Augsburg in 1686. And most of Kerry's exiled serve, not Poland or the Emperor, but Louis. The grand-daughter of the saviour of Europe, Clementina Sobieska, will become the wife of the Old Pretender, son of Mary of Modena and James II. Their son is the famous Charles Edward Stuart, "Bonnie Prince Charlie". The cause of the Pretenders is the overthrow the monarchy of the Georges and the restoration of the Stuarts to the throne of Britain and Ireland. The wisdom of Kerrymen's participation in the Pretender's project, and their continued participation in the wars of France, will be the subject of increased soul searching as the new century grows old. We need only consider the fate of the gentle Palatine people at the hands of Louis, who, for being German and Lutheran, are driven out of their homes after Louis's forces attack the Palatinate in 1689; they will arrive as refugees in Ireland in 1709, and some will settle in Kerry.

---

145 Thomas D'Arcy Magee, *The Irish Writers of the Seventeenth Century* (Dublin 1846).

The Eighteenth Century

"She did not die; but she lived to feel, without exhaustion,
all the agony of dissolution; to be the spectatrix of her own
funeral, and the conscious inhabitant of her own sepulchre"
John Philpot Curran to Edmund Burke, 1795

"The Brightness of Brightness,
I met upon the way in loneliness; Crystal of crystal in
her grey-fleckt blue eye shining;
Sweetness of sweetness in her voice without repining;
Redness and whiteness in glowing cheeks were blending…"
Aoghán Ó Raghaile, 1670-1726

"I bequeath and leave … five pounds to the Guardian and
friars of Irrelagh Abbey for praying for my soul; which legacy
I leave to my son, Cornelius, to discharge"

Will of Col. Donogh MacGillycuddy
(of the Confederate War, obit.1696),
Kerry Evening Post, 17 May 1893

The Dispossessed, the Poets and the Rapparees

Readers of eighteenth-century literature and folklore know the desolation that overwhelms Ireland in the aftermath of the Boyne and Limerick, and how feelings remain raw through the course of the eighteenth century. The defeated find a voice in the extraordinary output of poet Aoghán Ó Raghaile (c.1670-1726) from Sliabh Luachra, the semi-mythical and indeterminate region east and north-east of Killarney. Ó Raghaile's life has witnessed a trilogy of defeats – Cromwell and Kinsale preceding the Boyne/Aughrim/Limerick. He laments the loss of his MacCarthy patrons, occasionally hurling defiance at the new planters, and he writes vision poems (*aisling*) looking forward to the coming of the Pretender – a second Stuart Restoration.[146]

Ó Raghaile's patrons were the MacCarthys, and latterly the Kenmares.[147] He planned, we think, to be a *file* (poet) to the MacCarthys ("The princes my forbears served before Christ died"), writing the classical syllabic metres of the bards which only the scholars could understand. But his world has changed, and his poetry changed with it, and now he has to write the songs of the people. With the Big House gone, and the planter's hospitality not up to scratch, he becomes the first of those poets of poverty:

> "My heart is withered and my health is gone,
> For they who were not easy put upon,
> Masters of mirth and of fair clemency,
> Masters of wealth and gentle charity,
> They are all gone. MacCaura Mor is dead,
> MacCaura of the Lee is finished;
> MacCaura of Kanturk joined clay to clay
> And gat him gone, and bides as deep as they."[148]

But it is an honourable poverty, and he dreams of a return of the Stuarts who as Scottish kings are descended from the Gaels of Ulster and can unify Ireland as never before. The poet's heart lifts at the prospect: "The Brightness of Brightness, I met upon the way in loneliness ...".

Many of the dispossessed become the rapparees of Irish song and legend, some of them having enjoyed a fleeting career as members of the James's Parliament – if we

---

146 The subject of the Aisling is Ireland as the abandoned female who asks of her hero the redress of her wrongs.
147 When a connection of Ormonde (Honora Butler of Kilcash) marries the third viscount Kenmare, Ó Raghaile marks the occasion with a poem: *Epitalamium do Tuighearna Chinn Mara.*
148 Translated by James Stephens.

are to believe their detractors. Kerry schoolmaster and diarist Humphrey O'Sullivan placed the rapparees' origins in earlier times:

> "These rapparees were poor Irishmen who were plundered by James I, King of England, by Oliver Cromwell and by William of Orange. They used to fight with *ropairí* or short spears, and it was from the word ropaire that they got their name."[149]

The government passes anti-tory legislation in 1703 and 1707 to tackle vagrancy and French recruitment, aimed against:

> "tories, robbers and rapparees ... all loose, idle, vagrants, and such as pretend to be Irish gentlemen, and will not work nor take themselves to any honest trade or livelihood, but wander about demanding victuals, and coshering from house to house amongst their fosterers, followers and others".

What is to be done? They are "to be sent ... on board her Majesty's fleet or to some of her majesty's plantations in America". A separate clause attempts to deter, against "Papists of this kingdom (who) do frequently keep private intelligence with the French and other enemies to her Majesty and her kingdoms (on account of which) several parts of the sea-coasts are infested and often insulted by French privateers, chiefly manned by Irish papists". The legislation provides that, "A presentment may be made at the assizes for the compensation paid out by grand juries, which will be recouped by the Popish inhabitants of the area".[150]

Famous rapparees include Eamon an Chnoic (Ned of the Hills, Upperchurch, Co. Tipperary), a comrade of "Galloping Hogan" who acted the scout for those who blew up the siege train during the first siege of Limerick. The most blood-thirsty rapparees are to be found in the region of Glenflesk, just east of Killarney, territory of O'Donoghue. William, son of Sir Francis Brewster, sometime Lord Mayor of Dublin, has bought a large estate in Glenflesk, but finds no peace there. In late 1696 this William Brewster is attacked at his house by a mob of about 500 under O'Donoghue's command. O'Donoghue proceeds to strangle Brewster "with my cravat and his Irish thumbs ... forcing blood out of my ears".[151] William Brewster's sister Lucy has married Rev. James Bland, later Archdeacon of Limerick and Dean of Ardfert; Bland has arrived in Ireland as chaplain to the Lord Lieutenant and he has chosen

---

149 *The Diary of Humphrey O'Sullivan – Amhlaoibh O Sullleabhain - 1827-1831*, ed. Tomas de Bhaldraithe, Mercier 1979, p.23.
150 2 Anne, c. 13 (1703), 6 Anne, c.11 (1707)
151 Brian de Breffny, "Brewster of Kerry", *The Irish Ancestor 1971*; Sir Wm. Trumbull to the Lords Justice, 10 Nov.1696, in Eamonn O Ciardha, *Ireland and the Jacobite Cause, 1685-1766, A Fatal Attachment* (Dublin 2002), pp. 91-2.

Killarney as his parish; he arrives there in the same year as the attack by O'Donoghue on his (Bland's) brother-in-law Brewster.[152]

The family of O'Connnell from the very south of Kerry becomes connected with the Black O'Donoghues of Glenflesk: Máire ní Dhuibh (Black Mary) O'Donoghue, is grandmother of the Liberator, Daniel O'Connell; that lady's father, Daniel O'Mahony of Dunloe, is "the great and terrible Papist who ruled South Kerry with his four thousand followers", to quote Froude.[153] What happened was that on the vast Petty estate in the South, the Grand Leases of 1696 – perpetuity grants – were given to some of the leading tenants after Petty's death, and one of these was O'Mahony of Dunloe, who seems to have turned his tenants into a gang of desperadoes. How precarious is the grip of government we infer from a note written by the governor of Ross Castle some years later:

> "There are several Irish gentlemen that live near this place who have refused the oath are imprisoned at Trally, such as Sir Nicholas Browne, called Lord Kenmare, Colonel Maurice Hussey, and his two sons, MacCarthy Mór and others, who are very poor ... I shall be very glad to find that effectual care is taken to repair this place and some stores put in here, which is a matter of greatest importance for securing the Protestants and keeping a footing in the country ... Some Irish gentlemen have very freely taken the oath, and others will, but the proprietors and idle persons and such as served King James and are entirely disposed to assist the Pretender or any Popish interest, or take any feasible opportunity of rebellion ..."[154]

A Williamite in Tralee:
Letitia Coningsby as Lady Denny

How completely different is urban Kerry from the haunts of Aoghán Ó Raghaile, and how complete the change in the parliamentary representation as the victors fill the seats in the Protestant Parliament – where Catholics will be excluded until Catholic Emancipation over a century later.

The general election of 1692[155] – the year a Jacobite invasion threatens these islands from the Netherlands – sees the great Whig families of Denny, Blennerhassett and FitzMaurice

152 "Old Kerry Records" in *Kerry Evening Post*, 27 April 1910; the descendants of the Blands will reside at Derryquin, near Sneem.

153 Mrs Morgan John O'Connell, *The Last Colonel of the Irish Brigadr*, 2 vols. (London 1892), vol. 1, p. 7.

154 Colonel Hedges to Secretary Dawson, Ross Castle, April 1708, quoted in M.A. Hickson, *Old Kerry Records*, Series 2, p. 117.

155 *Journals of the House of Commons*, amending *Kerry Evening Post* 15 July 1914.

make a clean sweep of the county and borough seats; and they and their network (Mullins making a first appearance for Dingle) will remain in charge for much of the century to come. Sir Edward (whose wife Mary Maynard was left alone with the Jacobites) becomes MP for the county in 1692 and '95; Sir Edward's cousin, John Blennerhassett of Ballyseedy (the one who quietly left the county after a peaceful transfer of Ballyseedy to Charles MacCarthy Mór), is returned for Tralee in 1692, later Dingle and Kerry. In 1692 the Petty interest is joined with the FitzMaurice by the marriage of Petty's daughter to Thomas FitzMaurice; FitzMaurice is returned MP for the county (his brother William returned at the same general election for Dingle). Thomas is a very brutish individual, if we are to believe the autobiography of his famous grandson, Prime Minister Shelburne, but his marriage takes his family decidedly into the government fold. The start is his creation as first Earl of Kerry. The honour necessitates his transfer to the Irish House of Lords, his seat in the House of Commons going safely to a member of the Cromwellian family of Sandes. The FitzMaurices will govern Kerry through the Penal era, Ross Castle the Governor's centre of operations.[156]

William FitzMaurice (1694-1747),
second Earl of Kerry, Governor of Kerry
(by Stephen Slaughter, private collection)

156 The Crosbies continue to be governed by their native Irish sympathies and the MacGillycuddy marriage alliance; however a daughter of Anne Petty marries Sir Maurice Crosbie.

A future Lady Denny arrives in Tralee in 1700 as the wife of Edward (son and heir of Sir Edward Denny and Mary Maynard). The bride is Letitia Coningsby, daughter of Sir Thomas Coningsby, author of the Treaty of Limerick. This autumn day the customary welcome given to a Denny, mainly the illumination of houses, helps everybody to consign the events of the siege to a distant corner of memory. Later in the night the Denny Bible is brought out and her arrival is carefully recorded beside the date, 3 October 1700:

> "She made hir entry with divers gentillmen of quality, and about 200 horse of the tennaunts, and Shee and hir husbund received with much joye in the Castill of Tralee by the father Coll: Edward Denny, and the mother Madam Denny and by all the noble relations."

The arrival of this fascinating lady, Conningsby's daughter ("my excellent mother-in-law" to the famous philanthropist Arabella FitzMaurice) marks an important change in Denny politics: from the courtier and then royalist, to clear association from this point with the Whig elite. Coningsby was the first to come to William's aid when the King was wounded in the shoulder by Jacobite gunners the day before the Boyne. He helped stanch the blood.[157] Later Coningsby wrote the military and civil articles of the Treaty of Limerick. In the first two decades of the new century he continues a powerful figure in the governments of London and Dublin, serving on both privy councils.

The Penal Code is further strengthened. The Banishment Act has impacted the ordinary Catholic clergy: "The Kerry parish priests registered by the government in 1704 were all middle-aged man, and as they died off no others were allowed to take their places ... unregistered priests were to be transported, and if they returned hanged". [158] It is 1720 before Fr Denis Moriarty is consecrate Bishop of Ardfert and Aghadoe (Kerry) – more than fifteen years after his nomination by the Pretender. Some reduction of the Act's severity is arranged by foreign intermediaries. The Pope – no friend to French power – intercedes with King William to lessen the impact of

---

157 The tradition of Coningsby helping to stanch the wound of William at the Boyne is repeated in the latest *DNB* ((Oxford 2004) where the Coningsby entry is from the pen of a Denny descendant Rev. Canon A.E. Stokes. Coningsby's mother was one of the Protestant Loftus family of Rathfarnham Castle, Dublin, and related by marriage to the descendants of Richard Boyle, Earl of Cork.

158 Jeremiah King, *History of Kerry, or History of the Parishes in the County,* 1908-14, pp. 278-9.

the Banishment Act, and receives a positive response.[159]

The project of anglicisation (begun seriously in Tudor times) can be renewed. Many of the old Gaelic placenames are replaced, for example Baile and Ghóilin with Burnham (the place of origin of the Mullins family), Tirnacush (Ir. Place of the Hollow) with Dicksgrove (of the Merediths), and Tullygarron with Chute Hall. More and more the O' will be dropped from the start of Irish surnames.

Emergence of a Kerry Convert constituency –
Reign of Queen Anne

It is one of the ironies of Irish history that the most systematic series of anti-Catholic laws is imposed during the era of Anne (1702-14), herself the daughter of a Stuart. The most infamous is "An Act to prevent the further growth of Popery" (2 Anne, 1703, c. 6), which provides that Catholics should be given leases of only thirty one years; the infamous gavel clause forces the subdivision of Catholic estates among the sons, with the additional refinement that if one son converts he is entitled to turn out the father. Two other Acts are the ban on Catholic schoolmasters (1709, 8 Anne c. 3, which also punishes the sending abroad of Catholic children for education), and we might mention here the removal of the vote from Catholics by the Act of 1727.

To some, strategic conversion to the Established Church is viewed a necessity after the exclusion of Catholics from the professions and Parliament, and as a means to allay the danger of estate subdivision under the gavel clause of the Popery Act of 1703. Sir Stephen Rice and two other advocates appeared before the bar of the Irish House of Commons to put the Catholic case for mitigation of the Popery Act,[160] yet Sir Stephen's sons, Edward and James, convert in 1716-7 and 1720.[161]

For those unwilling to convert, a common feature of the century is the "Friendly Discovery": a Protestant neighbour registers an estate in his own name but gives it back to its rightful owner. Hugh Falvey of Faha, near Killarney, is described as "the conforming kinsman who saved the property of the O'Connells, and, I rather think, of other Catholic families in Kerry".[162] The

---

159 Patrick Fagan, *Catholics in a Protestant Country, The Papist Constituency in Eighteenth-Century Dublin* (Dublin 1998), p. 56.
160 Fagan, *Catholics in a Protestant Country*, p. 58.
161 *The Convert Rolls*; the Rices do not appear to have converted in order to inherit their father's property: see Timothy P. O'Neill, "The Rices of Mountrice: solicitors' records of an epigonal family", in *Journal of the Kildare Archaeological Society*, vol. viii, part 3, 1996-97, pp.352-354, p. 354.
162 Mrs Morgan John O'Connell, *The Last Colonel of the Irish Brigadr*, vol. 1, pp. 53-6.

O'Connells seem always to have benefited from the protection of the Dennys, the knights of Kerry, and others of the old Kerry families;[163] near Tralee, Rev. John Day prevents the filing of a Bill of Discovery against land in Tonevane belonging to one Casey by himself filing one.[164]

The very old Donogh MacGillycuddy (whose will extract appears at the beginning of this chapter) ordered five pounds sterling be paid the friars at Muckross Abbey to pray for his soul. He it was who brought his family and the estate through the Williamite-Jacobite wars as through the wars of the 1640s. He and his sons fought for James, but his son and heir Cornelius, MP Ardfert, dies childless in 1712, then a generation (or more – the genealogists disagree) is skipped to find a successor, Denis. This MacGillycuddy marries Anne Blennerhassett in 1717 and converts to the Established Church in the following year. The bride is daughter of the very Williamite "Black Jack" Blennerhassett, one of the "Galway Prisoners of '(16)88' " who tried to escape to the North where the Protestant garrison prepared to resist King James.

When Denis and Anne's son and heir, Cornelius MacGillycuddy, contemplates marriage to a Catholic in 1743 a lawyer advises him as follows:

> "I am of opinion, yt you can't w'th safety marry a Papist. Such a marriage is attended with very many legal disabilities, such as to be deemed a Papist, unless the lady shall conform within ye year and day after ye marriage ...".

Cornelius heeds the advice and instead marries Catherine Chute in 1745.[165]

We remain in the Killarney district to look at the contrasting experiences of the two great houses there, the Kenmares and the Herberts. Valentine Browne, Lord Kenmare, grandson of James II's viscount, succeeds his father as third Viscount and makes alliance with the Catholic Butlers of Tipperary when he marries (1720) Honora Butler of Kilcash. But by then the marriage of a sister has got the Kenmare estate into a terrible state: she was brought up in England as a Protestant before marrying John Asgill, who is described by the editor of the Kenmare papers as one of the contemporary land sharks.[166] Due to the activities of Asgill, the estates are

163 O'Connell, *The Last Colonel of the Irish Brigade*, vol.1, p. 115.

164 *R.I.A.*, Day papers, ms. 12w9, Rev. Day to Charles Casey, 13 April 1769.

165 Brady, *The MacGillycuddy papers*, Mr Keatinge, lawyer, Dublin, 7 Jan. 1743, to Cornelius MacGillycuddy, p. 199.

166 MacLysaght, Edward, (ed.), *The Kenmare Manuscripts*, Irish Manuscripts Commission 1942, Introduction, x. Richard Hedges of Macroom is listed as another land shark.

encumbered with debt when the 3rd Viscount comes of age in 1716 (his father dying in exile four years later), and a special Act of Parliament is required in 1727 to sell parts of the estate (chiefly the woods of Bantry) to restore solvency.[167]

Valentine's other sister, Frances, appears more circumspect. Frances changes faith with her marriage in 1723 to Edward Herbert of Kilcow (Castleisland) and later Muckross. They become the first owners of Muckross. (Edward Herbert's father did not appear on the list of those attainted by the Parliament of James II.) Edward will win not only a bride from the Catholic Kenmares, but the estate of the MacCarthy Mór as well. He is "a dedicated farmer and an excellent manager", his prosperity over at Castleisland founded on a long tenancy under Lord Powis (Henry Arthur Herbert, of Oakley Park), lineal descendant of the Elizabethan planter in Kerry; but he yearns for land around the Killarney lakes.[168] Lord Kenmare's sister is certainly in love with him, if we are to believe their granddaughter:

> "Mr Herbert when young married the daughter of Lord Kenmare, a Roman Catholic lady, who exemplified the force of Love by going off with him privately, and marrying him against her religious prejudices, and against the injunctions of her only brother Lord Kenmare whom otherwise she so dearly loved that she lost her senses at his Lordship's death some years after, and never retrieved them to her own death."[169]

So, we may assume that Frances's support helps Edward's rise to real property and influence culminating in a seat in the English Parliament as MP for Ludlow (1754-70). He is part of an important property deal of 1733: the Castleisland estate of Lord Powis is leased for ever at a yearly rent of £1900, and a fine of £6000 on entering, to a group of leading Kerry landlords, including our Edward Herbert of Kilcow, Sir Maurice Crosbie of Ardfert and John Blennerhassett of Ballyseedy.[170] Next, the move to Muckross in the estate of the MacCarthy Mór, where in October 1735 wife Frances describes their abode as "a sad cabin" – though Edward has plans to build "a tolerable house".[171]

---

167 The recovery is credited to the efforts of Lord Kenmare's aunt Madame da Cunha; the forfeited estate was vested in the Chichester House Trustees; the claim of the child heir Nicholas was allowed, but Asgill bought a life interest.
168 Valeri Bary, "A Strange Account of the Last MacCarthy Mór", in *The Kerry Magazine*, 2002, p. 36.
169 *Retrospections of Dorothea Herbert 1770-1806* (London 1929-30, edn. 2004) p. 1.
170 *Registry of Deeds*, 14013393441 (date 1749); *House of Commons Journal*, vol. 5, p. 198 (date 1753).
171 Kenmare Papers, Frences Herbert to Kenmare, Muckross, 10 or 16 October 1735.

We look a generation ahead. Having probably underwritten many of MacCarthy Mór's debts, the families become united in marriage when a daughter of Edward and Frances marries Florence MacCarthy Mór. The MacCarthy Mór has converted to the Established Church, and when a son, Charles MacCarthy Mór, dies mysteriously on Putney Common in London in 1770 the entire MacCarthy estate transfers to the Herberts.

Maurice ("Hunting Cap") O'Connell of Derrynane once had an experience of Edward Herbert that left a sour taste - or so his nephew Daniel O'Connell later related. Daniel wrote how,

> "when the estate of 'Tomies on the Lake' was offered for sale, he ('Hunting Cap') agreed to purchase it... and that thereafter (our Edward Herbert) the ancestor of the present Mr Herbert sent him a communication to this effect, that if he (my uncle) became the purchaser, he (Mr Herbert) would immediately file a Bill of Discovery against my uncle and deprive him of the estate".

Here is no friendly discovery, but the real thing, Herbert, naturally enough, becoming the owner of the property.[172]

The O'Connells of Derrynane, as well-known smugglers, are no friends to the government in the person of the collector of excise. Yet their freedom to live in the old way is helped by the planter families, most of whom live in the North of the county. There is the well-known exchange between historian Charles Smith and Hunting Cap, when Smith, on a visit to Derrynane, stated his intention to write about the survival of the O'Connell estate. Hunting Cap asked him earnestly to not do so, so that he and his family might continue undisturbed outside the reach of the Penal Laws. In 1767 a jail break in Tralee by a band of notorious outlaws, the family of O'Connor "Laidir" (Ir. strong), leads to press allegations of Excise collusion with criminals, to the prejudice of the family of Derrynane. A letter from Kerry in the *Freeman's Journal* charges that this "gang of freebooters" has been "already reprieved at the request of the excise men, who suggested that they would make excellent spies in the business of the revenue"; there are plans to use them "on board the revenue cutter on the Kerry coast".[173]

---

172 Letter to the press, dated 19 November 1839, from Daniel O'Connell, reproduced in *Last Colonel of the Irish Brigade*, vol. 2, p., 269.
173 *Freeman's Journal*, 24-28 November 1767; for more of this see Mrs Morgan John O'Connell, *The Last Colonel of the Irish Brigade*, vol. 1, pp. 112-118.

War of the Spanish Succession (1701-1715)

Still in the reign of Anne, a colony of those Palatines who fled Louis arrives in Kerry in 1709. Some settle on the Southwell estate at Rathkeale, others on the Oliver estate around Kilfinane. A colony settles in North Kerry. They have names like Fizzel, Glaizier, Switzer, Benner, Heck, Young, Barkman, Delmege and Bovenizer:

> "In the year of seventeen hundred and nine/
> In came the brass-coloured Palatine/
> From the ancient banks of the Swabian Rhine."[174]

It is hoped that their settlement will assist the project of converting Ireland to Protestantism, at the same time improve living standards and agricultural practices. Arthur Young, the agriculturalist, encounters them when he visits the estate of Arthur Blennerhassett, near Tralee, during the second half of the century.

When the Palatines arrive the War of the Spanish Succession is in progress. This war is the upshot of another phase of foreign imperialism on the part of the king whose actions forced the Palatines to leave the Palatinate: Louis XIV. Americans know it as *Queen Ann's War*, a war that will occupy Kerry's Wild Geese and extend the Jacobite era to the middle of the eighteenth century.

The war begins in 1701. King James dies in exile that year, raising hopes that Louis will recognize William. No chance. Louis recognizes James's son by Queen Mary of Modena, a personage we know as the Old Pretender. What has this to do with the Spanish Succession? Only this: the Spanish king dies about the same time, and Louis gets involved in Spanish affairs just as he did in Irish, this time nominating his own grandson as the rightful heir to the Spanish throne; so Kerrymen will fight on a Spanish front (with the Duke of Berwick, the man who burned Orrery's mansion in Charleville, Co. Cork) as well as the better-known fronts in Germany and the Netherlands, and in the Italian satellite kingdoms of Spain and Austria.

The threatened invasion of Scotland by the Pretender in 1708 is said to have intensified Protestant fears, but the last four years of Queen Anne (1710-1714) bring the Tories back to power, and with them a soft-pedalling of Penal Law enforcement. Dean Jonathan Swift is working in London as a propagandist for the Tory government when he becomes well acquainted with Lord and Lady Kerry (Anne Petty and her brutish husband Tom FitzMaurice). They are residing at

174 rhyme collected by Patrick Weston Joyce of Glenosheen, Kilfinane, in
   Mainchin Seoighe, *The Joyce Brothers of Glenosheen* (Kilfinane 1987), p.5.

her brother Shelburne's house in Piccadilly. Swift's Journal to Stella concentrates on Anne:

> "We have struck up a mighty friendship, and she has much better sense than any other lady of your country. We are almost in love with one another; but she is most egregiously ugly, but perfectly well bred."[175]

In Kerry some admirers of the Tories begin to feel more comfortable. Sir Thomas Crosbie (the founder of the Ballyheigue line), MP in King James's Parliament, is said to be enlisting men for the Pretender, using the excuse that he is sending them to fight the Moors in North Africa; he refers to the Pretender as King James III. The Penal Code remains in force and invasion remains a threat. The accession of George I coincides with the Jacobite rebellion in Scotland of 1715, followed by the attempted invasion of Scotland by Ormonde in 1719. .

The Williamite colony around Tralee consolidates its position by intermarriage. Jane Denny, sister-in-law of Letitia Coningsby, marries the Blennerhassett heir at Ballyseedy. He is the "Great Colonel" John Blennerhassett who represents Tralee or Kerry in the Irish Parliament from the reign of Anne to the third George, becoming Father of the House. He must wield a huge political influence. Moving down a generation, in 1740 Thomas Denny, son of Sir Edward and Lady Letitia, marries his Blennerhassett first cousin, Agnes. Thomas's brother, Arthur, has already strengthened the colony by marriage (1725) to a granddaughter of the Cromwellian Petty: this lady is Arabella FitzMaurice, who becomes the well-known Dublin philanthropist Lady Denny after her husband Arthur, described as "a good sort of man", dies young in 1741. His young widow, Arabella, becomes the famous Dublin philanthropist Lady Denny, but before she goes to Dublin she helps raise her brother John FitzMaurice's small son at their father's house in Lixnaw; the old man is that brutish twenty-first Lord and first Earl of Kerry already met in these pages, while the little boy is the future prime-minister, Lord Shelburne, later the Marquess of Lansdowne.

A formal political expression is given to this family-political coalition in 1727 with a kind of sharing of the electoral cake. This *Indenture Tripartite* also brings in Sir Maurice Crosbie of Ardfert who is married to Anne FitzMaurice, sister of the young widow Arabella (Lady Denny). The compact will help avoid election polls together with their atmosphere of heightened excitement and the inevitable duels, thereby bringing to Kerry the kind of Hanoverian calm that prevails

175 Jonathan Swift, *Journal to Stlla*, 4 May 1711.

internationally. The leading figures of the family compact, the Great Colonel John Blennerhassett, already mentioned, and Sir Maurice Crosbie, began their parliamentary careers in the reign of Anne.

Lady Arabella Denny, by Hugh Douglas Hamilton, c. 1762. Resident of Blackrock, Co. Dublin, widow of Arthur Denny (d. 1742) of Tralee Castle, she founds the Magdalen Asylum in 1766 and is given the Freedom of the City. Her Tralee funeral in 1792 is remarkable for the keening of "twelve widows who each received two suits of black yearly and donations at festivals from her Ladyship since the death of Col Arthur, her husband" (K.E.P. 3 April 1909).

From the 1730s Kerry MPs sign up to the powerful "Munster Squadron" under parliamentary undertaker Henry Boyle, of Castlemartyr, Speaker of the House of Commons. Speaker Boyle is a member of the famous Boyle clan of Richard Boyle (Earl of Cork), and so we associate the Munster Squadron with the narrow Protestant nationalism of the eighteenth century. When Speaker Boyle and his followers raise the flag of Protestant patriotism in 1755 by refusing to agree London's "previous consent" to the disposal of the Irish budget surplus, the parties to the Indenture Tripartite give their enthusiastic support.

Kerrymen in the Irish Brigade

Before we consider the War of the Austrian Succession (1740-1745), we recall the two great military heroes of the previous conflict, the War of the Spanish Succession, on whom Europe depended to curb the expansion of France. One was Prince Eugene of Savoy, a soldier in the service of the Austrian empire with a distinguished record against the Balkan Turks. But the great victories are more associated with his ally Marlborough (John Churchill, who took Cork from Roger MacElligott), with our Irish Brigade usually on the losing side: Blenheim (1704), Ramillies (1706), Oudenarde (1708) and Malplaquet (1710).

Roger MacElligott of Ballymacelligott commanded one of the new regiments in the French service (created after the second great wave of Wild Geese departed at the end of the Irish wars), "of which rank and file generally was of Kerry origin".[176] MacElligott used to be Colonel in Clancarty's Regiment, which was largely composed of Kerry and Cork recruits, and he drew from Clancarty's to found his own Regiment. [177]

Daniel O'Mahony of Killarney was highly decorated by France. In 1702 he was at Cremona, a town in the north of Italy, where he led a successful resistance to Prince Eugene and the Austrian assault. As hero of the day "O'Mahony of Cremona" was selected to bring the news in to King Louis in Paris, where the King in person decorated him. A song commemorating the victory, "The day we beat the Germans at Cremona", began to be sung in Killarney.[178]

There are Kerrymen in the coalition that opposes the French. Many of the McElligotts will serve in the armies of Austria where they will be styled "Barons of Trughenackmy", after their native barony.[179]

---

176 Maurice G. McElligott, "Some Kerry Wild Geese" in *The Irish Genealogist*, vol.2, no.8, Oct. 1950, pp. 250-255, p. 251.
177 John Cornelius O'Callaghan, *History of the Irish Brigades in the Service of France* (1870), p. 140.
178 O'Callaghan, *Irish Brigades*, pp.204-217.
179 McElligott, "Some Kerry Wild Geese", p.252.

The Pretender, Austria: War of the Austrian Succession
(1740-1745)

Until the second half of the eighteenth century the support of the Pretender continues crucial to the survival of the Catholic Church in Ireland. It is the Pretender who nominates Denis Moriarty as Bishop of Ardfert and Aghadoe in 1705. Before nominations for appointment to the Irish hierarchy reach the Pretender, his advisers, such as Viscount Clare, vet the names, which are then forwarded to the Pope for the necessary papal brief. In the middle of the century, Dingle MP Robert FitzGerald is participating from Ireland in Pretender nominations – a very anomalous arrangement given FitzGerald's membership of the exclusively Protestant Parliament; however, as the grandson of Honora O'Brien (sister to Viscount Clare) he has a strong sense of his Jacobite heritage.

What Austria can offer is diplomatic intervention to achieve some mitigation of the Penal Laws. The War of the Austrian Succession (1740-1745) finds Britain in alliance with Catholic Austria. Britain and Austria are enemies of France, which positions Austria as a powerful intermediary with Britain on behalf of Ireland; Austria herself has a Protestant minority, so Britain is as much concerned for this minority as Austria for the welfare of her co-religionists in Ireland.

Robert FitzGerald (d. 1781),
Knight of Kerry
(courtesy Sir Adrian FitzGerald)

General John Sigismund Maguire, of Ballymacelligott and related to Roger MacElligott, serves with great distinction under the Austrian empire. Maguire's ancestor came to Kerry from the North at the outbreak of the 1641 rebellion, then married a MacElligott. Young Maguire followed his MacElligott kinsmen to Vienna and proceeded to make his name in the Austrian Succession and the Seven Year Wars. Field Marshal Ulysses Maxmilian Browne, originally from Camus, near Bruff in County Limerick, is in the Austrian service in time for the attack by Prussia on Silesia, and becomes a Count of the Holy Roman Empire.

The attack on Silesia by Frederick the Great of Prussia is the action which triggers the War of the Austrian Succession, and though the Austrian empire has exerted a tyrannical rule from Vienna over subject races in Bohemia and the Balkans, yet it is difficult to construe Frenderick's action as other than international aggression, aggression directed against the young heiress to the Austrian throne, Maria Theresa, and tearing up the agreement (the Pragmatic Sanction) drawn up to protect her succession. Britain quickly takes the young Queen's part and scores a famous victory at Dettingen in 1743 (King George himself in command). On the other side, the Irish Brigade wins a famous Irish victory at Fontenoy (in modern Belgium) in 1745 as part of the army of Marshal Saxe; prominent at Fontenoy is the Regiment of Clare which includes many Kerrymen.

In the same year as Fontenoy the Young Pretender (Bonnie Prince Charlie) launches his doomed invasion of Scotland and England. In reality, there is little enthusiasm in Kerry by 1745 for the Bonnie Prince Charlie's mission to restore the Stuarts, though when news arrives of his adventure, sentiment is probably divided. The Prince has set out from Rome to France, then on to the west coast of Scotland. Of the "Seven Men of Moidart" who accompany him, four are Irish, one being Col. John William O'Sullivan of South Kerry. This O'Sullivan went to Europe as a seminarian, before exchanging the soutane for the sword and service in the War of the Austrian Succession. The Scottish expedition proves a disaster: the insurrection is defeated when Bonnie Prince Charlie is defeated at Culloden in 1746. When all is lost it is O'Sullivan who grabs the bridle of this dazed master and forces him to leave the field. The Prince escapes to the Isle of Skye, assisted by Flora MacDonald, before making his way back to France. Bonnie Prince Charlie will appear once more a few years later - in London, of all places. He will show his face in one of the Jacobite taverns near the inns of court and the courts of law down near the River Thames. Then he will disappear for ever.

The European Enlightenment:
A Desire for Détente

"Was it for this the wild geese spread
The grey wing upon every tide ..."
W.B. Yeats, *September 1913*

Change in Continental Europe and in Kerry

Many of the old certainties are revisited and questioned in the era into which we now travel (say the third quarter of the eighteenth century), and part of the credit for this must be conceded to a movement known as the European Enlightenment, now entering its glory phase. There occurs a kind of détente in religious animosities and a reassessment of the Europe divided into two camps by the Reformation and Counter-Reformation. Coeval with the Enlightenment is the fall away of the Irish Brigade, leading to its eventual disbandment during the 1790s. The Continental colleges are reformed, making their activities less antagonistic to their host countries and to the Irish hierarchy, and more palatable to the British government; the new college in Paris, the Collège des Irlandais (built 1769-75), is symbolic of the change. The Irish cease to call for the restoration of the Stuarts, and the British begin to think of a more racially and religiously inclusive Empire. Poets, priests and schoolmasters reveal themselves openly in something called the Court of Poetry; the most beloved is the wandering poet, labourer (spailpín) and schoolmaster from Sliabh Luachra: Eoghan Rua Ó Suilleabhain.[180]

    Literature and philosophy have begun to reevaluate the importance of human emotions. Jean Jacques Rousseau's *Nouvelle Heloise* (1761) and *Emile* revisit and revaluate the importance of childhood and the upbringing of children. Oliver Goldsmith's *The Vicar of Wakefield* (1766), a tale of placid acceptance and charitable response in the midst of poverty and adversity, will occupy a place on the shelves of Kerry homes for centuries. Goldsmith's *Vicar* and his *Deserted Village* inspire the German lyric poet and dramatist Goethe who further popularises the genre with *The Sorrows of Young Werther* in which we find the central character reading the poems of *Ossian*, the pseudo-Gaelic romance written by Macpherson that swept the literary world in the 1760s. The bogus *Ossian* has at least convinced readers of the value of the Gaelic past as a souce for inspiration, meanwhile the suicide of the hero at the end of *Werther* prefigures the many incidents of early death among artists and the literati around the time of Napoleon – the Romantic age. The Romantic age may be a few years off, but the cracks have begun to appear in the world of classical learning founded on Latin and Greek, and in the world of the Baroque courts which played host to our generations of Wild Geese.

---

180 Eoghan Rua Ó Suilleabhain is said to have served under Rodney in one of the sea-encounters with the French in the Caribbean during the War of American Independence. Of courts of poetry, the most famous is that convened by poet and public house owner Seán Ó Tuama in the village of Croom on the Maigue river.

Leaders of the Enlightenment, such as Diderot and D'Alembert with their famous *Encyclopaedia*, promulgate a view of Catholicism as a hostile agent in society with a historically dysfunctional relationship with scientific discovery. Voltaire, the great French philosopher and historian, campaigns against the criminal code, which he associates with the Catholic Church, crowning his campaign when he forces a reinvestigation of the judicial murder of a man named Calas after a trumped-up charge that he murdered his son for converting to Protestantism. Protestant Frederick the Great of Prussia has become the symbol of enlightened rule: he welcomed religious exiles like the French Huguenots (some of whom settle in England and Ireland) after their banishment from France when Louis XIV revoked the Edict of Nantes.

Even the reforms under Catholic monarchs, like Joseph II of Austria (successor to his mother Maria Theresa), antagonise Rome, Joseph claiming as much control over church affairs as any Protestant monarch. The Papacy is an embattled secular power in Italy, distracted by the responsibilities of running the Papal States which it still owns. The Society of Jesus (the Jesuit order) is expropriated and expelled by all the Catholic monarchies, including Austria, Spain under Carlos III, and predictably France.

The Kerry bishops of this period, Nicholas Madgett (1753-74) and his successor Francis Moylan, are Gallican in outlook (the term recalls the independent record of the French church in its dealings with the Papacy) – more concerned to be on good terms with the government than with acting as standard-bearers of resistance to the remaining penal restrictions under King George. The Pretender's control over Irish church appointments will loosen (he is getting older and soon he will die), and the claims of George III (1760) to succeed to some of the rights enjoyed by the Pretender begin to look more and more plausible. The Pope has winked at similar power in the hands of the Catholic monarchs, and in Kerry the government tolerates the anomaly of Lord Kenmare nominating not only the parish priest of Killarney but the rector as well!

Irish bishops have begun to reoccupy their sees since as early as the second quarter of the eighteenth century. Finding the supply of priests from the Continental colleges inadequate, they ordain candidates here at home – though requiring them to present themselves at a Continental college and undertake a seminary education. Soon there is an overabundance of priests and many fail to comply with the requirement to go to a college, those who do generating problems of indiscipline and taking up the places of clerical students. Indiscipline becomes rampant at the colleges and in Ireland, necessitating a papal decree in 1742 restricting Irish ordinations to twelve priests per lifetime per Irish bishop,[181] and another in 1751 closing the novitiates of the regular clergy in Ireland. The new Irish College in Paris will restrict places to clerical students.

The Brigade is down but not out. Kerrymen will continue to enter continental European armies up to the time of the Seven Year War (1756-63), but thereafter recruitment will diminish steadily. Among the reducing number are grandsons of Capt. O'Connell of the Boyne, who go to Europe in time for the Seven Years War. And they take opposite sides! One is the future Count Daniel O'Connell (b. about 1745) who in 1769 joins the Regiment of Clare in the service of France. A few years older is his first-cousin, Morty "Moritz" O'Connell (b.1738) who becomes a Baron of the Holy Roman Empire and Grand Chamberlain to a number of the Austrian emperors from, and including, Joseph II. The two O'Connell cousins remain life-long friends.

Important challenges continue to face the efforts of the Georges to bring Kerry under the rule of law and order. Smuggling continues to impede the revenue, and the control of smuggling continues in the hands of the Whiteboys, wool leaving the country, brandy coming in, criss-crossing Kerry in a highly organised web of land communications. However, the illegal trade also helps neutralise the effects of the Penal Laws, since, in order to govern wisely Kerry's elite has learned to collaborate with and benefit from it; and the benefits of smuggling are enjoyed well beyond the old south of the county, the historic county of Desmond. The Danish Silver Robbery at Ballyheigue in 1730 reveals the involvement of some of the county elite. Johan Heitman, the Captain of the *Golden Lion*, a Dutch East Indiaman, finds himself in difficulty when his ship runs aground at Ballyheigue. He receives what he believes to be friendly assistance of Sir Thomas Crosbie of Ballyheigue Castle (son and namesake of the MP who sat in King James's Parliament). The gold is stored in the Castle, but Crosbie has caught a chill during the rescue and dies as a result. Later, his wife and the local gentry appear to connive at the robbery of the gold. Some of the participants in these events are government law enforcement officers: they include John FitzMaurice, who later inherits the earldom of Shelburne and is father of the Prime Minister William, 2nd Earl.

A kind of convergence of opinion appears around the issue of Irish commerce. The bulk of legitimate commerce with the continent is in the hands of Catholic merchants, who

---

181 Walsh, T. J., *The Irish Continental College Movement* (Dublin and Cork 1973), p. 79.

continue to exploit their excellent connections with exiled Jacobites. Dublin politicians aim their protests at London and the commercial and constitutional discrimination suffered by the Protestant nation and Ireland generally. The workings of the Irish Parliament are hampered by means of a fifteenth-century statute called Poynings' Law, while commerce labours under the Navigation Laws passed to protect shipping monopolies with the colonies.Under William, Ireland was hit with fresh trading restrictions, particularly on woollen goods. One wing of the Irish elite begins now to view Catholics as fellow citizens.

A number of Kerry gentry have made successful attempts to introduce the growing of flax and the linen industry. (Lord Orrery, zealous for improvement and the spread of Protestantism, tried it at Charleville in the previous century.) The credit for introducing flax to Kerry is given by contemporaries to Robert FitzGerald, MP Dingle. Flax and the linen industry are associated with the founding of Charter Schools, which were set up for the promotion of Protestantism. Linen appears to have been part of the curriculum of the Charter school at Castleisland (constructed 1750-1763), founded by "Robert FitzGerald, Esq., counsellor at law, on behalf of himself, Sir Maurice Crosby, Arthur Crosbie, Esq., John Blennerhassett, Esq., Richard Meredith, Esq., Edward Herbert Esq.", who donated "about 26 acres of land, most of them worth 20/- per acre", having arranged "a subscription of £40 per annum from the neighbouring gentlemen, towards the support of this school".[182] An industry for long associated with the North of Ireland now effects something of a transformation in the rural South, with scotch mills and bleach greens appearing throughout Kerry.

Kerry and the Seven Year War (1756-63):
arrival of the Whiteboys

This latest war is known in America as "The Great War of Empire" on account of the enormous imperial gains made by Britain at the cost of the French, with new territory stretching from the rice fields of India to the snowy steppes of Canada. The career of William Pitt the Elder, hero of the parliamentary opposition and the street agitators, now reaches its apotheosis, when this sickly but inspirational orator prime minister emulates in the political arena the achievements of his generals in the Year of Victories, 1759. One of the generals, James Wolfe, dies at the moment his army takes Quebec from the French – and Quebec will have a transformative effect on British rule in Ireland. In India, Clive defeats the French at Plassey and wrests India from them; he returns to accumulate

182 Michael Quane, "Castleisland Charter School", *J. K.A.H.S.*, 1968, p. 25-40.

a scattered estate in counties Clare and Limerick where the modern University of Limerick is centred on Plassey House.

The war is remarkable for the "Diplomatic Revolution" which brings Britain to the side of Frederick the Great of Prussia. It is Frederick who ties down Britain's enemies in Europe, enabling Britain to conquer her new empire overseas from the French. The Prussian alliance will stress the Protestant character of the struggle. The novelist Thackeray later captured this change in his novel, *Barry Lyndon*:

> "Now, somehow, we were on Frederick's side ... and I remember, when the news of the battle of Lissa came even to our remote quarter of Ireland, we considered it as a triumph for the cause of Protestantism, and illuminated, and bonfired, and had a sermon at church, and kept the Prussian King's birthday; on which my uncle would get drunk – as indeed on any other occasion."

Frederick will be placed in the Protestant pantheon alongside Gustavus Adolphus and Charles XII of Sweden, and the more recent William of Orange; the royal houses of Prussia and Sweden are intermarried and both are associated with the defense of the Reformation during the wars of the seventeenth century. Are we, then, back to the era of religious wars? Not quite. British policy from now stresses the inclusiveness of the new empire, and George III, who comes to the throne in the course of the war (1760) proclaims his wish to be a king to all his people. Yet there are factors at play that jeopardise the new, more open empire. One is the Americans, who will be asked to foot some of the bills for the conquest of Quebec and whose heritage is hostile to Catholicism. The other is the growing Scots influence in London since the Scottish Act of Union of 1707 and the defeat of the Stuart in the campaign of 1745-6; many of the Scots belong to the Calvinist tradition and to that extent will try to maintain the new empire free of Catholic influence.

The other side of the Diplomatic Revolution sees France make alliance with Austria; the Austrian princess Marie Antoinette (Maria Teresa's daughter) becomes a pledge of this novel arrangement with her marriage to the future Louis XVI (both will go to the guillotine during the French Revolution). As if to confirm the religious character of the war, Spain – no longer Habsburg since the Spanish Succession war, but now Bourbon – comes in on the side of France in the so-called "Family Compact". The principal negotiator for Spain is the son of a Kilmallock man, Ricardo Wall, born in Nantes in 1694. We need again to balance the scales: Wall, Prime Minister of Spain under the great modernizing king Carlos III, has lent his enthusiastic support to the removal of the Jesuits from that country.[183]

In 1759 the southern coast of Ireland again becomes the potential landing ground for a French invasion. In the event, a small French squadron lands at Carrickfergus in the North of Ireland. Yet most of the occupying army in Ireland is stationed in Munster and Connaught, and in Munster two years later the Whiteboys signal their arrival with an insurrection against rents and tithes. (Historians will use the term Whiteboy to cover the many phases of rural insurrection in the Irish South.) Kerry and the South generally is tillage country; since earlier in the century pasture has been removed from the obligation to pay tithe, but Kerry remains exposed to the tithe system. Protestant fears of the Whiteboys are very ably voiced by leading parliamentary undertaker and Munster man, Henry Boyle, now Earl of Shannon, whose return to Cork in 1766 is reported in the press: "On Thursday last was presented to the Earl of Shannon, from the principal Inhabitants of the City an Address of Thanks for his steady adherence upon all occasions, to the Protestant Interest."[184]

Kerry does not take the lead in the Whiteboy campaign. Dominic Trant, son of Dominic Trant of Dingle, informs us that the campaigners of the 1760s were more active in Tipperary and Kilkenny than in Kerry, concentrating on "some alleged local grievances as to tithes and commons in the counties of Kilkenny and Tipperary".[185] Kerry has no incident comparable with the judicial murder of the Whiteboy priest Fr Nicholas Sheehy in Clonmel in 1766, the culminating event in Whiteboy activity in that region. A signal event nearer Kerry is the death of outlaw Art Ó Laoghaire in 1773; his shooting, at Carriganimma (between Milstreet and Macroom), while home on furlough as a captain of the Hungarian Hussars, is the upshot of a dispute with a local representative of law enforcement named Morris. The dispute is said to centre on an offer from Morris of £5 for Art Ó Laoghaire's horse; a Catholic can not own a horse of greater value than £5 under the Penal Laws, and has to accept an offer; Ó Laoghaire refused the offer, and so the quarrel began. The reason his fame spreads so widely is that the killing of Art is preserved in a famous lament – a keen (Ir. caoineadh), the

---

183 *William Flin's Cork Hibernian Chronicle*, 12-16 February 1778, has Wall's death: "On his estate in the Kingdom of Grenada, in Spain, in the 85th year of his age ... a native of this kingdom, Lieutenant General to his Catholic Majesty's service, and formerly Ambassador Extraordinary from the King of Spain to Great Britain."

184 *Freeman's Journal*, 26 April 1766.

185 Dominic Trant, *Considerations on the Present Disturbances in the Provinces of Munster, their Causes, Extent, Probable Consequences and Remedies* (Dublin 1787).

famous *Caoineadh Airt Uí Laoghaire* – attributed to his distraught wife; the riderless horse returns to the couple's dwelling with its blood-splashed saddle, then she goes to the spot where she finds her dead husband. Another detail: the wife is an aunt of the future Liberator, Daniel O'Connell.

Art Ó Laoghaire is said to be wearing certain Stuart tokens when he dies. But the era of the Stuarts is coming to an end. The Old Pretender dies in 1766 and in 1770 the Pope rescinds the Stuart prerogative to appoint Irish bishops. The Dublin authorities do not consider in the Whiteboys to be in league with the French. Meanwhile the Catholic leadership has created the Catholic Committee, which held its first meeting in the course of the Seven Years War, on 2 April 1760. The Committee, composed of aristocrats, is content to give to King George the role of appointment to the Irish hierarchy wielded to now by the Pretender. In 1762 the British look favourably on the offer of one of the Catholic aristocrats (Lord Trimbleston) to raise a Catholic force to land in Portugal to attack Britain's enemy, Spain. But the move is rejected by the Dublin Parliament.

The first cracks in the Penal Code: the role of Kerry

Inside Parliament, Lord Kenmare and the early Catholic Committee have a group of ad hoc allies. They include Robert FitzGerald, MP Dingle since the 1740s. FitzGerald broke with undertaker Henry Boyle's Munster Squadron back in 1753-5 to take the government side in the conflict over prior consent in the disposal of the budget surplus. Thereafter FitzGerald bypasses the undertakers entirely, going directly to government for political favours and to advance the cause of the Catholics. On 26 February 1762 he presents heads of a Bill to secure Catholic loans to Protestants, earning the following accolade in the Stuart Papers. "He is also one of the best friends and defenders the poor Catholics of this Kingdom have. He is a man of great credit and influence in the Parliament and kingdom."[186] During the 1760s FitzGerald remains in contact with his cousins among the Stuart supporters on the continent, most notably Charles, Marshal Thomond, hero of Fontenoy. When Lord Townshend comes as viceroy in 1767, beginning a second round of the contest with the undertakers, FitzGerald is squarely in the government camp, not just to exploit the better source of patronage, but because government at Dublin and London is in general favourably disposed to the removal of the Penal Laws.

The new pro-Catholic connection threatens to supplant

---

186 Fr Henry Dolphin, Dublin, to Charles O'Kelly, OP, Rome, 25 August 1764, in Patrick Fagan, *The Stuart Papers* (Dublin 1995, 2 vols.), vol 2, p. 246.

the Blennerhassetts and can deliver a key loyalist in the shape of the very influential Catholic leader, Lord Kenmare. Though Catholic, Kenmare has no separatist or ultramontane (Roman) prejudices to make him unacceptable to the Dublin and London governments – and he will dampen any talk of parliamentary reform. He and his convert support like to acknowledge Catholic Gaelic families like MacGillycuddy of the Reeks and MacGillycuddy's cousin O'Sullivan Mór. The Chief of the Reeks, the highest mountains in Ireland, exerts a special fascination. Probably many converts have been fostered in childhood among the Gaelic-speaking tenantry; on public occasions they like to claim *Milesian* (Gaelic) blood, with vague references to the Irish Brigade, a number of whose regiments are under local Old Irish commanders, O'Brien's (viscounts Clare), Clancarty's and MacElligott's included. Since the Restoration, the FitzGeralds and the Hicksons are related to the still-Catholic O'Briens, viscounts Clare, while Cornelius MacGillycuddy's marriage to Catherine Chute in 1745 produces important convert figures, including occupants of the shrievalty, for the turbulent decades ahead.

Robert FitzGerald's sisters' marriages have meanwhile raised a number of Cromwellian families to empathy with the cause of the Catholics; eight of these sisters ("the Ten Geraldines") are married throughout Mid and North Kerry to the likes of Herbert of Cahernane, Hewson of Ennismore (Cromwellian), Sandes of Sallow Glen (Tarbert) and Meredith of Dicksgrove. Previously the family has intermarried with the likes of Chute and Herbert (Elizabethan). Of the Hicksons, Christopher Hickson of Fermoyle (grandson of Honor O'Brien and the Knight of Kerry) and his wife (Elizabeth Conway, m 1745) are described M.A. Hickson as "devout Roman Catholics".[187]

Catholic recruitment to the British army continues to have support. Sir Boyle Roche (later MP for Tralee), cousin of Lord Kenmare, is a supporter of Catholic recruitment. Roche himself serves in America in the Seven Year War, and is captured by Indians in Canada before being released at the fall of Quebec in 1759. He returns to Ireland and embarks on a career in Parliament (MP Tralee 1775 and 1790), there gaining a reputation for malapropisms, or Irish "bulls". Here is a coherent statement from Boyle in the Irish House of Commons about the many Catholics who served with him in America:

> "Major Boyle Roche said, he thought himself obliged to say something on this point, as he had been lately on the recruit duty; on which his instructions were

187 *Kerry Evening Post*, 20 October 1880.

to inlist only Protestants (however in) the year 1757, when many recruits were raised in Munster, the officers inlisted a great number of Papists, who were sent abroad, and their conduct shewed that their religion did not influence them, so as either to behave remissly in action, or to desert, though in Romish countries, and fighting against those of their own religion. And every military gentleman in the house, who had served last war in America, could testify that there never was less desertion than from the Papist soldiers, and that no men behaved better or were more observant of discipline."[188]

The sons of Kerry's Protestant gentlemen can hope for officerships in the same army and in the same war:

"Eusebius Chute, Esq. of Obrennan, co. Kerry, whose death we announced in our last, was formerly a Lieutenant in the 9th Foot. In his early days and prime of life he saw a great deal of hard military service, and was present 'in many a well fought field'. In the year 1761, at the conquest of Bellisle, he received a severe and dangerous wound, a musket ball having entered under his eye and lodged in his head; though on this occasion he might have retired with honor, he did not quit the service of his King and Country. The vast effusion of blood brought on a debility of the whole frame, and a dropsy, still the spirit of the man was unsubdued; the year following, viz 1762, he fought at the storming of the Moro Castle, and the capture of the Havannah." (*Limerick General Advertiser*, April 29, 1806)

The Rise of William Petty, Earl of Shelburne

William Petty has succeeded his father to the title and estates of Shelburne just as the Seven Year War ends, having played his part as a soldier "in the Rochefort expedition and other raids on the French coast".[189] A career in high politics beckons, and a seat in the Lords, which is why he will visit his South Kerry estate on only a few occasions during his life; there, all along the ragged coastline of Dunkerron and Iveragh, the illegal trade is rife – surely an embarrassing anomaly for a politician appointed President of the Board of Trade in 1763, Shelburne's first ministry.

As a young President of the Board of Trade Shelburne

188 *Parliamentary Diary*, Oct.28, in *Freeman's Journal*, 28-31 October 1775.
189 John Norris, *Shelburne and Reform*, London 1963, p.7.

has come under the influence of the free trade philosopher Adam Smith, with whom he is said to have shared a coach journey from Edinburgh to London some years previously. And Smith's thinking has fed into Shelburne's by the time of the debates about the Peace.

> "Heretofore the extension of limits was the single point aimed at. But now the possession of territory is but a secondary point and is considered as more or less valuable as it is subservient to the interests of commerce, which is now the great object of ambition."[190]

William Petty (1737-1805), first Marquess of Lansdowne

However, the circumstances do not yet permit the implementation of Adam Smith's free trade principles: in his new office Shelburne must draw up a policy to restrain the colonists' push west across the Appalachian mountains where they will create new markets for their embryo industries (thus diminishing British exports to America). Shelburne's Proclamation of 1763 attempts to divert new settlement to places north, like Nova Scotia, at the same time protect the native American population between the Appalachian Mountains and the Mississippi.

In all areas Shelburne's politics are driven by the rational view, and this includes the advancement of the Catholics, the cause of which his son will be an eminent exponent. However, Shelburne makes himself unpopular among his political peers, initially for his proximity to the government of the recently crowned Geoge III and his Scottish minister the Earl of Bute. He is considered devious, and he keeps a distance. His biographers have looked for explanations in his childhood at Lixnaw, home of his grand-father Thomas FitzMaurice, the brutish twenty-first Earl of Kerry who married the daughter of the Cromwellian Petty. Contemporary critics blamed his partiality to the Catholic constituency which earned him the nickname "the Jesuit of Berkeley Square". According

190 Notes from a speech prepared by Shelburne moving the preliminaries of the Peace of 1763, in Norris, *Shelburne*, p.32.

to one observer, "he had no knowledge of the world, but a thorough persuasion of its dishonesty".[191] Shelburne returns to government in 1766, again under Pitt the Elder. But the Townshend duties undermine this administration, preparing the way for the long hegemony of Lord North and the debacles of British policy the early 1770s in Boston and throughout the colonies. Therefore, Shelburne is out of government until the end of the American trouble; meanwhile, in 1777, the future second earl of Glandore, John Crosbie of Ardfert, marries the heiress Diana Sackville, daughter of George Sackville, Secretary of State for the Colonies under Lord North during the War of American Independence.

---

191 Henry, Lord Holland, *Memoirs of the Whig Party During My Time*, edited by his son (London 1852-54, 2 vols), vol.1, p.39-40.

The Age of Revolutions - America

"… a few days ago at Oakpark, Col. John Blennerhassett, aged 84, Knight of the Shire for the county since the reign of Queen Anne and for many years the oldest member of the House of Commons."

Obituary of the Great Col. John Blennerhassett, of Ballyseedy, *Freeman's Journal*, 1 June 1775

"One step more still remains to be made – I mean the liberty of spilling their blood in defense of their King and Country."

Count O'Connell, Irish Brigade in France, 1778, aged 33, on hearing of the removal of some of the Penal Laws

Kerry and the American War of Independence

The great revolt brewing up against Britain in her American colonies since the Stamp Act crisis (1765) has to do with the failure of Britain to implement the principles of enlightened governance, including trade equalisation, in her American colonies. Colonial thinking has vestiges of the old Protestant interpretation of liberty unlikely to succeed in Kerry; however, the contest of arms and ideas reverberates in Ireland, which possibly explains those duels that distinguish the general elections of 1776 and 1783, particularly in Munster.

By the time of the Stamp Act crisis the Dublin and Munster press have penetrated Kerry, and the treatment of the important events that follow, like the Boston massacre, the Continental Congress, Lexington and Concord, and the Declaration of Independence on 4 July 1776, is generally sympathetic to the colonists. [192] Press propaganda is assisted by left-leaning Kerry lawyers who admire the role of lawyers at the head of the American revolt. The Munster Circuit ranks the first in Ireland, and from the 1770s its greatest talent is John Philpot Curran, of Newmarket in North Cork. His great oratory will be placed at the disposal of the parliamentary opposition during the 1780s, and later still at the disposal of the United Irishmen.[193] Munster is "Curran's Circuit".

Ireland is not a colony, yet she suffers the commercial and constitutional disabilities of a colony and can understand the American case. Many of Kerry's Jacobites in Europe are in sympathy with the colonists, and Irish regiments in France contribute to the forces sent to assist General Washington. Tom Trant, whose father is from Cahir Trant, near Ventry, is part of Walsh's Irish Regiment sent to help the Americans in 1780 against Rodney in the West Indies.[194]

The Blennerhassetts are instinctively Whig and pro-American. Great Colonel John Blennerhassett dies in 1775 (he is in Parliament since the reign of Anne) but he continues to wield his influence from the grave: in the 1776 general election Arthur Blennerhassett and Rowland Bateman are returned for the two county seats, their press publicity emphasising their desire to be the people's representatives.

When the war begins, the impact on Kerry is

---

192 See *The Cork Journal* of 28 May 1761 for Michael O'Connor, who delivers newspapers for one Swiney, of the City of Cork, defending himself against accusations that he obstructed the distribution to Kerry of the Bagnell's *Cork Evening Post.*

193 See for example Roderick O'Flanagan, *The Old Munster Circuit, Tales, Trials and Tradition* (London 1880) p. 1-2.

194 John Hayes, "The Trants: an Enterprising Catholic Family in Eighteenth-Century Cork", in *Journal of the Cork Historical and Archaeological Society*, 1981, 21-29.

immediately negative after Britain bans the export of provisions. Cork is the principal port. Lines of Kerry ponies laden with firkins of butter end their journeys at Cork after travelling along the great Butter Road from Kerry villages and towns. Buy Irish campaigns begin. There are few ties of affection between Kerry and America. Emigration to the colonies is a phenomenon of the next century, though convicts have been sent as indentured servants up to the time when the hostilities with the colonies begin. (From that point they are no longer accepted, and transportation to Australia from Ireland begins in 1791.) North of Ireland Presbyterians predominate in Irish emigration to America during the eighteenth century, swelling the Puritan exodus from England of the previous century when Massachusetts was founded shortly after the Plymouth Brethren landed on Plymouth Rock in 1620. Neither Presbyterian nor Puritan has exhibited an understanding of Catholicism, and in the middle of the nineteenth century there will be considerable antipathy to Kerry immigrants on the streets of Boston and New York.

In 1774 an oath of allegiance acceptable to Catholics is agreed, one declaring that the Pope has no wish to overthrow the Protestant monarch of Britain. Loudly proclaiming the virtues of the new oath is Fr Arthur O'Leary of near Dunmanway ("a wild Capucian of Cork"), who has trained for the priesthood in France and returned to wield his pen and his oratory in the service of British policy and Catholic loyalism. He even joins a famous liberal dining club in Dublin known as "The Order of St Patrick" where he rubs shoulders with up-and-coming legal individuals, many of them pro-Catholic, like Robert Day of Tralee and Richard Townshend Herbert of Cahernane (Killarney).

In the Quebec Act of 1774 Britain passes a pro-Catholic consitution for Quebec, the French territory taken over in the last war. The Act has the effect of making the American colonists somewhat nervous at the presence of Catholicism so near their borders. Their reaction is echoed in the Irish press, predominantly supportive of the colonists on the question of the Quebec Act and therefore hostile to the rise of Catholicism. A meeting in Tralee pretends that the Jacobite cause is being toasted: the meeting authorises a press advertisement to offer a reward of fifty guineas for information leading to the prosecution of "several Papists (who) have dared to drink Toasts and make use of expressions highly disrespectful to the illustrious House of Hanover".[195]

1775 is a significant year. In Europe the Regiment of Clare is amalgamated with other Irish regiments in a partial dismantling of the Irish Brigade. Recruitment to the Brigade

195 *William Flin's Cork Hibernian Chronicle*, 8 August, 1774.

has been falling off from mid-century, and there is no longer any real desire to bring down the Georges and restore the House of Stuart. In 1776 Francis Moylan, Bishop of Kerry, takes the oath of allegiance before one of the justices of the peace at Killarney, "with twenty other Roman Catholic Clergymen and sixty gentlemen, merchants and reputable farmers of that communion".[196]

The two county MPs, Bateman and Blennerhassett, vote against the Catholic relief Bill introduced in 1778, while Robert FitzGerald MP Dingle votes its passage into law.[197] The Act confers on Catholics the right to inherit and transfer property on equal terms with Protestants, and to practice their religion openly. The "gavel" clause of Queen Anne's time, which forced the subdivision of Catholic estates, is removed. A further Act will pass in 1782 permitting Catholics to sell land. Over in France in 1778 the brother of Hunting Cap O'Connell hears the news of the relief Act, and issues a qualified welcome, with "One step more still remains to be made – I mean the liberty of spilling their blood in defense of their King and Country"; but he adds that even in that scenario he would never join a war against his beloved France.[198]

Robert FitzGerald MP is forced out of Dingle to Valentia at this time and replaced by his nephew of the Protestant Townsend family, of Castletownshend, Co. Cork. It appears, on the face of it, essentially a family dispute. However, the Townsends are allies of Lord Shannon (Boyle), while the family of the Knights (notably Robert himself) remain Jacobite-connected and in touch with their cousins on the Continent. The current Knight is Maurice, known as the "Dingle Knight", nephew of Robert. His wife is Anne FitzMaurice, one of the Lixnaw family. They have no children and Anne – having "a very sufficient estimation of her social position and long line of ancestral descent" – taunts her husband relentlessly.[199] Anne may or may not be an anti-Jacobite, but she is determined to deny Dingle to Robert when he becomes Knight. The struggle intensifies when Robert marries for a third time and finally becomes a father on the birth of his son Maurice in 1772. Anne's jealousy knows no bounds; she compels her husband to change his will and leave Dingle to the Townsends. Subsequent to the loss of Dingle, Robert purchases land on Valentia, and this is the beginning of the Knight of Kerry connection with the island.

---

196 *Hibernian Chronicle*, 7 –11 March, 1776.
197 The division list is reproduced in the *Hibernian Chronicle*, 13 August 1778.
198 O'Connell, *Last Colonel*, vol. 1.
199 "Curiosities of the Peerages of Kerry", in *The Kerry Magazine*, vol. 2, October 1855, pp. 189-191, p. 191; see also "Petticoat Government" (pamphlet dated 1780) in *Kerry Evening Post*, December 1915.

Catholic chapel building and parish organisation press ahead. Chapel villages will appear, like Knocknagoshel, and Carrigkerry in neighbouring West Limerick. Bishop Moylan writes a typical report from Tralee in 1779 to his metropolitan, James Butler (the Second) of Cashel, "I have comfort in informing your Grace that my new chapel is growing fast - the walls will be finished, I expect, in a fortnight, and I hope to have it roofed and slated by the middle of August". He tells Rome that he has constructed chapels in Tralee and Killarney, only complaining the distances and inadequate roads which make the regular administration of the sacraments a difficulty.[200] Moylan has a friend in Paris in Abbé Edgeworth. With Edgeworth's assistance he helps Honora (Nano) Nagle devise a rule for a teaching order, later the Presentation sisters. They become established in Cork. The first Kerry foundation is in Killarney in 1793, in "three houses in New Street" given by Bishop Teahan. Miss Curtayne (as Sister Joseph) arrives from Killarney to found a convent in Tralee in 1809.[201]

The government is asking very little that the hierarchy is not prepared to give. Archbishop Butler and Bishop Moylan appear even to contemplate the suppression of the regulars (Franciscans and Dominicans), who have always been slightly outside the control of bishops and excessively zealous in the service of Rome. Butler and Moylan desire to please the British and smoothe the passage of the 1782 relief bill, but the bishops of the rest of Ireland draw the line at this effort at appeasement, so there will be no suppression of the regulars, and the 1782 Bill is enacted without it.[202]

Lord Charlemont's Volunteers 1779-1782

The gentry need to raise volunteer corps to replace the regular army deployed in America. Their role will be to defend the coast against America's allies France and Spain, and police the interior.

The overall leader of all the Irish Volunteers is the Armagh nobleman and aesthete, Lord Charlemont. The earliest muster in Ireland is said to be the one in Carbery, Bantry and Beare in West Cork in 1774. The corps take colourful names, some of them surviving in a modern football clubs, like *The Laune Rangers. The Dingle Volunteers* are formed in August 1779

200 Bolster, "The Moylan Correspondence", *Collectana Hibernica* 1971. No. 14. pp 82-142. Tralee, 2 May 1779; Rev Kieran O'Shea, "Bishop Moylan's Relatio Status, 1785", in Journal of the *Kerry Archaeological and Historical Society*, 1974. pp 21-36.

201 T.J. Walsh, *Nano Nagle and the Presentation Sisters* (Dublin 1959), p. 198.

202 Eamon O'Flaherty, "Ecclesiastical politics and the dismantling of the Penal Laws in Ireland, 1774-82", in *Irish Historical Studies*, no.101 (May 1988) pp.; 33-50, pp.40-41.

at a meeting chaired by Dominic Trant, to "assist in repelling any hostile invasion of this kingdom". The Kerry corps include many Catholics, a clear violation of the Penal Law statute prohibiting Catholics from carrying arms. In County Cork there are corps with names like the *Duhallow, Doneraile and Clogheen Rangers*, and the *Bandon* and *Mallow Independents.* The winners of the 1776 general election, Arthur Blennerhassett of Arbela and Rowland Bateman of Oakpark, form Volunteer corps. Bateman is the "handsome venerable Cromwellian" who commands the "Kerry Legion, composed of farmers and the shopkeepers and tradesmen residing at the Rock".[203]

John Paul Jones by Charles Willson Peale, from life, c. 1781-1784
(courtesy Independence National Historical Park)

---

203 Jeremiah King, *History of Kerry*, p. 230.

John Bateman FitzGerald, the Knight of Glin, forms the *Royal Glin Artillery*. (His father, the previous knight, married Mary Bateman of Tralee in 1755 and converted to the Established church at the same time.)

The well-known pro-American privateer and Scotsman, John Paul Jones, appears off Kerry in 1779, in the Shannon estuary and off the southern coast. Jones has been in Paris with the American representative to the French, Benjamin Franklin, and Franklin has been helping to fit out Jones to attack points on the enemy coastline. Jones leaves Lorient in the middle of August 1779 on board the *Bonhomme Richard* with two small frigates, a corvette and a cutter, and by the 23 August he is off the South West of Ireland, from where he sails north along the west coast, then around the top of Scotland.[204] Rev. Day, according to the historian Froude, alerts Dublin that Jones is off Ballinaskelligs. Some of his crew wander ashore only to be made prisoners and sent for a spell to the county gaol in Tralee. Today Jones's name survives in a kind of dance at Irish wedding celebrations, but, worried about a landing by Jones, Robert FitzGerald MP writes to Maurice (Hunting Cap) O'Connell in 1780 suggesting he form a Volunteer corps filled with the Catholic gentlemen of the southern baronies. However, Hunting Cap replies that, notwithstanding the danger from Paul Jones, the gentlemen of the South are still prohibited under the Penal Laws from bearing arms. He is polite, but no corps can be formed.[205]

Aside from drills, parades and displays, there is the campaign to support home industry. The press reports a Fancy Dress Ball[206] held in Tralee in 1780 in aid of the County Infirmary, all the roles well "supported" (i.e. acted):

> "Mrs Denny, a patroness of the charity, in an elegant fancy dress, and patriotic devices... Mrs Cameron, the Goddess Fame, sending her Mercury about distributing the characters of mortals to the world. Mrs Yielding, an Ambassador's Lady, a fine beautiful figure. Mrs Willoe, the Priestess of Apollo, a most beautiful figure, well dressed and deserted. Mrs Blennerhassett, a Quaker, very pretty... Mrs Gunn, a Turkish Lady, dressed quite in character, a fine figure inimitably well supported..."

---

204 Joseph Callo, *John Paul Jones, America's First Sea Warrior* (Annapolis 2006), p.xix.

205 Mrs Morgan John O'Connell, *The Last Colonel of the Irish Brigade*, vol. 1, pp. 264-6. Two years later Hunting Cap and his brother are alleged to have authorised the assault on a revenue official named Whitwell Butler; for the part of Dominic Trant in exonerating the O'Connells see *The Last Colonel*, vol. 1, pp. 307-313.

206 *William Flin's (Cork) Hibernian Chronicle*, 14 February 1780.

The Volunteers Espouse the Politics of the Whigs

Near the end of the American War the question of Ireland's commercial and constitutional disabilities is raised at a great assembly of the Volunteers at College Green, Dublin. Again Kerry is closely involved. Ireland has discovered a truly great parliamentary strategist and orator in Henry Grattan MP. Grattan's rise to prominence coincides with the temporary eclipse of Henry Flood, Kilkenny man and previous leader of the parliamentary patriots. Grattan has a key associate in a former class mate at the Middle Temple: Robert Day, of Lohercannon, Tralee.

Grattan asserts the rights of Ireland as a kingdom under the Crown in an important parliamentary address in April 1780; the ensuing legislation (to remove the power of the Irish privy council under the Declaratory Act of 1720) is prepared by another of his patriotic allies, Barry Yelverton of Kanturk. They argue that Ireland ceased to be a Lordship in 1541 when she acceded to the status of Kingdom under Henry VIII. Yet, far from being England's equal under the monarchy of the Georges, the Irish Protestant Parliament has been downgraded and the country has suffered under the Navigation Acts, the Cattle Acts and the destruction of her woolen trade.

Shelburne is back in ministerial office in 1782 as Secretary of State, and Grattan sends Robert Day to handle the final negotiations of Legislative Independence with Shelburne. Day is a somewhat reluctant envoy: his future is a career as Crown lawyer and later a judge, but Grattan respects his expertise in constitutional law, and Day possesses the additional advantage of being Shelburne's distant cousin. Day's work bears fruit: Legislative Independence is achieved (on top of Free Trade with the West Indies, granted in 1779), and the so-called "Grattan's Parliament" comes into existence, lasting until the Act of Union of 1800.

Shelburne, as we have seen, was raised at Lixnaw by his aunt Arabella, the wife of Arthur Denny of Tralee Castle. Arthur died young, then Arabella departed Lixnaw to become a famous Dublin philanthropist and founder of the Magdalen Asylum. Shelburne had a high estimate of his aunt, and it seems quite probable that he had a hand in the granting of the baronetcy to Barry Denny in 1782. Sir Barry is the nephew of Arthur.

The concessions made by Britain to Ireland, most notably Legislative Independence, are considered huge at the time. Yet Volunteers are not about to go quietly now that the American war is over. Grattan has plans to keep the Volunteers in existence to pressure the government for parliamentary and electoral reform. Now also Henry Flood returns to prominence and tries to steal a march on Grattan by questioning the value of what has been won: Has England truly renunciated her legislative power over Ireland in domestic affairs? As the crisis over Renunciation evolves, with Flood at its centre, Robert Day and, it appears, Thomas, Lord Kenmare (obit.1795), part company with Grattan.

Their parting of the ways is the background to an episode of disagreement leading to the expulsion of Sir Boyle Roche from the *Killarney Independent Light Horse*. Roche, Colonel of this corps, gained fame throughout Ireland for his many "bulls", or malapropisms, as an MP. (Sir Jonah Barrington preserved some of these for posterity.) Roche has tried to assuage the fears of Parliament about further demands for Emancipation, stating that Lord Kenmare has no wish to press for further relief legislation at this time. But the men of the *Killarney Independent Light Horse* object to this strange announcement and Boyle Roche has to place notices in the newspapers to "unsay" something attributed by him to Lord Kenmare, that is, that Kenmare instructed him to tell the great Volunteer Convention of late 1783, held in the Rotunda in Dublin, that Catholics were in no hurry to receive further relief. It was another mess for Roche, and an embarrassment for all involved.

During all the time of these constitutional debates among the Protestant Whigs of Ireland, Kerry has appeared determined to enhance her reputation for lawlessness. Organised crime is more than ever connected with smuggling, the leading organisers "regimented (and) convoying their goods in defiance of all opposition ... overcoming the small bodies of troops detached against them", in the words of Sir Boyle Roche. In 1784 , the year after the Treaty which ended the American war, we learn that "the merchants and tobacco manufacturers" of Limerick are presenting a petition to Parliament complaining "the great loss and damages they suffer from the vast quantities of tobacco landed and smuggled into the county of Kerry and its neighbouring districts". According to the presenter of the petition, Sir Harry Hartstonge (brother-in-law of the Speaker Edmund Sexton Pery), the contraband is "carried openly and at noon-day through all parts of the country". Sir Boyle Roche,

> "described the enormities committed by the smugglers along all the coast, and through all the tract of country which reaches from the river Shannon to the old Head of Kinsale, and which he called the grand mart of contraband trade. In this part of the kingdom that lawless description of men, armed and accoutered, and regimented, march in open day, convoying their goods in defiance of all opposition, frequently encountering, and generally from their numbers overcoming, the small bodies of troops detached against them. These excesses he thought called loudly upon the legislature to enact rigorous laws, which if rigorously put into execution, and if the members of the House were

unanimous in a desire of suppressing smuggling, would put a stop to the evil, and double the revenue of the state without laying one new tax on the subject".[207]

Not surprisingly, the Volunteers continue in existence as a kind of police. Among their activities are efforts to curtail a practice very prevalent in West Munster: Edward Orpen, at the head of the *Kenmare Volunteers*, assists his cousin the High Sheriff, Richard Orpen of Ardtully, to apprehend a "party which had forcibly and violently deprived Miss Cannan of her liberty, and detained her with a view of transporting her from some part of the Western Coast to France, in order to possess her fortune". The Orpens go "to the house of George Bland, Esq., situated opposite the harbour of Kilmackillogue", the abductors "then lurking at or near Kilmackillogue Harbour, on the River Kenmare"; they all cross to Kilmackillogue Harbour and rescue the young lady "in a mountain some miles to the southward of that harbour towards Beerhaven".[208]

Little wonder that in 1787 John Philpot Curran, normally in opposition but struggling now to comprehend the scale of disorder in Kerry, supports a complete review of law enforcement in the county. Curran has always had a good grasp of root causes, but he is appalled at the corruption and inactivity of the forces of law and order, which is why he invites Parliament to consider Kerrry a kind of separate jurisdiction – a "Kingdom":

> "The low and contemptible state of your magistracy is the cause of much evil, particularly in the Kingdom of Kerry. I say Kingdom, for it seems absolutely not a part of the same country".[209]

---

207 Speeches in the Irish House of Commons by Sir Henry Hartstonge and Sir Boyle Roche, *Freeman's Journal* 28 February-2 March 1784, 17-19 May, 1785.

208 *William Flin's Cork Hibernian Chronicle*, 21 July 1785; letter from Killarney dated 19 July.

209 *Parliamentary Register* Vol 7, pp. 41-42.

Rightboy resistance to Tithes and Catholic dues:
Kerry becomes a "Kingdom"

John Philpot Curran's application of "Kingdom" to the state
of Kerry belongs to the debates of early 1787 when the Riot
Bill is being debated, hence Curran's concern with the "low
and contemptible state of your magistracy ... particularly in
the Kingdom of Kerry". Curran is not the first to use the term:
The phrase "Kingdom of Kerry" ("from Newcastle to Tralee in
the Kingdom of Kerry") is used some years previously in the
diary/travelogue of Lord Chief Baron Edward Willes.[210]

Kerry outrages appear again and again on the front
pages of Dublin newspapers in the summer of 1786. Tithe and
priests's dues are said to be the root of the insurrection. But
there are other causes, principally direct and indirect taxation.
Hearth money collectors, tithe proctors and tithe farmers, and
revenue officers in pursuit of illegal whiskey distilleries, are
some of the human profiles conspicuous in this era, as well
as the strange institution known as the ecclesiastical court.
Baronial constables, introduced in the 1780s, are accused of
supplementing their incomes with corrupt payments, and in
the 1790s the new militia family tax will add to the people's
burden. The redress of these evils constitutes the programme
of radical politics at the time; and even those who suffer under
the weight of taxation and other imposts do not seek their
abolition, only their reform.[211]

From 1784 Kerry and parts of Cork take the lead in
what becomes known as the Righboy insurrection (though the
press will continue to use the term Whiteboy). In response, the
1780s becomes a great decade of Protestant reaction. Important
Catholic relief legislation has been passed, with the result that
a Protestant reaction has set in. Historian Louis Cullen has
written of "progressive repeal (of anti-Catholic laws) from 1778
onwards accompanied by a new zeal to enforce what was left
of them, and to create forms of extra-legal discrimination to
substitute for the fall of legal barriers".[212] Grattan's continuing
efforts to further reform the constitution have alarmed
the reactionaries, with the result that any further Catholic
campaign will be viewed as a threat to the landed settlement
and the power of the Protestant Ascendancy.

---

210 James Kelly (ed.), *The Letters of Lord Chief Baron Edward Willes to the earl of
Warwick, 1757-62* (Aberystwyth 1990), p. 60.
211 David Dickson, "Taxation and Disaffection in Late Eighteenth-Century
Ireland", in Samuel Clark and Jamse S. Donnelly Jr. (eds.), *Irish Peasants,
Violence and Political Unrest 1780-1914* (Wisconsin and Manchester 1983), pp.
37-63.
212 Louis Cullen, "Catholics under the Penal Laws", in *Eighteenth-Century Ireland*,
vol.1, 1986, pp.23-36, p.24.

Now begins the "Pamphlet War" of the 1780s, when a number of scribes debate the reform of the system of assessing and collecting tithes so as to ensure the health and continuity of the Established church. Among them is Dominic Trant, author of *Considerations on the Present Disturbances in the Provinces of Munster;* a more moderate pamphleteer is the Rev. Luke Godfrey, Rector of Kenmare.

The Duke of Rutland, Viceroy of Ireland 1784-1787, embarks on a tour of the South in the late summer of 1785 to see conditions for himself. He visits Lord Kenmare in Killarney and stays at Ardfert Abbey with the new Governor of the county, Lord Glandore, and his English Countess, Diana (née Sackville). Rutland's tour yields one of the iconic images of the Rightboy era, Lord Kenmare "dragging them (the insurgents) from the very altars of the Popish chapels to which they had flown for concealment and protection".[213] For a taste of what Kenmare has to contend with, the following is from Moyvane in the *Dublin Evening Post*, which inter alia states tithe to be the principal grievance and introduces the figure of Tom Langan, aka *Captain Steel*:

> "We are so pestered with Whiteboys in this county that we can attend to nothing else. Not a night passes without a meeting of several hundreds. The Duagh Boys, though the last who took up arms, have this week made a formidable appearance under the command of Captain Smart, Captain Speedwell of Listowell, Fearnought of Liseltin, Washington of that place, Steel and Slasher, Critchall of Ballylongford, who make, I assure you, our gentlemen of fortune very serious; be assured they have reason, for all law ceases but what the Whiteboys like; not a process to be served, not a cow drove, not a man to be removed from his farm, this season on pain of hanging. A gallows is erected in the Square of Listowell, another in Ballylongford, and one at the river near this house."[214]

Robert Day, who is Glandore's legal estate agent, is to the fore in legislative measures to curtail the Rightboys. As MP Tuam he will take a prominent part in the debates to introduce the rural constables for six southern counties (including Kerry) in 1787. The Magistry bill, which contains the reform of the magistracy as well as the new baronial police (the "Barneys"), is believed to be the earliest experiment in rural policing in the world. They

---

213 Rutland to Sydney, 26 September 1786, quoted in J. A. Froude, *The English in Ireland in the Eighteenth Century*, 3 vols; vol. 2, p.516.

214 *Dublin Evening Post*, Thursday, 6 April 1786, letter from Moyvan (sic), county Kerry, dated March 18.

become the object of much derision, even violent animosity, when they receive no real protection from central authority and rely almost completely on the county Governor:

"In 1786 a most formidable Insurrection of the Munster peasantry under the name of Whiteboys but afterwards assuming ye name of Rightboys made their appearance and spread with amazing rapidity through the counties of Tipperary, Limerick, Kerry and Cork; at first by nightly incursions demanding and taking arms wherever they could learn any were to be had. Afterwards they proceeded on ye Reforming or correction of allegd grievances which they pretended to have sufferd as well from their own Clergy in their exorbitant demands for fees and official duties as for the Extortions of ye Clergy of the Established Church in the cruel conduct of their Tythe farmers and Proctors. They dragd Indivls out of their Hses by night, made them first swear that they wod not pay more to Parish or Minr. than the sums and prices for tythes & duties wch. they pticrly. prescribed & then generly obligd them to go along wth them on their Expeditns. They became at last so bold as to appear & adminr oaths in open day, & at the Chappel on Sundays. One whole summer the Inhabts of these counties, but chiefly the coy of Cork, lived in constant alarm and terror; several & chiefly of the Clergy were obligd to keep an armed Guard by night in their Houses, sometimes forced to seek Shelter from home being menaced wth a visit from them. They had one day what they calld a Review in that county and mustered in and about Skibbereen (near the parish of Drinagh) some thousand strong mounted and armed. At length the Archdeacon Tisdall, who had been their chief object as a very active magistrate, did on the very day of the Review, take one of their captains, Captain Right (a Tim ? Driscol), Prisnr. and with a party of soldrs. lodged him in Jail. Several others were taken in different parts of the county. Mr. Cox of Dunmanway was particularly active as was also the Revd. J. Townsend, Clonakilty. Their outrages were more atrocious in other parts pticrly. about Cork. By their regulations as to Tythes the Clergy were cut down one Half in their value – 4s for pots. wch were worth 8s, 2s for Wheat or Barley, & 1s for Oats by the acre. They found it extremely difficult to set Tythes on any terms; & were it not for the countenance of Mr. Townsend & Counsr. Townsend, my friend the Revd. David Freeman who has favour'd me with this detail wod not have been able to set even at the low rates wch. he submitted to. Their own priests many of them suffered in person and income, but chiefly in the latter – marriages 5. 5d, instead of £1.2.9 &c &c".[215]

215 R.I.A., Day Ms. 12 w 14. Robert Day, *A Short History of the Whiteboy Insurrection of 1786*.

When he returns to Dublin, Rutland sends the army into Munster in the summer of 1786 under the command of Lord Luttrell. The effect is "as favourable as could have been expected", however "If any serious opposition be made to the troops, it will arise in the county of Kerry, whither he is proceeding". Why might this be? "The smugglers in that quarter are very numerous and are all in possession of arms, and it is reported they threaten resistance, (however) that I much doubt".[216]

The new provocation in the Rightboy era is the excessive demands being made by the Catholic priests, who some believe are beginning to wield a power marked by several degrees of overconfidence. The *Dublin Evening Post* of 26th August 1786 reports that a priest of Tralee, Rev. Cahill, returning on horseback to the town, was stopped by six men near the church at Rath. They demanded the return of a crown which he charged for the granting of a marriage licence, in contravention of Captain Right's sliding scale. Rev. Cahill managed to beat off his attackers with his strong whip, and as he "put spurs to his horse" the men empty their pistols in a failed attempt to bring him down. The same issue reports "Proceedings and regulations as entered into by the Roman Catholic clergy of the county of Kerry at their late meeting dated Killarney, August 12, 1786". The Kerry clergy are "anxiously desirous to remove, as far as depends on us", all pretexts "for tumultuous risings which disturb the peace of the country". They desire "not to put their parishioners to the expense of making entertainments for them at stations of confessions, christenings, weddings or funerals (so as) to avoid not only extortion, but every vigorous exaction in the collection of their dues". The signatory is Bishop Francis Moylan.

A priest named Nicholas Neilan of Causeway makes an unusual (and very effective) magistrate in the decade of the 1780s. Fr Neilan remains still active in 1811 when he is picked out for special mention from the bench at the assizes at Tralee. It is difficult to know now if his predicament as a priest made him the object of any exceptional antagonism, or is it only because he is so effective when so many magistrates quietly opt out of their duty? We learn years later, that "He was obliged to barricade his windows and make garrison of his house and have arms in it ... and ultimately to take refuge in the town of Tralee".[217]

---

216 Rutland to Pitt, Black Rock, 13 September 1786, in *Correspondence between the Right Honourable William Pitt and Charles Duke of Rutland Lord Lieutenant of Ireland* (Edinburgh, London 1890).

217 Evidence of Daniel O'Connell to the Select Committee of the House of Lords, 9 March 1825.

The French Revolution and Kerry

"Lord Kenmare, though himself a Catholic, hunted down the insurgents of Kerry, 'dragging them from the very altars of the Popish chapels to which they had flown for concealment and protection'."

(Report of the Irish viceroy, the Duke of Rutland,
26 September 1786)

*Robert Day (1746-1841), principal tustee of the Denny estate from his
daughter's marriage to the 3rd Baronet, Sir Edward Denny, in 1795,
appointed Justice of the King's Bench (Ireland)) in 1798*

Kerry's High Tories come to power

The return to reaction in Irish politics and the use of the term Protestant Ascendancy coincide with the accession to power in Kerry of the convert, pro-Catholic connection around Lord Glandore, MacGillycuddy of the Reeks, the Hicksons, Lord Kenmare and Robert Day. They will be known in the nineteenth century as the High Tories, but sometimes they identify themselves as the Geraldines; Jacobite by descent, they are forced into reaction by the times in which they live. When the Catholic cause becomes linked with the French Revolution, the Dublin Parliament makes grudging relief concessions in Acts of 1792 and 1793; the new governing party of Kerry is compelled to temper its enthusiasm for the Catholic cause, and help pull the country back from the brink revolution.

The High Tories have risen to prominence during the American war, taken power in the early 1780s, and will continue to control politics through the French Revolution and into the early years of the new century. William Pitt the Younger and Edmund Burke are their inspiration. Their opponents, the Blennerhassetts, who do not seem to have the same commitment to the Catholics, are already past their best when the "Great Col. John" Blennerhassett MP, of Ballyseedy (Father of the House), dies in 1775. Meanwhile the Shelburne interest remains absentee and fairly irrelevant in county politics.[218] Shelburne's cousins at Lixnaw, governors of Kerry in the first half of the century, are a declining influence for the same reason: the third Earl has begun to pursue his personal and artistic interests in London in the 1770s, and in the early 1780s he sells off the estate. The way is clear for a successor to the governorship of Kerry; in the 1780s the honour devolves on the Geraldine/convert figure of John Crosbie, Earl of Glandore; he will retain the position through the Revolutionary period, his prestige and popularity contributing conspicuously to peace and good order. He is Governor of Kerry from 1785.

The new party wins the two County seats in the general election of 1783, displacing Arthur Blennerhassett and Rowland Bateman.[219] The Rightboy agitation is brought under control with a mixture of harsh eighteenth-century penal measures and the assistance of the priests; the same measures will be applied to manage the comparatively peaceful delivery of Kerry from the Rebellion of 1798. Extremely loyal to Pitt the Younger, Prime Minister in the wake of the loss of

218 A brother of the Earl succeeds to a seat for County Kerry in 1762 on the death of John Blennerhassett Jr.
219 Their replacements are Sir Barry Denny (detached from the anti-government side during the 1780s) and Richard Townshend Herbert of Cahernane.

America, they decline to take the side of the Irish and English opposition during the Regency crisis of late 1788/89).[220] The opportunity for loyalism is great consequent on the removal of the parliamentary undertakers, including one the principal "rats" of that crisis, Lord Shannon (Boyle). And electoral reform is out of the question.[221]

As they suspend their advocacy of the Catholic cause the High Tories are able to point to their achievements, including those of Robert FitzGerald's time, and the gains of 1778 and 82. Many believe that Emancipation has been achieved, or at least that degree of "equalisation" feasible for the present, and that a far greater urgency attaches to problems around rent and tithe. Anglicanism is on the rise again in England, waking up from its long eighteenth-century slumber and preparing to battle for the souls of the Irish in the century to come.[222] Meanwhile, unable to read the future, the Catholic hierarchy is content to support the governing party, and so it preaches respect for lawful authority.

The French Revolution: an Introduction

The storming of the Bastille prison in Paris is usually taken as the beginning of the French Revolution. Observers in Ireland and Britain believe they may be witnessing the kind of constitutional change that occurred in England in 1688: a limited monarchy with an elected assembly able to curtail the power of the king. Then it all goes horribly wrong. The extremists take over. They nationalize the Church in 1790, perpetrate the September Massacres in 1792 and invade the Low Countries at the same time. England declares war to liberate Holland after Louis is executed in January 1793. The Reign of Terror begins and Robespierre presides over a bloodbath.

Opinion in Britain and Ireland becomes quickly polarised. The Whig opposition and the street radicals admire the Revolution and hold meetings and set up corresponding societies to advance the revolutionary programme, chiefly the reform of Parliament. But the Whigs are split, and the case against the Revolution and in favour of France's monarchy is put by Edmund Burke in his *Reflections on the Revolution in France* (1790), a thundering rejection of the European

---

220 Glandore is given one of the Masterships of the Rolls as his reward.
221 Commons Journal, vol. XI, P. 221; 12 March 1784. A petition of the Freeholders of the County of Kerry convened in the county court house at Tralee on Saturday 31 Day of January, 1784, complaining, among other matters, that "a few peers" control politics in Kerry.
222 A headline convert of the 1780s is John Butler who resigns as Bishop of Cork to marry in order to succeed to the title and estates of Dunboyne; in the resultant reshuffle (1787) Francis Moylan ends his tenure as bishop of Kerry (1775-87) to assume Butler's place in Cork, Moylan's native county.

Enlightenment that has brought all this about. (Its best known passage places Louis's Austrian Queen, Marie Antoinette, on a romantic pedestal where Burke considers she belongs: "It is now sixteen or seventeen years since I saw the Queen of France.") Burke's roots are in the Blackwater Valley in the district just east of Fermoy. In the present emergency he departs the Whigs to join Prime Minister Pitt, splitting the Whigs and taking a section of the party with him. The upheaval is slow and traumatic, the final rupture coming in 1794 when Burke and the Duke of Portland cross the floor of the House to coalesce with the Tories. This is when Portland issues an invitation to our Irish Jacobites to leave France and come over to England to form a new Irish Brigade: *Pitt's Irish Brigade*. Count Daniel O'Connell, the "Last Colonel" of the Irish Brigade, accepts the invitation.

Despite the transfer of the likes of the Last Colonel, and others, to the side of Britain (or perhaps because of it), a percentage of Kerry opinion (how large it is not possible to say now) prefers Charles James Fox, the charismatic leader of the liberal, pro-French wing of the Whigs. Fox's cousin is the Irish rebel Lord Edward FitzGerald (son of the Duke of Leinster and born in Leinster House, our modern Parliament building). The acrimonious split in the Whigs reverberates in Kerry, affecting the general elections for years into the new century. The leading Whig is the young Lord Lansdowne, son of the prime minister of 1782. He embraces the cause of Catholic Emancipation, while the High Tories, as long as the war against France lasts, move in the direction of reaction – hostile to Catholic Emancipation and reform, and more and more identified – fatally – with the repressive policies of Pitt. Copies circulate in Kerry of Thomas Paine's *Rights of Man*, the rebuttal of Burke's *Reflections*, proclaiming that the ills of society are attributable to privilege, and that a new society can only be built on popular democracy.

Some Kerry exiles with direct experience of the Revolution are disaffected from bloody revolution for the rest of their lives: When King Louis is guillotined in January 1793 he is attended by Abbé Edgeworth whose correspondent is his former college comrade at Toulouse and later Bishop of Kerry, Francis Moylan. Louis's Austrian Queen is next up: her brother, the Austrian Emperor, appeals to James Louis Rice of Dingle to save the Queen of France, his sister. James Louis, using money from his brother-in-law, the Paris banker George Waters, arranges a ship at his father's warehouse in Nantes to spirit Queen Marie Antoinette away to safety in Dingle. The plan never takes effect and the Queen is executed.

Francis Thomas, third Earl of Kerry, who departed Ireland to engage with artists and architects, has been living in France for a number of years. He flees the Revolution back to

England, but his great wealth is left behind. The young Knight of Kerry, Maurice FitzGerald (b.1772, son of Robert), is said to be carried along by the early, relatively bloodless, phase of the Revolution. He will shortly forge his lifelong identification with conservatism when he takes his seat for Kerry in the Irish Parliament in 1795. First, however, he will require a spell in the new Kerry Militia (embodied under the legislation of 1793) to make him shed his liberal principles. Of his flirtation with revolution, his guardian writes that, "a young politician fresh from Greece and Rome is a Jacobin by inclination", however, the Militia "will, I trust serve to correct him, to wean his mind from the filth and abomination of principles which every gentleman is now ashamed of".[223] Lord Kenmare, as far as we know, is never smitten by the appeal of revolution; on the contrary, his family suffers by the Reign of Terror: the brother of Kenmare's first wife, Arthur Dillon, colonel proprietor of the Wild Geese Regiment of Dillon, is guillotined as an aristocrat on 13 April 1794. Family loyalty in the service of the Franch monarchy has proven a liability. An uncle Dillon became Bishop of Toulouse in 1758, a diocese that played host to an Irish college that trained many young Kerrymen for the priesthood and the Irish mission. The Dillon tragedy will be compensated by the reward given Lord Kenmare by King George: Kenmare's Jacobite title will be recognised by the Crown in early 1798 just before the outbreak of the great Irish Rebellion.

A very young Daniel O'Connell witnesses the violence while a student at St Omer in the Low Countries. A number of O'Connell's family served King James at the time of Aughrim and the Boyne, and young Daniel is appalled at the new France now emerging; for the rest of his life he will reject the use of violence to achieve political ends, at the same time rejecting French republicanism. His uncle, also Daniel, leaves the service of the Irish Brigade and crosses over to England to help organize Pitt's Irish Brigade. It is a time of changing alliances, and he is "The Last Colonel of the Irish Brigade" met with earlier in this chapter.

The Impact in Ireland: the 1790s

In Ireland the standardbearers of the French Revolution are the United Irishmen, who travel over and back to France throughout the 1790s. The "French disease" is caught by the Catholic Committee when Wolfe Tone becomes its secretary, forcing Lord Kenmare and the aristocrats to secede in late 1791. Kenmare's effigy is burned in Dublin and elsewhere; his opponents among the movement's democrats say that Kenmare

---

223 National Library of Ireland , FitzGerald Papers (copies), Robert Day to Lord Glandore, 25 May 1793.

was "born for slavery" and lacks "the spirit either of the Gael or the Saxon in his composition".[224] Kerry rallies to his support, supporting signatories from all the Kerry baronies appearing in the press.[225] But the tide of history is with the followers of Wolfe Tone. At the end of 1792 – the year in which a Catholic relief act admits Catholics to the Bar – the new, radicalised Catholic Committee convenes a great meeting at Taylor's Hall, Dublin and decides to bypass the Irish Parliament and go over to England to lay its further demands at the feet of the King. The High Tories of Kerry take great offence; an obvious parallel springs to their minds in the time when Sir Stephen Rice went to London to represent the Jacobite case just over a hundred years previously, when the crowd chanted "Make way for the Irish ambassadors".

Barristers are the principal conduits of revolution, which is hardly surprising in view of Wolfe Tone's membership of the Bar. There is a rich crop of Kerry or Kerry-connected barristers. Thomas Addis Emmet and Arthur O'Connor are top of the list. O'Connor is a relative of the O'Connor Kerry clan (after whom the northern barony of Kerry is named) and lives near Bandon. We will meet him again. Thomas Addis Emmet is admitted to the United Irishmen on 7 December 1792, and he travels the Munster assize circuit during the remainder of the decade. John Collis – "Citizen Collis, the Counsellor" to Judge Day – takes the United Irishman oath 23 April 1793; he is the Society's secretary for a time. Is he the same "Counsellor Collis" who makes a two-hour speech in Tralee in April 1806 congratulating His Majesty for installing a pro-Catholic Whig ministry?[226] The Killorglin barrister Harman Blennerhassett has, according to Professor McDowell's list, an address at Aungier St., Dublin and is admitted to the United Irishmen on 4 January 1793. Barrister Dominic Rice, of Eustace St ("little Dominic Rice, the barrister"), the Catholic activist who attended the Catholic Convention in Taylor's Hall, Dublin, in late 1792, and numerous Tralee meetings after 1800, is admitted to the United Irishmen on 4th January, 1793. [227]

The Emmets' father, Robert Emmet Sr, held the very privileged position of State Physician, so it comes as no surprise that the actions of his sons send shock waves through the Irish establishment. Their mother was from Kerry, a Mason, the daughter of James Mason of Ballydowney who kept a smuggler's shop in Killarney, where he is said to have operated an exclusive

---

224 Madden, *The United Irishmen*, vol. 3. pp. 5.
225 *Faulkner's Dublin Journal*, 10-12 January 1792.
226 N.L.I.,Talbot-Crosbie Mss. June 1799; *Lim. Gazette* 25 April 1806.
227 R. B. McDowell, "The Personnel of the Dublin Society of United Irishmen 1791-4" in *Irish Historical Studies*, vol. 2 (1941-41), pp. 12-53: Dominic Rice, Eustace St., barrister, admitted 4th January, 1793, p.45.

trade in brandy and other contraband.[228] The Masons are also associated with Kilmore cove near Ballyduff, which overlooks Ballybunion from the south. Emmet's full Kerry descent has only been scratched at the surface by his recent biographers, who know more about his father's ancestors, so we should defer to the greater knowledge of our Kerry historians of bygone days. Mary Agnes Hickson and Jeremiah King are clear about Emmet's origins in the Elizabethan settlement of Kerry. Through the Masons his ancestry went back to the Blennerhassetts and the founder of Killorglin, Jenkin Conway. A Catherine Blennerhassett, Emmet's ancestor, was sister of the famous "Black Jack" Blennerhassett, one of the "Galway Prisoners of (16)88' ", connecting the Emmets inextricably with the Protestant state in Ireland.

> "Thus Robert Emmet had not only scores of Kerry cousins, Blennerhassetts, Hewsons, Hilliards, etc. etc., but he was likewise the direct descendant of the Elizabethan grantee of Killorglin, the Patriarch Jenkin Conway, who it is to be feared must have had something essentially radical and revolutionary in his Welsh or Norman blood, seeing that he was the common ancestor of Harman Blennerhassett, Robert Emmet and Daniel O'Connell!" [229]

In Kilmainham with Robert Emmet as he awaits execution is another Kerryman, Christopher Hickson, first-cousin of the father of Mary Agnes Hickson (and a Catholic), who "signalised himself by knocking down a Mr. Simpson, their Jailer, who was ill-treating the captives".[230]

The many-times Provost of Tralee, William Rowan, counsellor at law, knew the Emmets in earlier days when they were all law students in London – days when it was still fashionable to talk revolution. Provost Rowan's son, historian/ Archdeacon Arthur Blennerhassett Rowan, expands a little on his father's circle at this time, which included the ill-fated barrister brothers Sheares, whose father was from West Cork:

> "The Emmets (in virtue of their Kerry cousins through their Mason mother) were his intimate associates – 'John Sheares' his personal friend, - 'Bagenal Harvey' his intimate at the Temple – of 'Curran's' unhappy home he knew many a painful anecdote from his intimacy in the House ..."[231]

---

228 T.J. Barrington, *Discovering Kerry* (Dublin 1976), pp.103, 218.
229 Jeremiah King, *History of* Kerry, p.226.
230 *Kerry Evening Post*, 24 July 1880.
231 Archdeacon Arthur Blennerhassett Rowan, "*Tralee and its Provosts Sixty Years On, with introduction by The Last of its Provosts*" (Private Collection, only 24 copies printed", 24 printed 1860; Introduction, p.ii.

Provost Rowan's grand-daughter (daughter of the historian-Archdeacon) writes about her grandfather's frequent contact with his cousin Archibald Hamilton Rowan at the time when the two attended Oxford. Archibald will be one of those behind the publication in December 1792 of "An Address from the Society of United Irishmen to the Volunteers of Ireland" (signed William Drennan, Chairman, Arch. Hamilton Rowan, Secretary). The rebel Rowan and Provost Rowan part their ways when the future Provost takes his degree in 1787, "after which there are no letters from his cousin".[232]

The Curran of Provost Rowan's youthful circle of acquaintances is the great advocate John Philpot Curran, and father of Emmet's lover Sarah. As an MP in the 1780s he became a distinguished parliamentary critic of government on issues like the baronial police and the

John Philpot Curran as Master of the Rolls, courtesy National Gallery of Ireland

burdens of rent and tithe on the shoulders of the Irish peasantry. On the outbreak of war with France in 1793 he supported Britain, but from 1794 he returned to opposition when government introduced coercive measures, and in that year we find him in the first of his great trials, as advocate for Archibald Hamilton Rowan and William Drennan. Later he will defend the brothers Sheares.

And so we witness a great fragmentation of opinion among the governing elite coincident with an epidemic of the French Disease among Kerry-connected members of the legal profession. It all bears out something Daniel O'Connell told a select committee of the House of Lords in 1825: that it was elements within the ruling elite itself that brought revolution to Kerry, and that there was no dissention in Kerry on religious lines.[233]

---

232 *Kerry Evening Post*, 19 October 1898. The first of the Rowan family in Kerry is George Rowan of Maghera who fought for King William. He married Mary Blennerhassett.

233 *Report of the Select Committee of the House of Lords* 1825, Daniel O'Connell, 9 March, pp. 123-171, p.142. O'Connell instanced the popularity of Tralee Parish Priest Fr Egan (obit. 1801), how the new Chapel of Tralee was built "to a considerable extent with the money of the Protestants" and how they expressed their particular admiration for Fr Egan with a monument: "There is a monument erected to the Reverend James Egan (PP Tralee 1787-1801) with an inscription upon it ... the monument remains in a very conspicuous part of the Catholic chapel of Tralee."

Government responds; Barry Denny's death, the flight of Harman Blennerhassett

How to head off revolution in Ireland is the challenge the government faces at the beginning of the 1790s, and it responds with a policy of rapprochement with the Catholics. But the new relief Bills of 1792 and 1793 are enacted only after very acrimonious debate in the Irish Parliament, though Lord Glandore is very much in support in the House of Lords. The right to train for the Bar is conceded in the Act of 1792, and admission to the county grand juries and the vote in parliamentary elections in 1793. In Kerry four Catholics are immediately promoted to the Grand Jury, three of them from Lord Kenmare's Killarney region: Daniel Cronin, Thomas Galwey, Maurice ("Hunting Cap") O'Connell and Daniel Mahony.[234]

What one hand gives, the other appears to take away. In 1793 Militia legislation is passed and a militia embodied. The legislation is greeted by the militia riots of that summer in which Dingle is involved. Much of the rioting is inspired by the old Defender movement. The Defenders were formed in the North to protect the Catholic community after the outrages of the Protestant Peep O'Day boys in the 1780s, before sweeping out of the North in the middle 1780s to mingle with the displaced Catholics of South Ulster who were settling in North Connaught. Now as a more country-wide movement during the nineties, the Defenders encourage opposition to the embodiment of the Militia, while at the same time they help revive the old campaign against rent and tithe. They disseminate misinformation, that the militia Bill includes forced recruitment and mandatory service overseas – in Flanders, for example. In reality the Bill provides for substitution and buying out of the draft. And there is no overseas service. The Dingle disturbances take place in June when a number of Defenders are killed. The *Limerick Chronicle* (26 June 1793) reports "riots" during which "the elegant mansion of W.T. Mullins, Esq. was totally demolished"; the Bishop, Dr Teahan, mentions the Dingle disturbances in a pastoral, and appeals for calm.

The leading modern biographer of Tone has found that, in the period up to the Rowan trial Tone was not a separatist; he could even live with the grudging passage of the Catholic relief Act of 1793, and its aftermath in the shape of the Convention and Militia Acts; moreover, the movement Tone headed, the radicalised Catholic Committee of the post-Kenmare secession, was increasingly at odds with the United Irishmen, whose Northern Dissent membership retains an abiding fear of Catholic tyranny (and has a far greater empathy than Tone with the labouring poor).[235]

---

234 *Limerick Chronicle*, 21 August 1793
235 Marianne Elliott, *Wolfe Tone, Prophet of Irish Independence* (Yale 1989), p. 228.

As the government crack-down begins to take effect, Tone is forced to leave for America; the American example of independence teaches him the need to go to France and help arrange the invasion of Ireland for the purpose of establishing an Irish Republic.

Towards the end of 1794 disaster strikes Kerry with the death of Sir Barry Denny in a duel. Denny has only recently inherited the baronetcy, and during the previous decade his father, though a natural Whig, was drawn into alliance with the High Tories. France's Reign of Terror and the Irish government's crackdown on the United Irishmen set the scene for the duel; more locally, there is the reemergence of the rival Blennerhassett interest. The fatal duel takes place during a Kerry by-election campaign in October 1794 to replace John Blennerhassett, sitting MP for the county, who died suddenly in Mallow. Sir Barry Denny interferes on the side of Henry Arthur Herbert of Muckross, causing a challenge from the candidate planning to take Blennerhassett's seat for Blennerhassett's faction: John Gustavus Crosbie. The two meet at Oak Park where Crosbie kills Sir Barry with a single shot to the temple.

Harman Blennerhassett is,, apparently, intimately connected with John Gustavus Crosbie ("I was one of the counsel attending John Crosbie's election, I believe in 1793 (sic)").[236] Harman, like the Emmets, is a direct descendant of Black Jack Blennerhassett of the Williamite army (above), and destined to become one of the revolutionary barristers of the 1790s. His activities are shrouded in obscurity, but by the time he decamps for America in 1796 he has married his own niece, Margaret Blennerhassett, and sold the entire estate of the Killorglin Blennerhassetts to Thomas Mullins (later Lord Ventry). In America this "tall, lanky, near-sighted Irishman", amateur scientist and subscriber to Rousseau's wilderness utopia, settles on an island on the Ohio River, which is named Blennerhassett Island. There he builds an Irish country mansion (complete with serpentine walks) and indulges his scientific interests, with his own lab and a solar telescope. Next he associates with Vice President Aaron Burr, who, having shot Secretary of the Treasury Alexander Hamilton in a duel in 1804, and now part-ostracised by official society, has formed a conspiracy to lead the secession of certain western territories from the United States. Burr is captured for his conspiracy and when the case is tried in 1807 Harman and his collaboration with Burr feature prominently.[237] However, there is insufficient evidence for a conviction.

---

236 *Kerry Arch. Magazine*, Oct. 1916. p.40
237 Nancy Isenberg, *Fallen Founder, The Life of Aaron Burr* (New York, 2007), p. 293.

The name of Mullins (Lord Ventry) is worth watching from this time, most immediately the career in property and politics of Thomas Mullins (1736-1824). The family is well intermarried with the Blennerhassetts. In 1780 Mullins's daughter Arabella became the wife of Richard MacGillycuddy, a natural member of the High Tory party and High Sheriff of Kerry in 1793. Another blow to the High Tory group is the appointment of Lord Fitzwilliam as viceroy at the beginning of 1795. Fitzwilliam appoints an opposition nominee (George Sandes of Greenville, Listowel) as high sheriff for 1795-6 with scant regard for the solid work in embodying the Militia done by the likes of Richard Townshend Herbert of Cahernane, Robert Day, Glandore and others. Soon there are complaints that Sandes is appointing some surprising new faces to the Grand Jury.

The Lansdowne heir, Henry Petty FitzMaurice, although an absentee like his father Shelburne (1st Marquess of Lansdowne), is an admirer of French and radical ideas. In the years before the Revolution the first Marquess played host at Bowood to some leading radicals, like the dissenter and Unitarian scientist Joseph Priestley who wielded the pen in a kind of pamphlet war against Bishop Horsley, leading advocate of the Anglican High Church and opponent of the French Revolution. Young Henry is sent to be educated at the University of Edinburgh, centre of the Scottish Enlightenment, and soon he is preparing for his good showing among the Kerry populace after 1800; they will be the long years when he and the Whigs are in the political wilderness and Petty FitzMaurice receives the new Catholic petitions to Parliament. The long running trial of Warren Hastings from the 1780s has helped prejudice Kerry on to the side of the Whigs, not least the eloquence of the great Irishmen Burke and Sheridan, the leading prosecutors and critics of the misrule of India under Hastings. Although Burke decamps for the Tory benches, Charles James Fox (Burke's and Pitt's great opponent on the French Revolution) continues a hugely charismatic popular leader of the Whigs.

On the other side, the High Tories of Kerry find it increasingly difficult to shake off identification with the repressive regime of Camden, who has replaced Fitzwilliam in March 1795. One of the party, Robert Day, is in a particularly difficult position as Chairman of the Kilmainham Quarter Sessions near Kilmainham prison where some of the leading Defenders and United Irishmen are held. Now also the conservative consensus with the Catholic Church is breaking down. Edmund Burke, the great exponent of continuing the programme of Catholic relief in the teeth of events in France and Ireland, dies in 1797, the same year in which Robert Day takes public issue with Bishop Hussey of Waterford (a correspondent of Burke) who has denounced the flogging of a militia man named Hyland for refusing to march to Protestant church service; Day considers Hussey an ingrate after the government favoured him with appointment as the first President of the new government-sponsored college at Maynooth for the training of priests.

Failed Descent at Bantry Bay; the Slide into Chaos

While Wolfe Tone and Arthur O'Connor are in France plotting invasion, Lord Kenmare has been sharing with the Knight of Kerry the view from Killarney, that "...the alarm about the French invasion is very great here".[238] A French fleet under Lazare Hoche appears in Bantry Bay at Christmas 1796, but storm conditions prevent landing. The escape is considered providential; there is talk of the same "Protestant wind" that brought King William over to Torbay a century before, and the wind that scattered the Armada a hundred years before that again. Richard White of Bantry House reports the fleet to Dublin Castle. Now comes Bishop Moylan's finest hour. Transferred from Kerry to the see of Cork in 1787, in time for the whole course of the Revolution, Moylan issues a Pastoral letter in early 1797 condemning the French attempt to land at Bantry Bay. British propaganda (including Robert Day from the bench of Kilmainham court) has found a bishop who is prepared to stand by the government. The Pastoral is given a huge welcome.

After General Lake has dragooned Ulster there are accusations that the Kerry Militia Regiment serving there has been infiltrated by rebel sympathisers, the Regiment becoming "as deeply implicated as any" in the United Irishmen. Six of the Kerry Militia and some local Orange men are shot and killed in Stewartstown, Co. Tyrone in 1797. The occasion is 12 July, the day when the townspeople "ornamented with orange ribands" commemmorate the Battle of the Boyne. One report states that three men of Lieutenant Gunn's detachment "stopd these men and took from them the Orange cockades" (and) "it was not without much bloodshed the disturbance was appeased".[239] What an unfortunate day for the Kerry Militia to be billetted on the homes of Tyrone Orangemen! On the following day there is a fresh outrage when Lord Blayney arrives to chastise

238 FitzGerald Papers, Lord Kenmare, Killarney, to Maurice FitzGerald, 2 December 1796.

239 National Archives of Ireland, Herbert Ms. M/1859/34. Lieutenant Gunn's Statement of his Transaction at Stewartstown, 12 July 1797; Historica Mss. Commission, Dropmore; Report of the Mss. of J.B. Fortescue, vol. 3 1899, Earl Camden to Lord Grenville: Nov. 3, 1797, p. 389; Padraig O Concubhair, "The Kitcheners of 1798 – The Kerry Militia", in *The Kerry Magazine*, no. 10, 1999; see more in *The Kerry Evening Post*, 19 Nov. 1892.

the "Kerries": his men kill three of them after they run into a barn to escape. Blayney's actions force an immediate inquiry, at which Glandore and a number of other commanders preside: it finds against the Kerry Militia for its conduct on the 12th, but against Blayney also for the events of the 13th; the command is subsequently removed from Blayney by order of the Irish Lord Lieutenant, Camden.

In late 1797, after the brutal pacification campaign of Lake in Ulster, the first number of Arthur O'Connor's newspaper, *The Press*, makes its appearance. But it is not the only newspaper doing the work of revolution in West Munster. In September 1797 Robert Day is sent down to Cork to clear the jail and arrange prosecutions. He conveys the results of his deal with "Mr. Driscoll'" of the *Cork Gazette*, a deal containing an undertaking by O'Driscoll through his attorney,

> "that he will no longer continue, or even revive in any way, the *Cork Gazette*, he is satisfied to be put under the following restriction. That the Attorney General do suspend the prosecutions now against him with discretionary power to pursue them, if, at any future day he (Driscoll) shall publish or be concerned in the publishing of the *Cork Gazette*, or any other newspaper of that complexion". [240]

The feared Rebellion happens in 1798. The principal centres are in Leinster and some of the counties of the North. Kerry remains relatively calm. But not entirely. Two sons of Richard Orpen of Ardtully, Horatio Townshend Orpen and Richard Orpen Esqrs, are brought before court martial in Limerick on 6 August, by order of Morrison, Brigadier-General of the Limerick/Kerry district, and charged with tendering the oath of the United Irishmen. At their trial the charge is thrown out, though not entirely to the satisfaction of Judge Day:

> "Messrs Orpen the tithe farmer of Doc. Godfrey, would proclaim Glanerogh and force the oppressed, harrassed and broken-down peasantry on the Lansdowne estate into rebellion." [241]

The High Sheriff, Collis, is arrested in June 1798, mistaken for a rebel when somebody finds a letter from him to a Limerick merchant named Arthur, and because Arthur is a rebel the

---

240 National Archives of Ireland, Rebellion Papers, 620 32 136.
241 Goddard Henry Orpen, *The Orpen Family* (London 1930) p. 175; Maurice Lenihan, *History of Limerick*, p.406; Talbot-Crosbie Mss. *N.L.I.* Robert Day to Lord Glandore, 22 Feb. 1798.

High Sheriff is thought to be one also.[242] He is soon released. The greatest single outrage in Kerry occurs in August when three yeomen are murdered in Castleisland barracks: "The rest of the corps had gone the day before to the races of Tralee and imprudently left to those unfortunate men the charge of all the arms and ammunition which they lost with their lives."[243]

In August 1798 the French, under General Humbert, finally land in Ireland, a pathetic and doomed expedition in the North West, at Killala in Co. Mayo. This time the Kerry Militia plays a distinguished part, in the Battle of Ballinamuck and the subsequent recovery of the town of Killala. It is in this Connaught campaign that two of the up-and-coming commanders of the Kerry Militia earn their reputations and found careers as Members of Parliament: Maurice (Knight of Kerry) and James Crosbie (Ballyheigue) – both distinguish themselves, as far as we can see, at the pursuit after Ballinamuck through counties Mayo, Sligo, Leitrim, Roscommon and Longford, and in the forced march to join General Trench at the taking of Killala.

Incredible to us today, the families of the Militia accompanied their men folk at a safe distance, so the arduous campaign must have been attended by at least some domestic comforts. The Kerry historian James Franklin Fuller informed his readers that his own father was born on the Connaught campaign of the Kerries that year: "my grandfather, Captain Edward Fuller ... was followed from place to place at a safe distance by his wife Elizabeth, daughter of 'Parson Jack' Blennerhassett, Rector of Tralee; and hence it came to pass that my father was born at Carrick-on-Shannon when the 'Kerries' were quartered in that town."[244]

Finally, there is the predictable activity from the hill-side men of the West Limerick/Kerry border region. But what is interesting here is some discernible continuity with Jacobite loyalties in previous generations, and with the tradition of rural campaign of that region. Gerald FitzGerald of Ballydonoghue (brother of John Bateman FitzGerald, Knight of Glin) is described as "the most prominent United Irishman in West Limerick", with Nicholas Sandes his Kerry collaborator.[245] The Knight's grandfather is described as "an active supporter of the Jacobite cause"; another ancestor is saturated in the Gaelic traditions of the locality.[246] The poet and scribe Micheal Ó Longáin, an associate of the United Irishmen, is connected with Glin; he is from near Cork city but his father used to be agent for the Glin estate, while his cousin Tom Langan is the

242 National Archives of Ireland, Rebellion Papers 620/38/100,145 a.
243 *Day papers, RIA Ms 12w11.* Robert Day to the county of Kerry Grand Jury, 26 September 1798.
244 "The Old Kerry Militia", in *Kerry Archaeological Magazine,* July 1919, p. 30.
245 J. Anthony Gaughan, *The Knights of Glin (Kingdom* Books 1978), p.90.
246 Gaughan, *Knights of Glin,* Jacobite note attached to pedigree of Thomas, Knight of Glin, obit.1731/31.

Captain Steel of the Rightboy campaign of the 1780s (above), now "in charge of the United Irishmen in Glin parish and surrounding districts".[247]   The following are arrested and sentenced to transportation to Botany Bay: Gerald FitzGerald, Nicholas Sandes, Phil Cunningham of Moyvane, Bill Leonard of Aghanagran, Marcus Sheehy of Duagh, Micheal Óg Ó Longain, and Pat Galvin.[248]

Why Kerry pikes remained in the thatch during the 1798 Rebellion is best answered when taken with another question: Why did Kerry erupt in the years after the Rebellion was crushed? Was Kerry's fire drawn in 1793 at the time of the anti-militia riots? Or did the governing elite gain the experience it needed in the Rightboy year of 1786 to be able to anticipate and deal with disturbances? As we will see, the decades immediately after 1800 produce an important phase of rural agitation, particularly in the north of the county; and Dublin will become convinced of French involvement. The campaign in Kerry to carry the Act of Union, immediately after the Rebellion, may be one of the factors in this fresh upsurge of violence. The Union campaign becomes very bitter and does nothing at all to help the Tories in their struggle to govern the county. We will look at this in the next chapter.

With the newly independent United States of America no longer available as a destination for Irish prisoners, the decade of the French Revolution has seen the introduction of transportation to Australia: the first ship for Botany Bay has set sail in 1791. Many a transportee is held in the old Jail of Tralee before transfer to the new prison at Kilmainham in Dublin, before embarkation for the journey to the southern continent.

---

247 Gaughan, *Knights of Glin*, p. 95.
248 Tom O'Donovan, "The United Irishmen and Limerick", in *The Old Limerick Journal*, no. 34, Summer 1998, pp.6-9.

The Napoleonic Age: the turn of the Nineteenth Century

"I am proud to consider myself a typical man of that minority. We, against whom you have done this thing, are no petty people. We are one of the great stocks in Europe. We are the people of Burke; we are the people of Grattan; we are the people of Swift, the people of Emmet, the people of Parnell."

(William Butler Yeats, Irish Senate, 11 June 1925, on a Bill to make divorce illegal)

Prologue to the Bleak Age:
An Acrimonious Campaign to pass the Act of Union

When a legislative Union of Ireland and Britain is forced through the Irish Parliament in 1800 – not at the first attempt – it draws the curtain down on the Anglo-Irish experiment in nation building that culminated in the creation of Grattan's Parliamen. Grattan is powerless to prevent it, Burke is dead, and the Kerry political leadership embraces the Union to protect its property and privilege. Lord Kenmare and the Knight of Kerry are persuaded that if they support the Union, Emancipation will soon follow.

The Union proves a catastrophe for British rule in Ireland. Emancipation is reneged upon, or postponed as long as the war with Napoleon lasts, and politics become once more polarised along religious lines. What a come-down from Yeat's idealised view of eighteenth-century Irish nationalism and the kind of inclusive state he envisaged with Irish statehood in the twentieth century!

Yet out of the Protestant community itself comes the most charismatic rebel leader of all in the figure of Robert Emmet – charismatic because young, and highly intelligent, and republican in the classical sense of the term. And nobody does more to propagate the legend of Emmet in his own day than the poet and song writer Thomas Moore, whose father, like Emmet's mother, came from Kerry; and Moore is one of a group of poets and artists including Keats and Shelley who spread the gospel of national liberation throughout Europe and the World at the beginning of the nineteenth century.

As Chief Secretary, Robert Stewart, Lord Castlereagh, manages the passage of the Act of Union. He is a Co. Down nobleman who entered the Irish Parliament with a liberal reputation in 1790, long before the repression of later years when poet P.B. Shelley wrote the famous lines, "I met Murder on the Way/He wore a Mask like Castlereagh/Very pale he looked and grim/Seven Bloodhounds followed him". Castlereagh has found a number of allies to help carry the Union in Kerry. Lord Kenmare and Thomas Mullins win promotion in the peerage for their Union support: Kenmare, a viscount since 1798, becomes an earl, and Mullins is raised to the peerage as Baron Ventry. Notwithstanding the notorious bribery used to pass the measure, it is important to remember that the Union brings an important advance in electoral reform. Two of the three pocket boroughs of Kerry are abolished – Ardfert and Dingle – while Tralee, which survives, has its representation reduced to one: Compensation of £15,000 each is paid to Lord Glandore and Townsend for the liquidation of Ardfert and Dingle, and Glandore is elected one of the representative peers at Westminster.

Returning to the campaign itself, a Kerry anti-Union campaign cathes fire when St John Mason, a first-cousin of the Emmets, publishes an inspirational address (propagating in effect the republican message of the Emmets) in the *Kerry Evening Post*, signing it "St. John Mason, Killarney, 24 Feb. 1799", and heading it, Address to the "Men of Kerry".[249] It denounces the foreign occupation of Ireland, "A Convulsed and struggling country, bearing upon her chest the incubus of 40,000 men, proclaiming themselves her protectors".

Judge Day, recognising once again a challenge from a member of his own profession (Mason is a barrister), responds with an address from the bench in Tralee at the opening of the Spring Assizes. The following extract comes from his manuscript original:

> "Government has indisputable evidence of the pious labours of certain virtuous <u>Citizens</u> to organize this county, & you yourselves can not be strangers to the fact. A Mine is laid amongst you & a single spark will suffice to produce a frightful explosion. … On my progress yesterday to this town several hand-bills were put into my possession of so daring and flagitious a nature as to astonish and stupify me, some in manuscript, some in print, some posted on chapel doors and other places of public resort, some circulated with great industry, some reprobating tythes, taxes and even rents, some reprobating Union, all under different forms and pretences tending and drifting to one and the same object, to agitate and excite 'the men of Kerry'. It is easy to trace these impudent and mischievous libels to the hive whence they issue. Composed in all the jargon, phraseology and pompous vulgar slang of the Jacobin school, made up of the stolen shreds and scraps of their vile vocabulary. It is easy to trace them to the execrable society of United Irishmen; possibly to the Irish directory itself now distributed among the prisons of the capital and issuing its traeasonable mandates throught their grates."[250]

To counter the rebels, a pro-Union declaration is finally agreed after a campaign to collect signatures among all shades of moderate opinion:

---

249 Republished in *Kerry Evening Post*, 7 April 1909.
250 Royal Irish Academy, Day papers, Ms 12w11, Charges to Grand Juries, Tralee, 18 March 1799.

"That an incorporation of the Kingdom of Great Britain and Ireland by a Union of their legislatures would be a measure of the greatest advantage to both, tending to promote the commerce and industry of Ireland, to allay the political and religious distinctions of the country, and to encrease the strength, the security and the resources of the Empire."[251]

The government has recovered a valuable ally in the form of the Catholic hierarchy of the South. Lord Castlereagh promises that Emancipation is part of the union package – a case of Where the Irish Parliament has failed, the Westminister will deliver. Dr Moylan (formerly Bishop Kerry but now of Cork) is among those taken in, believing that,

"Nothing in my opinion, will ever effectually tend to lay those disgraceful and scandalous party feuds and dissentions and restore peace and honour among us, than the great move in contemplation of the legislative Union and incorporation of this kingdom with Great Britain."[252]

The Irish viceroy, Cornwallis, brings important influence to bear on Maurice FitzGerald, the young Knight of Kerry, still at the beginning of his long career in politics. The Knight wavers but lives to regret his decision to cross to the government side, writing the following to his friend the Duke of Wellington many years later:

"From the time that Mr. Pitt abstained from giving practical effect to the Union as it was explained to me by Lord Cornwallis, by settling the religious question and pensioning the Catholic clergy as Lord Castlereagh proposed, and for which they were eager, I have never ceased to calculate on the question of Repeal (of the Union) being sooner or later taken up as an angry and national question".[253]

The Union comes into effect on 1 January 1801. Right from the beginning it is opposed by the young Daniel O'Connell, who, as we will see, will part company with the Knight over repeal of the

---

251 FitzGerald Mss., signatures in favour of Union; month somewhat unclear but appears to be May 11, 1799.
252 Rev. Dr Moylan to Sir J.C. Hippisley, 14 September 1799, in *Memoirs and Correspondence of Viscount Castlereagh*, edited by his Brother, Charles Marquess of Londonderry, London 1848-9, p.399.
253 Hartley Library, University of Southampton, Wellington Papers, ms WP1/1239/10; letter from Mce. FitzGerald to Arthur Wellesley, first Duke of Wellington, 6 December 1832.

Union many years from now. For the present, O'Connell lets the issue slip for a few years, raises it again in 1810, then drops it until the 1830s, then drops it again until the serious repeal campaign and the "monster" meetings of the early 1840s. During all the intervals there are other important fish to fry. Now, in 1801, there is no end in sight to the international war with France. A young Corsican of military genius named Napoleon Bonaparte has overthrown the Revolution. A politician as well as soldier, he will prepare a compromise with the Church and draw up a famous legal code that endures to this day. For now he reinvigorates his country with a string of victories that help the creation of a new French empire.

Robert Emmet and Kerry

A Peace with France – more accurately, the preliminaries of a peace – is realised in late 1801; then the formal Treaty (Peace of Amiens) follows in March 1802. Francophiles flood across the Channel to the Continent (Lansdowne's son, Henry, among them) in a renewal of the great love affair of the leisure classes of these islands with the nation of France.

Tralee continues to undergo an extensive redevelopment, which includes a new Georgian quarter centred on Day Place and the covering over of parts of the river still visible; a number of small private banks make their appearance, and there is even talk of a canal to link the town with the port.[254]

George Canning (b. 1770) becomes the MP for the town when he purchases the seat from Judge Day in time for the 1802 general election. Recently married, the son of an Irish actress from Co. Derry, he has dabbled in poetry and journalism where he has earned a deserved reputation for excoriating the anti-war voices in Parliament and the press. Tralee becomes his private route to enter Parliament following his stand-off with Pitt over Pitt's support for PM Addington's softer prosecution of the war with Napoleon. (It is a friendly stand-off: Canning has composed the rhyme "Pitt is to Addington what London is to Paddington", and with the agreement to purchase Tralee complete he organises a famous Dinner for May of 1802 for which he composes the famous toast to Pitt, "The Pilot who weathered the Storm".)

---

254 All the travel writers remark the transformation of Tralee over the next
 fifteen years or so, much of the credit for which will be given to Judge Day
 and Sir Rowland Blennerhassett, founder of Blennerville.

Robert Emmet, courtesy National Gallery of Ireland

Canning (like Pitt) resigned the government when the king reneged on Emancipation as part of the Union, and though he is a determined opponent of electoral reform (under the terms of which a rotten borough like Tralee would be surely abolished), he has played a distinguished part with Pitt in the campaign to abolish the trade in African slaves. Canning will part company with the Ultra Tories for all of his life on the Catholic issue. We view Canning, then, on the moderate wing of the Tories, somebody whose pro-Catholic principles will exclude him from government for two decades to come. Kerry's High Tories are Canning-ite; and though their allegiance to the cause fades in the years immediately ahead, they are shoulder to shoulder with O'Connell in the period when the campaign has a fighting chance at Westminster ten years from now.

War resumes in May 1803, and shortly after it does young Robert Emmet unchains his famous Rebellion in Dublin with its long consequences for Ireland down the nineteenth century and to the foundation of the Irish state in the early twentieth. The single greatest outrage of the rebellion is the death of the Chief Justice, Lord Kilwarden, who is dragged from his carriage in Dublin city and piked to death. As Kilwarden dies he asks that due process be given his killers. Emmet is condemned to death, makes a memorable speech from the dock, and is hanged in Thomas Street, Dublin in September.

Emmet's youthful idealism will have an immense bearing on the direction of nineteenth- and twentieth- century nationalism. His picture will hang in many Kerry homes and public houses over the next two centuries. In the years immediately ahead Kerry's apparent inactivity in 1798 will be followed by a new phase of rural violence in the northern baronies of the county. The hectoring performance of Emmet's judge, Lord Norbury (at least in the republican account of the trial), more than balances the humanity of the murdered Kilwarden, and Emmet does the rest when he denounces a court system at the service of the oppressor:

> "but where is the boasted freedom of your institutions, where is the vaunted impartiality, clemency, and mildness of your courts of justice, if an unfortunate prisoner, whom your policy and not justice is about to deliver into the hands of the executioner, is not suffered to explain his motives sincerely and truly, and to vindicate the principles by which he was actuated."

He does not defend himself against the charge on which he has been indicted, and he declares his innocence in the historic context of the struggle for his country's liberty. The speech is a brilliant success, and his words become disseminated throughout the world.

The role of Emmet's Kerry first cousin St John Mason in the Emmet rebellion remains obscure. He escapes Dublin after the rebellion (23 July) and is arrested at Nenagh, following which he spends a number of years in jail at Kilmainham, from where he petitions the young Marquess of Lansdowne, Judge Day and others for his release, complaining of "the indescribable barbarity of (Superintendent) Doctor Trevor", and of "George Dunn, the protected instrument of our barbarous Superintendent". Day writes back to say that he has "waited on Sir Evan Nepean (Chief Secretary to the Viceroy) and had a long conference with him upon my case".[255]

Thomas Moore (1779-1852) - Lord Lansdowne – the Romantic Era

Robert Emmet is perhaps the most charismatic figure of Irish nationalism, his youthful genius and idealism inspiring the hearts of his fellow countrymen at home and abroad over the next two centuries, and defining Irish nationalism as a matter of separating Ireland from Britain by means of an Irish Republic. If Napoleon surrounds himself with the romance and trappings of ancient Rome, the *Irish Melodies* of Thomas Moore sing the tragic fate of Emmet, surrounded by images of Ireland's past and the suffering and sacrifice of her people. Moore is the son of Kerryman John Moore (possibly from Knockanure) who owned a general store in Aungier St., Dublin. He will become the "Bard of Erin" but he knows little or nothing about his Kerry origins:

> "When I came indeed to be somewhat known, there turned up into light a numerous shoal of Kerry cousins (my dear father having been a native of Kerry) who were eager to advance their claims to relationship with me; and I was from time to time haunted by applications from first and second cousins each asking in their respective lines for my patronage and influence." (Moore, *Memoirs*)

When a friend and fellow student at Trinity with Emmet, Moore survived the famous visitation of the college conducted by Lord Chancellor Clare (John Fitzgibbon) just before the outbreak of the Rebellion of 1798. Moore and Emmet were listed for appearance before the Chancellor, but Emmet left the college to escape the discovery of his revolutionary intentions.

Moore departs for London in 1799 to attend the Middle Temple, there abandoning the Law to win fame as a poet and song writer, playing the piano and singing his songs to his own accompaniment. He mingles with the literary and artistic set, including Byron, and Barbara Godfrey, wife of the Marquess of Donegall (Chichester); Lady Donegall is daughter of Kerry clergyman Rev. Luke Godfrey, Rector of Kenmare. Moore is introduced early to Whig peer Lord Moira, a supporter of the Catholic cause during the 1790s, and settles near Moira's mansion

255 British Library, Bexley (Vansittart) Mss. 31229, ff. 161; Haliday Pamphlet, R.I.A., St John Mason Esq. Barrister at Law.

in Derbyshire. The phenomenally successful *Irish Melodies* appear between 1808 and 1834 using the airs heard at Belfast's Harp Festival and published by Edward Bunting in 1797. The *Melodies* contain a number of Emmet-inspired songs, including "She is far from the land where her young hero sleeps" concerning Emmet's lover, Sarah Curran, daughter of the advocate John Philpot Curran. Sung very rarely today are those inspired by the history and legends of Kerry and its hinterland, such as "St Senanus and the Lady", inspired by St Senan of Scattery Island, and "Desmond's Song", from the story of the "Love Lost" Earl of Desmond.

George Canning, (1770-1827), MP Tralee 1802-06, PM 1827 (by Charles Turner after Sir Thomas Lawrence, courtesy Nat. Portrait Gallery, London). Pro-Catholic but otherwise on the conservative wing of the Tories, Canning defines Kerry Toryism in the early nineteenth century

Napoleon in these years appears invincible, though his victories against the Austrians and the Russians are somewhat undone by the leadership genius of Pitt and the naval victory of Nelson at Trafalgar in late 1805: Trafalgar gives immortality to Nelson and a new name to a street in Tralee (Nelson, now Ashe Street). But Pitt dies in January 1806 and the Whigs come to power. Moore becomes a friend and protégé of the young Lord Lansdowne, Henry Petty-FitzMaurice (1780-1863), one of the Whigs' rising stars. Lansdowne is a product of the University of Edinburgh where his father (PM Shelburne) sent him during the golden age of the Scottish Enlightenment: he will become the perfect nineteenth-century Whig (liberal) though his role as a Kerry absentee landlord will make him the subject of much criticism. Lansdowne gets his first taste of power as Chancellor of the Exchequer in the brief Whig administration of 1806-7 which takes power on the death of Pitt. This so-called *Administration of All the Talents* is committed to peace with France and liberty for all. The forces of reaction think differently. One Kerry Tory calls them "the sworn friends of Arthur O'Connor and the panegyrists of the French Revolution".[256] The party fails to take a seat in Kerry but is a force to be reckoned with for the next general election. The *"Talents"* are in power for little more than a year, but in that time they abolish the slave trade and bring in a bill to permit Catholics to become officers in the army and navy. This Catholic Officers Bill is the measure on which the King dismisses them.

The Duke of Wellington – Judge Day –
the Rise of Lord Ventry

From 1807 Britain finds a hero who can match Napoleon. He is Arthur Wellesley, an Irishman from Meath – we know him by his title, the Duke of Wellington – and his successes will copper-fasten the rule of the Tories in Kerry as elsewhere in Britain and Ireland. Already the tide of war has begun to turn in the Far East where Wellesley's elder brother, Richard, has extended British rule in Northern India and into Mesopotamia (modern Afghanistan) at the expense of the French. Kerrymen will sign up to serve in this new British Empire, and when they return on furlough or on half pay, Kerry evenings will be enlivened by their tales of the Far East. Among the very first are Stokes and Hickson.

Recently returned from India, Arthur Wellesley has come to take up the post of Chief Secretary for Ireland under the new "No Popery" administration of 1807. Wellesley needs to find a parliamentary seat. Tralee returns him, but he opts instead to sit for an English borough, Newport on the Isle of Wight. Wellesley has a number of personal associations with Kerry. His aunt was the wife of William Francis Crosbie of Tubrid; and he has an old acquaintance in William Ponsonby of Crotto. Wellesley probably got to know Robert Day when Wellesley was elected to the Irish Parliament as MP for Trim in 1790, and Wellesley was there in 1795 to welcome the young Knight of Kerry (Robert FitzGerald's son, Maurice) after his election for Kerry; roughly the same age, they became lifelong friends. When Robert FitzGerald, younger brother of the Knight, was killed in battle under Wellesley's command at Seringapatham

256 NLI, FitzGerald papers, Judge Day to Lord Glandore, Loughlinstown House, Wed. 16 April 1806.

in 1799, Wellesley wrote a letter of sympathy to the FitzGeralds. Now in 1807, knowing of his imminent departure for Dublin Wellesley writes to the Knight, about "availing myself of the appointment that may be offered to me of cultivating our old acquaintance and friendship".[257]

Arthur Wellesley (Duke of Wellington) when in India 1797-1804, by Thomas Hazelhurst, courtesy National Gallery of Ireland

For the brief period 1807-8, before setting off for the Peninsula, Wellesley is the effective prime minister of

257 *Civil Correspondence and Memoranda of Field Marshal Arthur Duke of Wellington*, edited by his son(London MDCCCLX). Harley, St 30 March 1807.

Ireland, and the South generates the lion's share of his correspondence: his desk fills with outrage reports from Limerick and Kerry about how the magistracy and the courts system are overwhelmed by the rural campaign. It is an all-out campaign, apparently influenced by electoral politics (locally and outside of Kerry) and the perennial rural conditions, but now also by an admixture of French revolutionary ideology. It will reach a peak of intensity in 1808, the year in which James Nowlan, the *Gabha Beag* (Little Blacksmith) is executed. Nolan is sentenced to death for attempted murder but uses his trade in an attempt to avoid death - a metal collar smuggled into Tralee jail which he wears to his execution under a cravat. Taken to Gunsborough Cross he is hoisted aloft to die by hanging (more usually slow strangulation). He is let down still alive, and said to be able to stand, when a messenger from Tralee Jail arrives on horseback waving a white flag and carrying the information overheard by the warden, that the Gabha Beag will never hang, because of a neck device. Then he is hanged again and dies. It is April 1808.[258]

Wellesley is faced with the reality that many of the magistrates in the northern baronies have succumbed to threats and blackmail and are to some degree in collaboration with the insurgents. He commends the exceptions, "Mr Oliver Stokes, Mr. John Raymond, and Mr. George Church", and announces "I have again written to the Commander of the Forces to accelerate the march of the Troops into the County of Kerry".[259]

So these are the concerns that occupied the great Duke of Wellington before his departure for the Spanish Peninsula. Even when he puts together a string of victories in the Peninsula, the pride attending his successes engenders no improvement in the Irish South West:

> "...The return of our army from Spain has reached us, but the effects it will have upon the country cannot yet be known. In Ulster, Leinster and at this moment in Connaught, all are apparent peace and industry. In Limerick, Tipperary and Kerry there is an actual rebellion that no effort of the civil power can put down. They have been and are, assisted by France. Observe my lord that in the parts of the country last alluded to they were nearly in profound peace during 1798, and suffered none of the horrors of a civil war practically executed upon them, as Leinster, Ulster and a part of Connaught did at that time."[260]

258 Micheal O'Ciosáin, *Cnoc an Fhomhair* (An Sagart), pp.104-107; notice of the Gabha Beag's execution is carried in the *Limerick General Advertiser* of 19 April, 1808.

259 National Archives of Ireland, SOC 1188/15 Arthur Wellesley, June 11 1808.

260 Hobart papers, P.R.O.N.I. T2627/1/787. Pollock, Clerk Of the Pleas, Irish Court of Exchequer, to Hobart, 4th Earl of Buckinghamshire, 29 January, 1809

With the magistracy and court system unable to cope, a special commission under the Insurrection Act is arranged for Limerick and Tralee in January 1809. The following account of the commission appears many years later. It includes the execution of the killer of Lieutenant Thomas Elliott of the Feale Cavalry. Elliott was one of those who captured Nowlan, the *Gabha Beag*, suffering injury for his trouble on the night of 12 November when his patrol surrounded a house at Ballyhennessy, later dying of his wounds. The killer is a deserter from the army, one John Welch:[261]

> "Some remarkable circumstances attended the execution of these men, especially the murderer of Mr. Elliott. A convict in jail, of the name of — received his usual pardon on condition of performing the function of Jack Ketch *(the executioner of the Duke of Monmouth, the defeated rebel of the battle of Sedgemoor)*. He fulfilled his duty on the 23rd of January, but, refusing to do the same next day, was instantly sent off under escort to undergo his sentence of transportation. Before he reached Killarney he again nerved himself to earn his miserable pardon, and asked to be brought back to execute the men to be hanged that day.
>
> Meanwhile the Sheriff, bound to have the sentence of the law executed, was in much agitation in the prospect of having to perform the hateful duty himself, while in the emergency the gentlemen serving in the grand inquest of the commission offered to participate in the odium by each putting a hand to the rope by which the murderer was to be launched into eternity; but before the hour of execution arrived the convict had been brought back to work out the remainder of the hideous task which was the condition of his pardon."[262]

The special commission quietens matters for a few years. A military barracks begins construction in Tralee in 1810, intended to provide a permanent base for the military in Kerry and to remove the grievance of billetting soldiers on the families of the town. At a later period the Tralee's Barracks will become the depot headquarters of the Munster Fusiliers, and then it will gain a darker reputation for outrages committed there in the course of the Irish War of Independence and Civil War of the early twentieth century.

---

261 Daniel Mahony, Killarney, 14 ? November 1808, to Charles Saxton, Esq., Dublin Castle; the burning of Oliver Stokes's haggard is reported in *Faulkner's Dublin Journal*, 10 November, 1808.

262 *Kerry Evening Post*, 10 March 1860.

The strength of the Tories has become somewhat fragmented with the rise of Lord Ventry (Mullins) as a power in the county. The cracks became very visible in 1803 when Lord Glandore was forced to share the governorship, and at the same time removed from the colonelcy of the Militia; in his place came James Crosbie of Ballyheigue, the creature of Lord Ventry. Ventry's rise to landed and political prominence in Kerry has been a feature of the closing years of the old century, Glandore describing Mullins as "a gentleman who by fortunate purchases has acquired a landed property in county Kerry second only to Lord Kenmare and worth £8000 per annum".[263] His property portfolio now includes the entire estate of his cousin Harman Blennerhassett, of Killorglin, and the estate of the Rowans at Castlegregory; in 1807 he secured a slice of the Denny estate in parishes west of Tralee.[264] He now sets about reviving the Blennerhassett interest, which includes the somewhat shadowy figure of Arthur Blennerhassett of Bath. Ventry is related through the Blennerhassetts to the Guns of Kilmorna and Gunsborough, later of Mount Kennedy in Wicklow; back in 1801 Judge Day feared "the combined treasury of Burnham and Mount Kennedy" in the run-up to the general elections of 1802.[265]

Even the convert credentials of the main Tory grouping are under challenge since the party's recent opposition to further Catholic Emancipation. Meanwhile Ventry's daughter Arabella is married since 1780 to Richard MacGillycuddy of the Reeks, giving Ventry an important convert connection by marriage. All of this leads to the carve-up of the county for the general election of 1812 between James Crosbie of Ballyheigue (for Ventry) and the Knight of Kerry, both of whom will remain in the County MPs for a good number of years to come. Nobody regards Crosbie as a plausible candidate for Parliament ("Colonel Crosbie whom Nature never destined for either a Governor or a Colonel and who can do nothing for the Country" [266]) though he is a popular officer in the Militia.

Lord Ventry is exploiting two factors. One is his claim to be a wealthy independent interest *not* under the thumb of government, or idebted for favours to government; second, the party he is ousting is split on the Catholic issue, while Ventry is undivided in his Protestant allegiance and more in tune

---

263 *NLI*, Lord Glandore to Pelham, Talbot-Crosbie Mss. 9 Oct. 1795 .

264 *Registry of Deeds*, memorial 584 477399170, deed of 19 Feb. 1807, purchase, by Thomas Lord Baron Ventry (1st Baron –Ed.), of Cappaclough for £20,286 from the Denny trustees under the terms of the Denny Act of Parliament of 1806 "for payment of Incumbrances" on the Denny estate

265 FitzGerald papers; Day, Merrion Square, to Glandore, 5 December 1801.

266 National Archives of Ireland, Rebellion papers. 620/64/160. 27 Sept 1803, Judge Day to ? from Tralee.

with the winds of reaction now blowing in Britain and Ireland. Ventry will lend no support to the Kerry petition to Parliament in 1808 which is of course handled by Lord Lansdowne and his Whig colleagues, and by a faction of the old party, notably the Knight.

Bible Society Crusade in Kerry

Regrettably, the Napoleonic era in Kerry is remarkable for the beginnings of a new polarisation of society along religious lines. For this the activities of the new Protestant Crusade must take some of the blame. How times change! As late as 1800 a still-young Daniel O'Connell can help set up a Masonic lodge in Tralee with the town's Rector, Rev. John Blennerhassett, and the lawyer advising the Quarter-Sessions, Stephen Henry Rice. Such a group will be unthinkable by mid-century. (The British in Ireland crowd more and more to the banner of Anglicanism, while the new France is more and more a secular society and very hostile to the Catholic Church.)

Despite the threat of societal tensions, Kerry in Napoleonic times remains a remarkably integrated society. Emancipation may be placed on the back burner, but among high society at the Assembly Rooms, and those new villas being built around the Spa and Fenit, all the talk is about cross-community cooperation and shared Irish (*Milesian*) ancestry. Moore's sentimental melodies are in fashion and the O has begun to be reinserted in surnames; most important of all, conversion and intermarriage have long since done the work of smoothing social intercourse. The popular town Rector, Rev. James Day (1805-18, grand-father of historian Mary Hickson) is married to a daughter of MacGillycuddy of the Reeks, who makes a very imposing figure in the town. Mary Hickson's own father is descended from the knights of Kerry. The children of the owner of Tralee, Sir Edward Denny, have, from his wife, Elizabeth Day, the blood the Knights and the viscounts Clare (O'Brien), which means of course the blood of the Rebel Earl himself. These new Dennys grow to adulthood with the new century; the boys become clergymen filling the rectories and vicarages around Tralee well into the second half of the century.[267]

The chosen battle ground of the Bible societies is education. Did Bishop Hussey of Waterford stoke the fires back in 1796 when he issued a famous pastoral letter condemning Protestant schooling? Judge Day thought so. Edmund Ignatius

---

267 See, for example, obituary in *K.E.P.*, 26 Sept. 1877 of "Rev. Henry Denny, third son of Sir Edward Denny, Bart ... Rector of the united parishes of Ballinahaglish, Clogherbrien and Annagh for half a century".

Rice appears to have been influenced by Hussey's pastoral to found his Irish Christian Brothers.[268] Rice, to the great surprise of commercial circles in his native Waterford, decided to spend his life educating the poor, opening his first school in New Street in 1802 and using the name suggested by Hussey: Mount Sion. Vows are taken in 1808 with a rule modelled on that of the Presentation sisters, and the papal brief establishing the order of Christian Brothers is granted in 1820.[269]

The Bible societies view the contemporary Catholic revival as a formidable challenge. Many moderates see no conflict at all, only a common desire to quell revolution by means of moral regeneration, whose benefits will be a higher life than addiction to drink and crime. The more zealous Tories are inspired by the moral regeneration movement of Mrs Hannah Moore who by 1800 is distributing her religious tracts far and wide. The anti-slavery Society, founded in 1787, has become identified strongly with Tory evangelicals. William Wilberforce convinced Pitt – in their famous conversation "at the root of an old tree at Holwood just above the steep descent into the Vale of Keston" – to introduce to Parliament the great measure of Abolition. There is criticism of some westernising evangelical activity in India at this time: opponents capitalise greatly when Indians massacre the British soldiers in Vellore in 1806 after the British tried to implement a policy of new turbans and the shaving of beards. It is important to recall these tensions not only in the context of the Protestant crusade in Kerry but for a greater understanding of the Indian environment facing our soldiers and civilians who serve there in the course of the nineteenth century.

Some of the new private initiatives in education have Indian evangelisation as their inspiration, such as the school system of Andrew Bell in Madras, and the system of Joseph Lancaster who visits Tralee and Limerick in Napoleonic times to found schools.

The Association for Promoting Christian Knowledge (APCK, founded 1792) is already active in Kerry. More recently, the Hibernian Society (founded 1806) has begun founding schools which are open to children of all religious peruasions. The Kildare Place Society (founded 1811) becomes the channel for disbursing grant assistance to the schools. The condition for grant assistance will be the formula of "reading the Holy Scriptures without note or comment". Good, say the fledgling Protestant Bible societies; bad, say the Catholic clergy now preparing to gain control of primary education. The conflict will generate a real controversy in Kerry ten years hence.

268 J.D. Fitzpatrick, *Edmund Rice* (Dublin 1945), pp. 85-99.
269 Fitzpatrick, *Edmund Rice.*

From 1808 to 1812 Tralee returns James Stephen, the famous anti-Slavery campaigner. A young Scottish lawyer who gave his best years in the West Indies, his sister is the wife of Wilberforce. Wilberforce, Stephen, Thomas Clarkson, Zacharay Macaulay (father of the famous historian) and others constitute the Clapham Sect (from the district in London where they live in a kind of evangelical colony), known also as the *Saints*; when Stephen is returned for Tralee, it is the Prime Minister himself, Spencer Perceval, who arranges the purchase from Judge Day and the Dennys. Stephen is very close to Perceval and is credited with initiating the Orders in Council, the counter-embargo on shipping to answer to Napoleon's blockade.

Dominic Rice and Peter Bodkin Hussey advance Emancipation with O'Connell

The rise of Daniel O'Connell to the forefront of Catholic politics happens against the background of Wellington's career in the Peninsula and the Bible Crusade in Kerry. He has collaborated in preparing the new petition to Parliament in 1805, becoming a visible leader in the heave against the old guard of the Catholic Committee from 1808 when the Emancipation issue is again permitted to be raised in Westminster. Yet for the foreseeable future, as the regime basks in the reflected glory of Wellington's victories, the Catholic cause is in a state of abeyance. The era may be summarised as the Rise of Emancipation to 1812, and its Fall from the defeat in Parliament at Westminster that summer, through the trial of its supporters in the Dublin courts over the next few years; then the campaign is postponed until the final struggle during the 1820s leading to ultimate victory.

We have seen how the O'Connells lived on terms of considerable amity with the governing elite of Kerry, in particular with those elements whose ancestors shared a common allegiance to James II at the Boyne. Daniel's future allies are the Whigs. But the Whigs must endure another decade or more in the political wilderness. For now the war has given O'Connell a fresh argument against the Tories on top of opposition to the Act of Union: the argument for Emancipation on the basis of Irishmen's participation in the struggle against Napoleon. Unwilling to make concessions, the Tory *win the war* mind set resents the fact that Napoleon can arrange a concordat with the Vatican while Britain is unable to reach a similar arrangement with the Irish Catholic leadership.

O'Connell's call for Emancipation on the basis of Irishmen's contribution to the war is echoed by his principal ally at Westminster, Maurice FitzGerald, the Knight of Kerry, who has severed himself temporarily from the governing elite in Kerry by his continued support for Emancipation: the Knight is solidly Tory on electoral reform, but he feels betrayed that the Union did not deliver Emancipation. At a Catholic dinner in 1811 the Knight promises, that "the progress of your Emancipation is rapid". He speaks in the aftermath of a British victory over the French at the far-away island of Java, in the East Indies, telling his audience that the fortress was taken by "50 Irish Catholics, and at their head (a gallant officer, a friend of mine) placed a Catholic officer!!" [270]

It is in the courts that O'Connell makes his great impression. There, his extraordinary temerity (helped by the fact of his exclusion, as a Catholic, from the highest positions in the law) is characterised by a willingness to attack, as Emmet did in his speech from the dock in 1803, an apparatus of justice in the service of the regime. With his organisation struggling to be heard against the drumbeat of war, he is accused of playing to the gallery of the rural agitators, raising and lowering the temperature in the rural areas as the occasion requires in order to secure his leadership and advance his cause.

We need to give the background to the important Dublin trials of the Catholic delegates. From the recurrence of the King's illness in 1810 there is the renewed prospect of power in the hands of the Regent, who is believed to support Catholic Emancipation. Catholic meetings take place to raise petitions and elect delegates to a national Catholic assembly. But the outcome is disappointment. In 1811 the national assembly is prohibited, and the first of the trials of the Delegates begins late in the year and continues in the next; a feature of these trials is the alliance with the liberal press, chief among which is the *Dublin Evening Post* with its courageous editor John Magee.

Excitement rises to a fever pitch in Kerry, but a division appears over the object of the campaign. Many who wish the campaign well are in favour of a negotiated agreement in which the government will retain the right to nominate Catholic bishops. Lord Castlerosse, son of Lord Kenmare, is probably one of these. But it is the extremists we read about: those who will press on for unqualified Emancipation. Barrister Dominic Rice, chairman the Catholic meetings at this time, has a background in the United Irishmen. Counsellor Peter Bodkin Hussey, father of the literary land agent Sam Hussey, is described as "a satellite of the Kerry Demosthenes, Councillor Daniel O'Connell, so well known at all the Dublin meetings for Catholic Emancipation".[271] He is so fiery he earns the names "Red Precipitate" and "Salt Peter". When Rice chairs a "Meeting of Roman Catholics and

270 *Limerick Evening Post*, 25 December 1811
271 Wellington Papers, Hartley Library, University of Southampton, T.Stoughton to Major General Sir Arthur Wellesley, 20 March 1808

Friends of Religious Freedom" in Tralee on Monday 20 January 1812, Hussey proclaims that, "The right of Petition has been procured by the blood of our ancestors".[272]

In May everybody is overtaken by events. Prime Minister Perceval is assassinated in the Houses of Parliament. In the political vacuum moderates on both sides hope for a government that will include Canning:

> "The most favoured conjecture here is that Lord Wellesley, Canning and that phalanx will come in, the first to be Minister and First Lord of the Treasury, and the second his Chancellor of the Exchequer; and in that case some concessions to be made to the Catholics; as the Army and Navy, which I think would be vary desirable. It would detach the most meritorious as well as the most formidable classes from the Body, who by mingling with Protestant society and detached from their Priests would insensibly reform without recantation."[273]

Instead, Lord Liverpool is made Prime Minister in June, sealing the return of the Ultra Tories. Canning introduces a motion in the Commons in late June to take into consideration in the session of next year the laws against Catholics; the motion is carried by a large majority, but is thrown out in the Lords.

Now the extremists seize the moment. The Catholics of Kerry meet again on 1 July at the New Chapel in Tralee, Lord Castlerosse in the chair, just as the Ultra Tories in the House of Lords are throwing out Canning's moderate initiative; among the resolutions passed, proposed by Kean Mahony, seconded by John O'Connell of Grenagh, is the following:

> "That, as Irishmen and as Catholics, we would deem the annexation of any conditions or stipulations to our freedom, as a wanton instrument to our loyalty and our honor, and as calculated to injure the religion which we have inherited from our ancestors, and to which we firmly and constitutionally adhere."[274]

The defeat of the Catholic motion in Parliament in 1812 (and the defeat of Grattan's Bill in the following year), has marked the semi-retirement of the aristocrats and the take-over of the movement by O'Connell, who forges ahead with a demand for unqualified Emancipation and prepares an ever-stronger alliance with the priests.

---

272 *Cork Mercantile Chronicle*, Friday, 24 January 1812.
273 National Archives Ireland, Herbert Mss., M/1859/68; Robert Day, 16 May 1812 to Richard Townshend Herbert, Cahernane, Killarney.
274 *Limerick Gazette and General Advertiser*, 11 July 1812.

In early August 1812 one of the Batemans disturbs a Catholic meeting in Tralee by tearing down the transparency used in an illumination, with the result that the assembled crowd "immediately proceeded to acts of violence, by knocking down some, and striking others of the most respectable gentlemen of our county". John O'Connell of Grenagh, the Liberator's brother, has words with a Richard Blennerhassett over the incident, causing Blennerhassett to make a number of attempts over the succeeding three months to arrange a duel – without success. But on 13 November on the road between John O'Connell's home and the town of Killarney John O'Connell is wounded when Maurice O'Connor of Tralee shoots him in the arm in retaliation for something John O'Connell has said.[275] The incident is witnessed by a Bateman and a Twiss, but when Maurice O'Connor is brought to trial it is decided that Maurice O'Connor's action can not have been premeditated, and he is acquitted.[276]

The snows of that winter force Napoleon's retreat from Moscow; and Tory confidence in ultimate victory is further boosted with the victory of Leipzig in the new year. In Britain it is the age of the Luddites – the machine breakers in the factories – while in Ireland O'Connell's has begun his extraordinary series of performances in the Dublin courts at the trials of the Dublin Catholic delegates which will culminate in his attack on the Attorney-General in the trial for libel of newspaper editor John Magee.

The struggle over the schools intensifies. According to Padraig de Brún, in 1814 the Hibernian Society "underwent a complete revolution, abandoned the preaching of the Gospel and distribution of religious tracts, and determined on confining its exertions to the establishment and support of schools, and the distribution of the Holy Scriptures".[277] But the Catholic hierarchy is unlikely to agree to share the hearts and minds of Kerry's youth with the Bible Crusade.

---

275 *Cork Mercantile Chronicle*, Friday, 24 January 1812.
276 *Limerick Gazette*, 1 December, 24 November, 4 December 1812, *O'Connell Correspondence*, 16 February 1813, 25 March 1813.
277 Padraig de Brún, "The Kildare Place Society in Kerry", in *J.K.A.H.S.*, 1979, pp.63-118, p.64.

Napoleon, 1814 (Meissonnier)

Era of Advancing Liberalism

"Orange Peel ... a raw youth squeezed out of the workings of I know not what factory in England, and sent over to Ireland before he had got rid of the foppery of perfumed handkerchiefs and thin shoes ..."
O'Connell on Robert Peel.

Sir Robert Peel (1788-1850)

Robert Peel, Kerry and Daniel O'Connell

It may seem strange to begin a chapter on nineteenth-century Liberalism – a concept founded on the most famous slogan of the French Revolution, Liberté-Egalité-Fraternité – with the figure of Robert Peel (1788-1850), the arch-Tory, from the party opposed to electoral reform and Catholic Emancipation. Yet Peel plays an important part in addressing the obvious societal tensions in Ireland from this time. The son of a Lancashire textile magnate, Peel arrives as Chief Secretary in 1812 and spends a very formative few years here on his path to the prime ministership of England. Toryism has been softened during the war as Britain found herself fighting alongside the Spanish and Italian patriots; and even if revolution is crushed again in Spain in 1820 the case for removing the causes of revolution here at home is incontestible.

Something about Peel will provoke O'Connell to draw on his great powers of invective: he says much about Peel's supposed Orangeism, and his smile is "like the silver plate on a coffin". Peel comes from New Money, and is therefore outside the circle of the wealthy inherited governing class; yet he is no moderate like Canning, but a Throne-and-Altar conservative and firm opponent of Catholic Emancipation.

While Chief Secretary, Peel forms a connection with the Dennys, and through them with the leading Tralee Tory of the middle years of the nineteenth century, clergyman-antiquarian Rev. Archdeacon Arthur Blennerhassett Rowan (b. 1800), editor and mainstay of *The Kerry Magazine*. While Rev. A.B. Rowan is recuperating in London in 1824 after a short illness he visits the wife of his uncle, the unfortunate Sir Barry Denny killed back in 1794.[278] She is now Lady Denny Floyd, having married General Sir John Floyd in 1805 (the second time for both). Some years prior to the visit of the young Tralee clergyman, Lady Denny Floyd arranged a visit to the Floyd home (Mansfield Street, off Portland Place) from Robert Peel, on which occasion Peel renewed acquaintance with one of Floyd's daughters, Julia. (Julia and her step-mother first met Peel, probably at some official function in Dublin at the time when General Floyd was serving in Ireland.) The meeting at Floyd's home initiated a courtship, and Peel and Julia Floyd (b. 1795) were married in June 1820, Julia becoming the great support of Peel's extraordinary political career. Archdeacon Rowan wrote it all up in a book, where he states that Lady Peel was "the favourite step-daughter" of Lady Denny Floyd.[279]

---

278 Sir Barry Denny's wife was Anne Morgel, daughter of a Co. Limerick attorney.
279 Archdeacon Arthur Blennerhassett Rowan, *Tralee and its Provosts Sixty Years On, with introduction by The Last of its Provosts* (Private Collection, only 24 copies printed", 24 printed 1860; Introduction, p.xi.

Archdeacon Rowan does much for the poor of Kerry in the course of the Famine, but his outlook is very conservative on political and church reform: he will not live to see the Disestablishment of his Irish Church, and before the *Kerry Magazine* makes its appearance he is writing from his home, Belmont (Tralee), to the editor of *The Standard* to blame the Oxford Movement for the drift to Rome of leading young Anglicans at Oxford under the influence of Pusey and John Henry Newman.[280]

Let us return to the course of events. Peel, "a tall commanding figure and a frame so strong as to endure the labours of prime minister at the rate of sixteen hours a day",[281] arrives in Ireland in 1812 as a young Chief Secretary to viceroy Lord Whitworth. He finds a country run by patronage at the top, and at the bottom wracked by rural crime – crime so endemic in places like North Kerry and West Limerick that Peel reverts easily to High Tory prejudice and the belief that the Irish race is ungovernable. Yet this remarkable man will shortly embark on a programme of administrative and legislative reform.

Peel arrives just in time to slip into the Dublin court rooms for one of the Catholic trials, where he catches his first sight of O'Connell. The preliminary business of the trials permits O'Connell and his fellow counsel to attack the packing of juries; when the preliminaries are over O'Connell takes centre stage to defend his Catholic organisation against charges of involvement with the rural campaign. In the following year at the trial of the editor of the *Dublin Evening Post*, John Magee, O'Connell attacks the Attorney-General, Saurin in a memorably long tirade lasting a number of hours:

> "I defy him to allege a law or a statute, or even a proclamation, that is violated by the Catholic Board. … I disdain his moderation; I scorn his forbearance; I tell him he knows not the law, if he thinks as he says; and if he thinks so, I tell him to his beard, that he is not honest in not having sooner prosecuted us – and I challenge him to that prosecution."[282]

Occasions like this cause the poet Yeats over a century later to reflect on O'Connell's influence on Irish society and Irish life: "His violent nature, his invective, his unscrupulousness, are the chief cause of our social and political divisions".[283]

---

280 Rev. A.B. Rowan, *Romanism in the Church, illustrated by the case of E.B. Browne as stated in the Letters of the Rev. Dr. Pusey* (Belmont 1847).

281 *Dictionary of National Biography*.

282 Seán Ó Faoláin, *King of the Beggars* (1938), 1970 edn, p. 162.

283 W. B. Yeats, *Tribute to Thomas Davis* (Thomas Davis Centenary address 1945, published by Cork Univ. Press 1947, 1965 reprint), p. 15.

Peel makes an important advance towards a professional police when he replaces the old "Barneys", the baronial police of the 1780s, with the new Peace Preservation Force (P.F.F., the "Peelers") of 1814. The legislation permits the Lord Lieutenant to "proclaim" a district without waiting from magistrates to request such, and then appoint a stipendiary magistrate; the payment of the stipendiary magistrate and the sub-constables will fall on the people. In 1817 a modification is introduced comprising relief from $\frac{2}{3}$ of the costs of a district proclaimed, to be paid by the county. The system is extended in 1822 in response to the Rockite disturbances with some provisions for stipendiary magistrates to act in a coordinated manner instead of individually.

The new police is greeted as yet another sign of a government bent on oppression. But this time opposition comes from an unusual quarter: one of the circuit judges. In 1814 Judge William Fletcher, speaking in Wexford, gives a famous Charge in which he refuses to blame the poor; instead he links the disturbances with underlying root causes, and when he lists these he includes the new police force of Peel. Feelings are running very high after the Catholic and Magee trials. In June 1814, after the defeat of Napoleon, the Catholic Board is suppressed, and the Insurrection Act, under which trial by jury is suspended, is renewed.

Daniel O'Connell
(print by Ray, 1813, courtesy National Gallery of Ireland)

These are bad days for the Catholic cause. O'Connell is tempted into a duel in February 1815 with John D'Esterre after O'Connell referred to "the beggarly corporation of Dublin". Judge Day tries to intervene (according to the press report Day pursues O'Connell to a personal rendezvous, and obtains certain assurances from O'Connell), but O'Connell and D'Esterre meet at Rathcoole, where O'Connell shoots D'Esterre dead.[284]

A number of voices respond to Judge Fletcher's criticism, including Judge Day in the course of an address to the Westmeath Grand Jury. Unlike Fletcher, Day praises the new police force and denounces the Catholic campaign as a major source of the disturbances. Day's choice of language is particularly severe, referring the Catholic campaign as "a flame which in my conscience I consider as originating and vomiting forth from the Dublin Crater, at Aggregate and other meetings, by Separatists and enemies to the British name and connection".[285] O'Connell now launches a scathing *ad hominem* attack on Day at an Aggregate Meeting of the Catholics of Cork in the South Parish Chapel on Friday 7 April. We recall that Napoleon has escaped from the island of Elba and taken over the government of France again; prices have risen and Kerrymen are in jubilant mood, the pig farmers and pig buyers celebrating with the slogan, "Hurrah for Boney that rose the pigs".[286] Here is O'Connell at the South Parish Chapel:

> "Let it be recollected that one great cause of the fall of the Bourbons and of the restoration of Napoleon, was the generally received opinion in France, that the Bourbon judges were partial and corrupt. The first and most popular act of Napoleon was his proclamation or decree from Lyons, restoring the former tribunals and judges. The Bourbon judges were said to be frightful partizans of the small faction of returned emigrants; it was said they prejudged every question that came before them; that they convicted before investigation, argument or trial; and even held out lures to the government to send victims to their tribunals, rather than want causes for trial, promising beforehand to get sure convictions."[287]

---

284 Six months later O'Connell and Peel arrange to meet in a duel, but the meeting never materialises.
285 Charge of Judge Day at Mullingar to the County Westmeath Grand Jury, *Freeman's Journal*, 25 March, 1815.
286 Sam Hussey, *Reminiscences of an Irish Land Agent* (London 1904), p. 23.
287 *Cork Mercantile Chronicle*, 14 April 1815; *Freeman's Journal*, 18 April 1815.

The moment passes. When the Duke of Wellington and the Prussians defeat Napoleon at Waterloo (near Brussells, 1815), Tory rule is copper-fastened in Britain and Ireland as well as throughout Europe The Holy Alliance ("Concert of Europe") of the Crowned heads of Europe (including the ultra-reactionary Tsar Alexander of Russia) is coordinated by the great Austrian chancellor Prince Metternich, ably assisted by England's foreign minister Lord Castlereagh. Historians refer to the next fifteen years as the Bleak Age. The end of the war brings a slump in agricultural prices, with shattering impact on Kerry and the South of Ireland, while demobilisation releases soldiers into the rural areas in time to fan the flames the unrest.

In 1815 the government introduces a Bill which greatly assists the curtailment of farm subdivision: the assistant-barrister of the county only has to authorize the removal of unprofitable under-tenants for the will of the landlord to be implemented. The Tenantry Act fuels resentment against government seen on the side of the powerful.

In 1815 Peel drafts a plan to assist Irish families willing to settle in Canada. Better known are his attempts at this time to reform the workings of the Irish grand juries, whose presentments (budgets) for roads and bridges are well known to be inflated by corruption, with the consequence that grand jury cess weighs very heavily on the shoulders of the Irish poor. (The situation gives rise to the phrase "Bad cess to you".) The appointment of county surveyors under the legislation of 1817 ensures a more transparent examination of the presentments passed by county grand juries, and from 1818 all grand jury presentments must be made to a full attendance of magistrates at the quarter sessions previous to the assizes. The nomination of Kerry's high sheriff is taken out of the hands of county politicians in 1818; henceforth the assize justices will take the names of three candidates for the government in Dublin to nominate one. The office will continue outside the grasp of Catholics until Emancipation in 1829.

A personal tragedy plunges Tralee into mourning in the summer of Waterloo, when a young man dies in a duel at the hands of one of those cantankerous attorneys who have been such a feature of the Revolutionnary age. Here is the story. Cait Áilinn (Beautiful Cathleen), sister of John Bateman FitzGerald of Glin Castle married the sometime provost of Tralee, Maurice O'Connor. Their son, Henry Arthur O'Connor, is shot dead by the much older Rowan Cashel, "gentleman attorney", in a duel at Ballyseedy in August 1815. The town of Tralee goes into mourning. Cashel is brought to trial with every confidence of a conviction, for he has a record of many duels and a disregard for the rule of law. But a Charge from the presiding judge, Judge Day, a Tralee native, in which the younger man is made equally culpable, helps bring in a verdict of Not Guilty. The rule of law is hardly enhanced by the turmoil that greets the verdict and the release of Rowan Cashel; and when the victim's family put pen to paper and petition Parliament, they allege that the judge and Cashel are members of the same political faction in the county's politics.

Partial Famine of 1817

After the dreadful summer rain of 1816 a partial famine returns in 1817, accompanied by typhoid fever and widespread distress. The potatoes turn to balls of soap and the turf is sodden, which affects the drying of clothes, which, added to the hunger and debility, provides very favourable conditions for the outbreak and spread of typhus. Typhus is the travelling companion of unemployment, starvation, poor housing, insanitary conditions, wet climate and lack of fuel. William Carleton has described the human suffering in his novel *The Black Prophet*, in which the scenes are based on the famines of 1817 and 1822:

> "The same agent that destroyed the harvest spoiled the turf. Seldom had such a multiplication of evils come together. In some of the former years, although food and bedding were deficient, the portion saved was of good quality, and fuel was not wanting; but in 1816 every comfort that might have compensated for partial want was absent. This description applies to the two years of 1816 and 1817. In mid summer of 1817, the blaze of fever was over the entire country. It had burst forth almost in a thousand different points. Within the short space of a month, in the summer of 1817, the epidemic sprung forth in Tramore, Youghal, Kinsale, Tralee and Colnmel, in Carrick-on-Suir, Roscrea ..."[288]

In February 1817 a mob leaves Tralee and attacks a brig at Blennerville containing corn for Limerick. They cause the corn to be re-landed and damage the brig.[289] A local magistrate calms the situation. Later in the year one of the circuit judges hears from Tralee that the fever epidemic has put "twenty six miserably bad cases in the new and old jail". (The new jail is being brought into use with some of the prisoners being moved from the old.) The Kerry Assizes are postponed to prevent the confluence of people and the inevitable spread of infection. Eventually the judges arrive in Tralee at the end of August, having reversed the circuit and come from Cork.

---

288 Quoted in Raymond Murray, *The Burning of Wildgoose Lodge, Ribbonism in Louth – Murder and the Gallows* (Armagh 2005), p. 39.
289 National Archives of Ireland, State Paper 1835/31; Tralee, 27 February 1817.

In 1817 Parliament authorises the construction of asylums for the lunatic poor. Bishop Sughrue writes from Killarney of "the extraordinary and unprecedented demand for admission of fever cases into our Hospital" and that "I shall strongly impress on the poor people what they owe to the munificence and humanity of Government in a year of such unexampled difficulties". Peel recommends that the famine relief committee send £40 to the Killarney Fever Hospital, which they do.[290] In the first half of 1818 it is reported that there is a steady increase of "applications for admission into the hospital".[291]

Private efforts to assist the relief of distress are remembered by former political opponents. When the dust settles on the general election of 1818 a Dinner is held in Tralee to honour Daniel O'Connell. O'Connell has this to say about his old rival, Judge Day, whose retirement from the bench has become known and whose grandson Edward Denny enjoyed O'Connell's support in the general election for one of the county seats (Denny lost):

> "Do you require testimony of his worth as a landlord –
> go and ask his happy tenantry, and they will tell you he
> is not an excellent, but the very best of landlords. They
> will tell you how he fostered and cherished them during
> the bad times, out of which I hope we are escaping,
> and their present prosperity speaks their praise with an
> eloquence that no eulogium can equal ... With these
> social virtues he retires from public life into the bosom
> of a society which will, I trust, render the remainder
> of his life happy, by bestowing on him that respectful
> kindliness which he deserves as an excellent landlord,
> a kind friend, and a good man (Loud and general
> applause)."[292]

Peel's experience in Ireland so confirms his intransigence that when he leaves in 1818 he continues to embody resistance to Emancipation. He is returned to Parliament for Oxford, a bastion of the Ultra Tories, and as MP he leads the opposition to William Conyngham Plunket's Emancipation Bill of 1821, which is lost in the Lords. He will continue to have an important

---

290 *N.A.I*, Herbert papers, M/1859/117 C. Sughrue, Killarney, October 18, 1817
   to Richard T. Herbert.
291 *Freeman's Journal* 2 June 1818: report from Tralee dated 30 May.
292 The occasion is a dinner for O'Connell in Tralee's Mail Coach Hotel,
   reported in the *Kerry Herald*, reproduced in the *Freeman's Journal*, 9
   November 1818.

impact on Irish affairs as Home Secretary from 1822, but by degrees his resistance to Emancipation begins to thaw, and he is ready to make the first the famous u-turns of his political life when he supports the enactment of Emancipation in 1829 (when his great ally Wellington also sees the light); he will make an equally great u-turn from 1835 by beginning the work to dismantle the Corn Laws, which are perceived to favour the rich agricultural interests over the poor of the industrial cities and towns. On the church issue, a young William E. Gladstone believes that there is no greater traitor than Peel; he says so and leaves Peel's party temporarily; but Gladstone will execute a *volte face* of equally breathtaking proportions from the 1860s to the 1880s, first to Disestablish the same Church of Ireland, then give the farmers of Kerry the ownership of their farms.

Maurice FitzGerald (1772-1849), Knight of Kerry
(courtesy Sir Adrian FitzGerald)

The 1820s: the decade of Canning, Griffith's Roads and Valentia's Slate Quarries

From the early 1820s there is a change of direction as we approach the end of the Bleak Age of the Congress of Europe and the repressive principles of Austria's Prince Metternich, ably assisted by Britain's Castlereagh. Change will come slowly. The insurrections in Europe in 1820 are ruthlessly repressed, but the international congresses begin to demonstrate an unease with the policy of assisted repression. Canning as Foreign Minister is the representative of the change. Nearer home, his sponsorship of Catholic Emancipation is crucial to keeping the issue before the Westminster Parliament. In 1827 he will be Prime Minister.

Pressure from liberal opinion, including artists like the poet Byron and those too young to have any memory of the outrages committed by the first years of the French Revolution, begins now to influence the direction of politics. Indeed Byron becomes one of the icons of the age when he dies in Greece assisting the revolution there in 1824.

King George IV (no longer the *Regent*), comes to Ireland in 1821, his visit symbolic of a thaw in relations between the two countries. O'Connell bends the knee to greet him, an action held against O'Connell by his opponents; but O'Connell has an important new ally now in William Conyngham Plunket, successor to Grattan (obit.1820) as the leading voice of the Catholics in Parliament and Attorney-General (Ireland) from 1822. Canning returns to the cabinet in 1822 on the death by suicide of his rival Castlereagh, and as Foreign Minister sponsors the freedom of South America, "calling the New World into existence to balance the Old". Men from Kerry go off to fight under Simon Bolivar in the *South American Irish Legion*. They include Morgan O'Connell, son of the Liberator, and Daniel Florence O'Leary of Cork whose people originated in the O'Leary homeland at the headwaters of the River Lee, near the border of Kerry.

From the beginning of 1822 a forward-looking viceroy takes up his posting to Dublin: Marquess Richard Wellesley (elder brother of Wellington). No sooner settled in at Dublin, a Protestant faction targets him in a Dublin theatre, the unusual missile used by the mob becoming the subject of Dublin wit in the so-called "Bottle Riot". Marquess Wellesley sends the civil engineer Richard Griffith to Kerry in 1822 to lay out three main lines of new roads as part of a strategy to foster trade and at the same time quell lawlessness. The new lines are Newmarket to Listowel, Newcastle via Abbeyfeale to Castleisland, and Newmarket to Charleville.[293] The roads assist

---

293 Seán Ó Lúing, "Richard Griffith and the Roads of Kerry", in *J.K.A.H.S.*, 1976, pp. 92-124, p. 92.

greatly the growth of commercial prosperity; by 1829 a traveller can report as follows:

> "At Tralee the eye of the stranger is immediately arrested by the number of the new grain stores that have been erected. I think upon inquiry I was told, that out of eighteen or nineteen which I counted, three of them only were in existence as recently as the year 1813, and those three were the smallest of them. Much of the corn stored in those granaries must be the produce of the lands which have been opened up by the formation of this road (Rathkeale-Castleisland) of Mr. Griffith's".[294]

Griffith reports from Tralee the campaign to link the town with the harbour by a canal. In the south of the county since 1819 the Knight of Kerry has been quarrying the slate beds on Valentia Island. Slate will be shipped to London for the manufacture of billiard tables and roofing. At its peak the industry will employ five hundred men and provide a valuable addition to the income of islanders during the Great Famine of the 1840s.

In 1822 Lansdowne is attempting to foster the linen industry and wondering if he should finance a scutch mill. In 1824 the Knight writes to the Irish viceroy's brother, his old friend the Duke of Wellington, of his plans for Valentia as the starting point of Atlantic steam navigation: "The passage to Halifax would be ten days, and to New York and Quebec fourteen days. The journey would be made once a fortnight or even once a week".[295] This project will fall victim to the money crisis of 1826, when the Knight and Daniel O'Connell will lose their investments. Another government road builder, Alexander Nimmo, springs to the Knight's defence:

> "I think the Irish people are more indebted to that gentleman for his strenuous and successful endeavours to induce Parliament and the Government to take up the subject of the improvement of Ireland, and to come forward with liberal grants or loans of public money for the encouragement of her trade, the fishing, the linen manufacture, the opening and improving the mountain districts by roads – and the coasts and harbours by piers, quays &c than to any other of the members of the British Legislature. The whole of the measures now in operation

---

294 Ó Lúing, "Griffith", p. 97.
295 Wellington Papers, University of Southampton, WP1/796/12 19 Jun 1824, Maurice FitzGerald to Arthur Wellesley.

for the employment of the poor in public works may be traced to the committee of which he was the most active member and drawer up ... arising from ... disease of the year 1817."[296]

The 1822 Famine – Captain Rock –
Pastorini's prophesy

Famine, meanwhile, has returned to Kerry in 1821 with the failure of the potato crop west of a line from Derry to Cork. Here is *The Limerick Chronicle* of Wednesday 8 May 1822. Tralee, May 4:

> "The condition to which the starving poor are reduced in the South West of Ireland is most grievous and appalling. In several (*sic*), potatoes have already risen to eight pence per stone, equivalent to two shillings three or four years ago! The people are famishing even at this early period of the season: our streets are thronged with miserable starving clamorous beggars, and swarms of naked, half-starved children, who from their numbers, appearance and importunity it may be supposed would devour all the provisions in a large town to satisfy the cravings of hunger; sickness and epidemic diseases follow close on the heels of famine. They are the natural result of bad food and starvation. Typhus fever of the most malignant kind, begins to rage ..."

It is now that Captain Rock makes his appearance on the Courtenay estate in Newcastle West. In July 1821 the son of Alexander Hoskins, agent on the Courtenay estate centred on Newcastle West, is killed, and in the same year Major Richard Going, Chief Magistrate of Police, County of Limerick, is murdered. Kerry witnesses an appalling crime in the murder of Major Collis on 21 Nov. 1821 at his home, Kent Lodge, near Spa. Baron Pennefather later sentences to death two men by the name of Coppinger, and a man named Costello to transportation. The circumstances of Major Collis's murder - shot a dozen times in the body, robbed of money and his wife threatened not to summon assistance - appals the county. Over in Meanus (near Castleisland) Francis Drew builds up the windows of his house to protect his wife and four children.[297] We might include here a murder which

296 FitzGerald papers, copy for the Knight of Nimmo's letter (to ?), letter dated Killarney, 31 August 1824.
297 National Archives, SOC 431/2295/22 Francis Drew, Meanus, to Charles Grant, November 25th 1821.

appals the whole of Ireland. One September night in 1823 some men wearing white shirts over their clothes enter the home of the Franks family, between Rockmills and Kildorrery. Husband, wife and son are killed. Mr Franks was agent for Lord Kingston, and it was said that he had dealt harshly with some of the tenants. Brothers by the name of Cronin are convicted for these murders. Daniel O'Connell successfully defends one O'Keeffe and Thomas Bourke put on trial for the crime; they are found not guilty. A few years later O'Connell consolidates his courts reputation ("The Counsellor") when he defends a group of men indicted as part of the "Doneraile Conspiracy" in 1829; a celebrated account of this episode appears in the historical novel *Glenanaar* by Patrick Augustine Sheehan, parish priest of Doneraile.

The Tithe Composition Act of 1823 attempts to addres the tithe issue with a fixed rate for each parish agreed by commissioners appointed by the land occupiers and the owners of tithes. The high constables will hand to the church wardens a list of the leading cess (grand jury charge) payers of the parish. This list of names will be posted on the door of the Protestant church, and they will convene in a special vestry to agree a rate calculated on the average of the seven years preeceding November 1821.

If the Bible societies have contributed to strained relations throughout Kerry, the Catholic poor await the fulfilment of the prophesies of Pastorini which have foretold the overthrow of Protestantism in the year 1825. In 1815 Thomas Spring Rice of Mount Trenchard intervened with the Bishop of Limerick, Dr Tuohy, to silence the parish priest of Glin, Fr McEniry, who was telling his congregation that "a large lady of Orangeism was to be sent from England, that would cut the legs and arms of Roman Catholics and allow them to bleed to death ...".[298]

No sooner back in Ireland having testified to the Lords committee of 1825 O'Connell has to depart his usual script about interdenominational accord. A certain Rev. John McCrea has been encouraging Mrs Talbot-Crosbie (Ardfert Abbey) with her efforts to found a school at Ardfert; and McCrea has controversial things to say about popular devotion at the nearby holy well, *Tobar Na Molt*. Tralee curate Fr Walsh is critical of McCrea's activities,[299] and at a Catholic meeting in Dublin O'Connell seizes on the controversy to discredit "Johnny McCrea". McCrea responds with charges of deliberate misrepresentation.[300]

Thomas Moore, the "Bard of Erin", visits Kerry during a tour of the South as a guest of the Marquess of Lansdowne in 1823. Lansdowne has persuaded Moore to come and live near Bowood, his mansion in Wiltshire. Up to the time of this tour of the South

---

298 Tom Donovan, "The Visionary, the Liberator and the Bishop" in *The Old Limerick Journal*, no.33, 1996.
299 Maurice O'Connell and Gerard Lyne, *The Correspondence of Daniel O'Connell*, Rev. M. Walsh, C.C. Ardfert, to Daniel O'Connell, Tralee, 22 October 1826.
300 *Kerry Evening Post*, 7, 14 May, 1828.

with Lansdowne, Moore has been a critic of rural insurrection, but now he sees the county in the aftermath of famine and the Rockite campaign. He meets the likes of O'Connell, who informs Moore that the draconian powers given land agents and land lords since 1815 have exacerbated unrest, on top of the fall of prices consequent on the defeat of Napoleon and the ending of the war. Moore returns to his cottage at Sloperton to write *A History of Captain Rock and his Ancestors*.

Education is the principal battleground for the souls of the Irish poor. Bishop James Doyle of Kildare and Leighlin (he is known as *JKL*) publishes tracts to counter the work of the Kildare Place Society and its sponsorship of the schools of the Hibernian Society. When the *Society* sets up a school in Killorglin Fr Luoney (Looney) claims, that the people

> "withdrew their children from those schools, and returned all Testaments, Tracts &c which they got there, when the dangers to the faith of their children, if left at these schools, was pointed out to them, and when in case of refusal, this deponent and his assistant clergymen, threatened to withhold the Sacraments of the Church from them".[301]

Back in Tralee, Judge Day's Hibernian School on Strand Road encounters the opposition of the parish priest, the later bishop of Kerry Fr Cornelius Egan.[302] Fr Egan claimes to have promoted education "long before any free schools were established in Kerry by either the Kildare Place or Hibernian Societies (when) I had five in Tralee, one establishment in 1809 and the other in 1812, both giving education to 500 poor children".[303] Fr Egan will do business with the Bible Societies on condition that separate religious instruction can take place during school hours, something which runs counter to the ethos of schools receiving assistance from the Kildare Place Society. Judge Day's school has implemented the Society's policy of reading the scriptures "without note or comment", by this means keeping students together in the classroom.[304] In Blennerville the story is the same. There, John Kirby, a Catholic employed by the Hibernian Society, has the unhappy experience of seeing his school lose all his pupils after he is denounced from the altar; he

301 *Chute's Western Herald*, 7 May 1828; affidavit of Rev. James Luoney of Killorglin.

302 Cornelius Egan, d. 1856. (born Lismicfinan, Killorglin), Principal of the Diocesan School, Killarney, and Professor of Theology there 1806-1811; Parish Priest of Tralee 1811-24; Coadjutor Bishop of Kerry 1824; Bishop of Kerry 1824-56.

303 N.L.I., FitzGerald papers, Dr Cornelius Egan, Killarney, to the Knight of Kerry, 6 March 1825.

304 Padraig de Brún, "The Kildare Place Society in Kerry", in *J.K.A.H.S.* (1980) p. 123-4.

claims to have suffered excommunication and been pauperised when the people withdraw their children.[305] Fr Egan denies the excommunication but owns up to having ruined Kirby's school at Blennerville (as Fr Luoney did in Killorglin): "This as well as all other such schools was opposed by me and the consequence was that Kirby had no pupils".[306]

What will resolve the religious divide in schooling? The answer proves to be a compromise involving the moderates on both sides. These include the liberal unionist from neighbouring West Limerick, Thomas Spring Rice MP. Bishop James Doyle makes it plain that he is in favour of shared education – he only protests at the proselytising activities of the Bible societies:

> "I do not see how any man, wishing well to the public peace, and who looks to Ireland as his country, can think that peace can ever be permanently established, or the prosperity of the country ever well secured, if children are separated, at the commencement of life, on account of their religious opinions."[307]

Spring Rice campaigns throughout the 1820s for integrated education, and his work comes to fruition in the Bill of 1831:

> "Even though Spring Rice was at first unsuccessful in getting his proposals implemented, the final 1831 Bill embodied these proposals, and Spring Rice had legitimate grounds for claiming that the Irish National School System was his ... The National Schools system was an Irish system, developed by an Irish elite in the circumstances of the religious debates during the 1820s in Ireland, and Irish social circumstances."[308]

The Emancipation Campaign reaches a Crescendo

O'Connell prefers to work with the Whigs, and he feels particularly at ease with the left wing of the Whigs, the likes of Sir Francis Burdett and Henry Brougham, exponents of prison reform, popular education, electoral reform and the cause of anti-slavery, as well as Catholic Emancipation. Crowding to that banner now are young politicians like Thomas Spring

305 *Kerry Evening Post*, 14 May 1828.
306 Egan to Knight of Kerry, 6 March 1825 (opt.cit.).
307 "First Report of the Commissioners of Inquiry into Education in Ireland, 1825", quoted in Jennifer Ridden, *Making Good Citizens: National Identity, Religion, and Liberalism Among the Irish Elite*, Ph.D thesis at the London University, 1998, p.107.
308 Ridden, pp. 112, 114.

Rice. Spring Rice burst on the political scene with his election as MP for Limerick in 1820. He is grandson of Tom Rice of Ballycrispin (Castlemaine) who bought Mount Trenchard. There is also Lord Lansdowne, Henry Petty-FitzMaurice, who feels that his and the Whigs' chance will surely come soon. Spring Rice, Lansdowne and the Knight of Kerry know that the wind is at their backs when they support O'Connell's campaign for Emancipation. In the case of the Knight, this will distract from the fact that he and his Tory party are opposed to electoral reform. And he and Spring Rice and Lansdowne are at one in opposing O'Connell's plan to repeal the Union.

O'Connell democratises the campaign for Emancipation by setting up his Catholic Association when the "Catholic Rent" of a penny can be contributed by each poor family: hence O'Connell as "King of the Baggars", the title of Sean Ó Faoláin's biography. Popular democracy has arrived and the priests, far closer to the people than the bishops, become O'Connell's chief organisers. They will marshal the crowds to the polling stations to defy the will of the landlords and return pro-Catholic candidates at future elections. It makes an unedifying spectacle, but this is still the era of open voting (the secret ballot is a thing of the future) and who will say it is any worse than the spectacle of voters driven to the polling stations by their landlords to vote for the landlord's candidate?

In 1825 Sir Francis Burdett, in cooperation with Plunket and Canning, introduce a Catholic Bill in Westminster, but without success. O'Connell is in London at the time and witnesses the debate. Separately, O'Connell testifies before a select committee of the House of Lords about disturbances in Ireland, where he appears completely at ease with the offer of domestic nomination to the Irish hierarchy, adding that agreement might be reached within three to four years; he further states that he favours payment of the priests and disenfranchisement of the 40/- freeholders.[309] He will shortly regret his contribution.

In the general election in June the following year, 1826, the Catholic Association scores a remarkable success in unseating a Beresford in Waterford. Kerry is next. The pro-Catholic Knight of Kerry is returned. But there is no clean sweep. Elected also is the very young William Hare, grandson of the new and anti-Catholic power in the county, Lord Listowel.[310] Ventry has abandoned Col. Crosbie of Ballyheigue, who is taken up by the Catholics who remember his pro-Catholic form when he was High Sheriff in the year of relief legislation

309 *Report of the Select Committee of the House of Lords 1825*. Daniel O'Connell 123-171, p. 160.
310 As William Hare, Cork magnate, the future Earl of Listowel bought the FitzMaurice lands in the early 1780s.

of 1792.[311] Even if Lord Kenmare has ensured the return of the Knight of Kerry, Kenmare is seen as part of an aristocratic cartel with Ventry and Listowel, neatly carving up the county in a deal which means the erosion of Catholic unity. Ventry, Kenmare and Listowel (as Lord Ennismore) were rewarded for their support of the Act of Union; now in 1826, though there is a poll, the result is very much fixed by themselves, the Ventry freeholders being brought like slaves to the polling stating to vote as Ventry dictates.[312] The election is memorable for a strange commitment by a faction among the Catholics not to press any further demands once Emancipation is granted: they become known as the Orange Papists:[313]

> "When the agitation for Catholic Emancipation was in full swing in 1826, a good number of Roman Catholic gentry, among whom was Peter Bodkin Hussey ("Salt Peter"), entered into a kind of informal agreement that if it was granted they would be satisfied, and refrain from further agitation. For this they were reproached by the extremists and were called "Orange Papists".[314]

Col. Crosbie has a premonition of trouble and spends the first days of the poll trying to calm his supporters gathered in Tralee town; but he is unable to prevent what occurs on the 25 June, when his supporters attack the Ventry freeholders and beat them back to Blennerville when they try to enter Tralee, and the military, apparently under orders from the sheriff, shoot and kill a number of innocent people near the Court House:

> "The day the Ventry voters were coming in to Tralee to poll they were met at Blennerville by the town's men, who were always great Crosbie-ites, and who attacked them so violently that they fled back to their mountains to save their lives. This was the commencement of what is now known as "the shooting election" of 1826." [315]

311 This means the break down of the old alliance of the O'Connell's with the High Tories of Kerry seen to such useful effect in the 1818 election when Daniel O'Connell was the ally of Judge Day and the Dennys.

312 The aristocrats were accused of concealing their true allegiance to the Established Church behind promises of support for Catholic Emancipation. This was particularly hard to take in the cases of Hare and Ventry: Hare's proclamation in favour of Emancipation was considered risible by his critics in the Kerry press, while Ventry was well known to be a promoter of the Protestant mission in the Dingle Peninsula.

313 *Freeman's Journal*, 5, 7, 8, 10 July 1826.

314 *Kerry Evening Post*, 19 August 1914. This offer drew a dismayed reaction from a section of the Kerry public: "did ever a willing and sincere disposition to befriend Roman Catholics emanate from the House and Lineage of Listowel's Earl? – or can any friend to our cause proceed from the Castle of Convamore?" (*Kerry Evening Post*, 29 August 1914)

315 *Kerry Evening Post*, 19 August 1914.

The Knight will pay a heavy price for his part in the carve up of Kerry in 1826: the loss of his seat will be an unfair outcome given his long history on the Catholic side, but understandable as we approach the reform of Parliament and the final solution of tithe issue.

When Canning becomes Prime Minister in April 1827, it looks like Emancipation will be finally enacted, but the UltraTories abandon him and Canning is forced to form a coalition government with some of the Whigs, including the pro-Catholic Lansdowne. Then those who have abandoned ship oppose some of his Irish appointments, though Canning succeeds in having leading pro-Catholic William Conyngham Plunket raised to Chief Justice of the Court of Common Pleas after Lord Norbury (Emmet's judge) is finally persuaded to resign. Tragically, Canning dies in August (he has been ill since taking the prime-minister-ship), and by the beginning of the new year the ultra-Tories are back in power. The great measure is finally passed not by the mild administration of Canning, but by a government under Wellington as Prime Minister and Peel at the Home Office. Both have become converts to the cause, but it is *events* that force the arch-conservatives to give way in the end – events orchestrated by O'Connell. O'Connell puts forward his own name as the candidate for Clare in 1828. A Catholic is about to contest a parliamentary seat, and the leading Agitator at that! There is huge support and the priests are everywhere. He is elected easily and presents himself at Westminster. When he refuses to take the oath required of an MP before he can take his seat, popular pressure in Ireland mounts to a dangerous level and the country threatens to become ungovernable. Wellington and Peel know Ireland only too well. Wellington sounds the retreat, the passage of the Emancipation Bill considered a prudent response to a threatened civil war. O'Connell takes his seat in Parliament: the exclusive position of the Established Church under the Glorious Revolution is at an end.[316]

316 The comparison with Eamon De Valera's actions in the twentieth century is striking. De Valera is also elected for Clare and he refuses to take the Oath to the King when he appears at the Dail in 1926.

First Years after Emancipation:
the overthrow of the Tories

Emancipation has not conceded everything: clauses in the
Act forbid the use of ecclesiastical titles by Catholic bishops
and cardinals. And Catholics continue to be excluded from
the highest appointments in the Law, including the lord
chancellorship. There will be no immediate plans to re-
establish the Franciscans in Kerry. Their historian has written:
"All friars in the country were to register, all novitiates were
to close, no further friars would be allowed to return from
the Continent and thus the religious orders would slowly die
out. Only female orders and diocesan congregations would
survive."[317] Opponents from the Protestant side are correct in
their predictions: there will be more demands; the concession
of Emancipation prefigures the undermining of the Anglican
church in Ireland, which is finally disestablished by Gladstone
in 1869; moreover, Emancipation is a distraction from the real
grievances on the ground, those of rent and tithe, which have
yet to be tackled.

O'Connell has become identified with the cause
of liberation internationally. More locally, there has been a
growing if restrained clamour since the Act of Union against
the continuing domination of Judge Day over the borough
of Tralee, and in particular over the continued Corporation
practice of returning outsiders to the Westminster Parliament.
Protests culminate in a petition to Parliament in the summer
of Emancipation following the elction of Robert Vernon Smith,
described as a nephew of the famous Sydney Smith, founder
of the *Edinburgh Review,* therefore a Whig but nevertheless
unacceptable to O'Connell and the Tralee democrats. The
petition talks of the "violation of your petitioners' constitutional
rights" which have been "usurped" (by the Denny family) "by
virtue of a marriage settlement executed upon the intermarriage
of the present Sir Edward Denny, Baronet, with the daughter
of Robert Day, esq. late a Judge of his Majesty's Court of King's
Bench in Ireland". Three thousand pounds sterling is alleged
to be the price paid by the candidate for the Tralee seat.[318]

The achievement of Emancipation has not
satisfied O'Connell. He tells a Tralee audience in late
1829 that absenteeism, a "great curse" in Kerry, is draining
£150,000 a year in rents out of the county (*Western Herald,*
24 August 1829). In 1830, to mark the latest French
revolution (which places on the throne Louis Philippe,

317 Patrick Conlan OFM, *Franciscan Ireland* (Cork 1978), p. 46.
318 *The Western Herald,* June 29, 1829: petition to Parliament against the Return
    of Mr Robert Vernon Smith.

"the Citizen King"), he attends another meeting in Tralee with "an address congratulating the French people on the attainment of constitutional liberty" (*Kerry Evening Post*, 9 October 1830).

At the close of 1830 the long hegemony of the Tories comes to an end when the Whigs come to power with Lord Grey as Prime Minister. O'Connell should be happy. Instead he increases the pressure: he will play down the demand for repeal of the Act of Union of 1800 if he can promote a raft of reform proposals of his own, which includes rebalancing the grand juries and the Irish corporations in favour of Catholics, and abolishing tithes. In 1831 he puts up candidates in the general election pledged to the repeal of the Union. In Kerry he unhorses his old ally the Knight of Kerry to take one of the county seats for himself. Has a failed investment in the Knight's Atlantic Navigation Company prejudiced him against his old friend? It represents the breaking of an old alliance with the faithful Knight, a Tory who has nevertheless been his constant ally in the struggle for Emancipation. Next year, when the Whigs bring in the Great Reform Law, his son Maurice O'Connell ousts Sir Edward Denny from the parliamentary representation of Tralee! The result is Maurice O'Connell 91, Sir Edw Denny 71. Old friendships count for little! More accurately, the peace which he patched up with the owners of Tralee when he supported young Edward Denny, son of Sir Edward, in the 1818 general election, is now torn up in the aftermath of the Reform Law. In Dublin, where O'Connell takes one of the two seats at the end of 1832, there is no friendship at all: the city is a bastion of the Orange prejudice; moreover, Catholics are still not receiving their due in appointments to high office under the Irish government of Stanley (the future prime minister Lord Derby).

In a diary entry of 7 January 1833 Judge Day, wounded at the ingratitude shown the Knight, and the loss of Tralee as well, is aghast at O'Connell's continued demands on the government. O'Connell and Edward Ruthven have just been victorious in the Dublin election.

> "M. 7th O'Connell the Dictator & Ruthven who were elected last week for Dublin are chair'd this day by the trades thro Dublin wth great parade.
> Whence the unprecedented Dominion of this upstart Agitator over ¾ of Ireland? From two simple causes – two promises wch he well knows he cannot perform, 1st a Repeal of the Union, wch. the Cabinet have declared thro' Lord Althorp in the H. of C. that England can never consent to, 2d the Extinction of Protestantism

in Ireland, or rather Establishment of the Holy Roman whereby He has acquired a complete ascendancy over the priests who lend themselves throu' Ireland as his devoted instruments with most fatal success. Meantime the Whig Govemt who would willingly yield up Ireland to Popery look on wth cold indifference & leave this unhappy country (the Clergy in particular) to mob-ocracy & O'Connell, to rapine, anarchy and assassinations endless, without a single effort to control or even a symptom of disapprobation."[319]

For now O'Connell will postpone agitation to repeal the Act of Union in order to pursue his other goals through an alliance with the Whigs, who are now about to change leaders and make Lord Melbourne prime minister. To the bitter end O'Connell will oppose the Tories, building a popular movement when the Tories return in 1840s, the era of his famous "monster" meetings.

Henry Petty-FitzMaurice (1780-1863),
third Marquess of Lansdowne

---

319 R.I.A. Day Ms. 12w17, Diary of Justice Robert Day.

Victorian Times

"As regards these men of Forty-Eight, I look on their work with peculiar reverence and love, for I was indeed trained by my mother to love and reverence them ... The earliest hero of my childhood was Smith O'Brien, whom I remember well – tall and stately with a dignity of one who had fought for a noble idea and the sadness of one who had failed ... John Mitchel, too, on his return to Ireland I saw, at my father's table with his eagle eye and impassioned manner. Charles Gavan Duffy is one of my friends in London, and the poets among them were men who made lives noble poems also ...The greatest of them all, and one of the best poets of this century in Europe was, I need not say, Thomas Davis."

Oscar Wilde, San Francisco, 1882

The Tithe War and Poor Law Unions:
the diary of Humphrey O'Sullivan

Queen Victoria (reign 1837 to 1901) comes to the throne as the
Irish Tithe War of the 1830s reaches its climax. 1838 will settle
the tithe grievance, and the same year will see the enactment
of the Poor Law which introduces the work houses, in time for
the Great Famine which commences in 1845.

The atmosphere of politics sours decidedly from the
moment when the Tithe War rekindles and the government
responds with emergency legislation. One witness, the son of
a Protestant clergyman in the district of Newport, near the
Limerick border in west Tipperary, writes: "In the neighbouring
parishes the same kindly relations existed between the priest
and his flock and the Protestant clergyman. But in 1831 all
this was suddenly and sadly changed when the tithe war ...
came on us".[320] Some of the principal incidents of this phase of
the tithe struggle include the affray at Carrickshock (Carraig
Seac, South Kilkenny) and one at Rathcormack (east of
Fermoy). Carrickshock is mentioned in the remarkable diary
of Humphrey O'Sullivan, a native of Glenflesk, near Killarney
(b.1780). His family moved to Callan when he was a boy,
Humphrey becoming a hedge-school master in the district.
He speaks first of the introduction by the government of the
Irish Church Temporalities Bill, providing for the abolition of
tithes (in favour of a tax on clerical incomes), the abolition of
ten bishoprics and the use of some of the money to salary the
Catholic priests:

> "It is said that the tithes will be taken from the ministers
> who will be left only with their glebe-lands ... the new
> tithe law has not yet been enacted, that is the law
> enabling a process to be served on a person by putting
> his name up on the Protestant church door."[321]

The "Battle of Carrickshock" (December 1831) has been
described as the beginning of the end of the Tithe War. When
the accused are acquitted Humphrey O'Sullivan's account is
brief but graphic: under 24 July 1832, "thousands of bonfires
on the hills of Ireland all around as far as I can see on Sliabh
na mBan".

Kerry is visited by the world-wide cholera epidemic of 1832.
Its symptoms are "dramatic dehydration and rapid death". Water
contamination is believed to be the cause. Dr Francis Crumpe of
the Kerry County Infirmary prescribes intravenous saline infusions,

---

320 W.P. Le Fanu, *Seventy Years of Irish Life* (London, 1914), p.44.
321 *The Diary of Humphrey O'Sullivan 1827-1831*, 22 February, 4 May 1832.

making Tralee "the one place in Ireland where the seeds of one of the modern treatments of cholera started".[322] Its ravages do not spare the county's wealthy and well off, especially when engaged in assisting the poor. The press reports the death "In Tralee, of cholera, Thomas Mawe, Esq. M.D." (whose) "incessant attendance at the Hospitals – from the commencement and during the period of the epidemic – together with his very successful practice on many private cases, caused a state of debility predisposing him for a death so sudden and so melancholy". To deepen the tragedy, Dr Mawe's sister and niece are reported dead of the contagion in the same week as Dr Mawe (*Limerick Chronicle*, 15 August 1832). Walter Prendergast, one of the directors of the branch of the Provincial Bank in Tralee, succumbes likewise (*Limerick Chronicle*, 8 August 1832). By May of 1833 the cholera has abated. Here is Kerry's Judge Day at home in Loughlinstown, South Dublin, writing a diary entry under Sunday 5th May 1833:

> "Providence in his mercy having in a great degree if not altogether deliver'd us of the pestilential Cholera wth. wch. it has pleased Him to scourge the whole World for their sins, it is now succeeded by another Epidemic, much more general than the other but comparatively of a mild character – none dying of it save who it supervenes in the case of another disorder, or where caught by persons of infirm state of health or decayd old age. For want of a better name it is call'd Influenza."[323]

Lord Melbourne (William Lamb) and Kerry

The benefits of Emancipation begin to flow under the governments of William Lamb, Lord Melburne, who comes to power as Prime Minister in July 1834 and is re-elected after a general election in the following year.

When Lamb was in Dublin as Chief Secretary under Canning's government in 1827, he formed an amorous liaison with the wife of the Kerry clergyman peer Rev. William Crosbie, Rector of Castleisland, fourth and last Lord Branden. She was Cecilia Latouche, of the famous Dublin Huguenot family of bankers. Rev. William prosecuted Lamb for "criminal conversation" – and lost. Melbourne's personality and unhappy marriage gave him some cause to stray. Described by his biographer as, given to "sad questioning scepticism", he was a somewhat reluctant occupant of high office. His wife was the unstable Caroline Millbank who became besotted with the poet Lord Byron and famously cut herself with broken glass at a London soiree in 1812 with Byron present. To Caroline is attributed the remark, that Byron was "mad, bad and dangerous to know".

322 Robert Fitzsimons and Tom Fitzsimons, "Asiatic Cholera and Staggering Bob: The Cholera Epidemic of 1832-3", in *The Famine in Kerry* (*K.A.H.S.* 1997), p.33.
323 R.I.A., Day Ms. 12w17.

With Melbourne's government O'Connell forms his famous Lichfield House Compact: he will postpone agitation for repeal, and promise Melbourne the support of up to 62 Irish MPs in exchange for the democratisation of the Irish corporations and grand juries; he requires a better deal for Ireland than the provisions contained in the great Reform law, and progress on the tithe issue. The junction of Irish MPs with the Whigs helps the Whigs to power, O'Connell becoming king-maker in a situation similar to Parnell's over fifty years later, though party discipline at this time is nothing compared to the time of Parnell and Parnell's exercise of it. O'Connell's good fortune is too much for his enemies whose detestation is given expression in the English press:

> "Scum condensed of Irish bog!
> Ruffian – coward – demagogue! Boundless liar – base detractor!
> Nurse of murders – treason's factor! Of Pope and priest the crouching slave,
> While thy lips of freedom rave;
> Of England's fame the vip'rous hater,
> Yet wanting courage for a traitor.
> Ireland's peasants feed thy purse,
> Still thou art her bane and curse ...
> Safe from challenge – safe from law –
> What can curb thy callous jaw?
> Who would sue a convict liar?
> On a poltroon who would fire?"[324]

O'Connell's alliance with the Whigs will prove fruitful. An excellent under-secretary assumes office, a Scottish engineer by the name of Thomas Drummond, during whose tenure the grip of the Orange party is broken and the benefits of Union as well as Emancipation begin to flow. Drummond insists on the promotion of Catholics to the magistracy and the police, and he rebuffs calls for the use of coercion; a national police force is set up under his supervision in 1836.

We associate the abolition of tithes with the name of Lord John Russell, Home Secretary under Melbourne. For years governments have tried to preserve and reform the system on which the Protestant church in Ireland subsists, seeing the union of the Anglican communities on both islands as fundamental to the union of Great Britain and Ireland. Under the new proposals tithe will be retained but reduced in value and charged at a fixed percentage – the existing rates variable from one district to another seen as inequitable. The term used is "tithe commutation". In

324 Quoted in Oliver MacDonagh, *O'Connell, The Life of Daniel O'Connell* (London 1991), p. 407.

addition, the yield of tithe which is deemed surplus to church needs will be appropriated to secular use – such as educational provision for the Catholic majority. The downside is that the system will continue in existence – and with it the original grievance of paying for the upkeep of another man's church – the church of the foreign oppressor. Kerry will continue to witness the spectacle of cattle and pigs being seized by the police and military.

Russell understands this, so his Tithe legislation of 1838 abolishes the system entirely: he converts tithe into a reduced rent charge, payable by the landlord. And arrears are abolished. To what extent the new law has the effect of raising the rent is a matter for research.

Russell's Poor Law is enacted in 1838, the same year as the Tithe legislation. The scale of distress has been shown to be considerable, and the existing situation where relief has always fallen on the shoulders of the poor is considered no longer sustainable. The new Law attempts to alleviate this situation by providing for workhouses in a network of poor law Unions to cover all Ireland, to be run by guardians. These Unions will be the only form of local government known to most of Ireland for the next sixty years. The Dingle Union, as an example, has 19 electoral divisions, yielding 21 guardians, with separate divisions for the registry of births and deaths and for the dispensary system.[325] Will the Unions bring a measure of local democracy? How do the Irish landlords react? Lord Lansdowne is ideologically hostage to the current philosophy of non-intervention, or allowing the rules of the market have their effect (the ultimate expression of this is when Peel finally pushes through the principle of free trade in legislation of 1846 to repeal the corn laws). We learn that at the time of the Poor Law Bill Lansdowne and his Bowood circle "fought unsuccessfully to prevent the able-bodied having a right to relief"; later, responding to the Great Famine, he favours the "workhouse test", or, implementation of the standard of destitution necessary before relief is granted.[326]

Legislation to reform the municipal corporations passes the House of Commons in 1835, only to be withdrawn for fear of defeat in the Lords. It becomes law finaly in 1840. The Municipal Corporations Act provides for the enfranchisement of all freeholders with a £10 rateable property; the old Corporation are merged in the new Town Council, and the last Provost, Rev. Arthur Blennerhassett Rowan, antiquarian, philanthropist, and grandson of Sir Barry Denny, bows out graciously.

325 Sean Lucey, *The Irish National League in Dingle, County Kerry, 1885-1892* (Dublin 2003), p.13, 14.
326 Gerard J. Lyne, *The Lansdowne Estate in Kerry Under the Agency of William Steuart Trench 1849-72* (Dublin 2001), pp. xxxvi, xxxvii (introduction).

O'Connell's reform policies are delivered by the time the Whigs are removed and the Tories return to power under Sir Robert Peel in 1840. O'Connell now recommences his campaign to annul the Act of Union. He promises 1843 will be the year of Repeal, and he holds his famous "monster" meetings, the last of which, scheduled for Clontarf, near Dublin, is banned by the government. O'Connell complies with the order, is brought to trial, convicted and sent to prison. His career is effectively over. He dies in 1847 at Genoa on his way to Rome.

The Great Famine (1845-52): the Background

It would be wise to place Kerry's experience of the Great Famine in the wider context of Britain and Ireland. The largely rural society of Ireland and the greater industrial society of Britain have each experienced the evils of the great uncontrolled Industrial Revolution which began in the second half of the eighteenth century. The industrial boom making England the "workshop of the world" is founded on the scientific revolution of the late seventeenth century, which is associated with the names of Isaac Newton and (of relevance to Kerry) Sir William Petty and Petty's colleagues in the Royal Society. The profit imperative has been given full rein by policies such as the Navigation Acts favouring English shipping, the first of these Acts dating from the time of Cromwell. The advent of William and the Glorious Revolution of 1688 established the hegemony of the commercial class and facilitated the creation of Britain's great empire overseas.

However, a yawning gap in wealth and opportunity has resulted: grinding poverty is the lot of those sucked into new industrial towns like Birmingham and Manchester, and a matching poverty the lot of those left in the regions. A property-dominated Parliament at Westminster has passed enclosure acts permitting landlords to take over commonage, further squeezing the rural poor already deprived by the factories of additional domestic earnings from spinning and weaving. Oliver Goldsmith witnessed the effects of depopulation: "Ill fares the land to hast'ning ills a prey,/ Where wealth accumulates and men decay/ Princes and lords may flourish, or may fade;/A breath can make them, as a breath has made;/ But a bold peasantry, their country's pride,/ When once destroy'd, can never be supplied" (*The Deserted Village*); and in the nineteenth century Charles Dickens in novels like *Hard Times* and *Oliver Twist* showed the insupportable misery of the new towns.

In Ireland there are two distinct though usually interconnected problems: absenteeism and estate subdivision.

Absenteeism is not always a guarantee of neglect, nor residence a guarantee against it (an estate may be well managed at a distance through an agent when the landlord is a semi-absentee, perhaps a Member of Parliament); however, in Kerry there are some notable examples of neglect on the part of absentees, some of them Whig/reform advocates in high politics. The defeat of an Irish Absentee tax in 1773 was "helped by a selfish conspiracy between five great Irish proprietors who resided in England – the Duke of Devonshire, Lords Bessborough, Rockingham, Milton, Upper Ossory – and their friends and connections in the Irish Commons. Edmund Burke was the penman of the conspiracy and drew up for those Whig noblemen a letter to Lord North protesting against the imposition of such a tax".[327]

Henry Arthur Herbert MP, (1815-1866). He and his wife Mary Balfour are the first occupants of the new Muckross House (artist George Richmond, courtesy Muckross House)

327 T. Dunbar Ingram, *A Critical Examination of Irish History being a Replacement of the False by the True from the Elizabethan Conquest to the Legislative Union of 1800* (London, New York, Bombay 1900), p. 296.

The Act of Union of 1800 accentuated absenteeism. Typically, absentees reside abroad, drain the country of capital and leave the running of their estates to agents. By neglecting to reinvest in their estates, farms are permitted to be subdivided in order to yield a regular rent and permit the sons of the tenantry to marry; marriages take place while sons are young – there being no reason to wait – and the blind eye is turned to further (unofficial) subdivision by the tenant, all contributing to the inevitable downward spiral to ruin. Population grows disastrously from 1800 as a result of subdivision and an fatal reliance on the potato, from approximately four millions in 1800 to eight and a half millions in the year the Famine commences, 1845.

The grant of the vote to Catholics has also played a part. Before Catholics could become freeholders they were sometimes cleared from estates to be replaced by Protestants. Back in 1783 Henry Arthur Herbert of Muckross, cousin of Lord Kenmare, was accused of clearing about "one hundred cottagers with their wives and children" from his estate near Killarney, "in order to change every acre of his ground into a freehold".[328] Ten years later all changed when the relief act granted Catholics the right to the vote. What resulted was the creation of numerous new freeholders (intended by the landlord to vote at his direction), at the same time an aggravation of the problem of farm subdivision. The Petty estate in the South becomes the subject of sell-offs to principal leaseholders:

> "The Connells, Mahony's and Hassetts have concluded their purchases from Lord Henry Petty, and thus converted all those extensive chattel territories into freehold. This may make a serious change in the constituency of Kerry against the next election, and those chieftains may march all the Redshanks of the Southern Mountains down upon the hustings."[329]

Just how the situation further deteriorateds can by gauged from the next report by the same observer, Judge Day, this time to the *Parliamentary Inquiry into Disturbances in Ireland* in 1824:

> "The 40/- freeholder in Ireland votes out of a lease, and that lease is of the smallest possible quantity of property, either perhaps a cabin or a very small piece of ground for a potato garden, and out of that, on which he barely subsists, it is, that this independent

---

328 *Freeman's Journal* 16-18, 20-22 November 1783.
329 FitzGerald papers, Judge Day, Merrion Square, 5 March 1807, to Maurice, 18th Knight of Kerry.

constituent is supposed to be entitled to vote; he is registered upon his positive affidavit out of this wretched holding as a freeholder worth 40/- a year; this surely is but a mockery of a freehold. He and his brethren are driven by the landlord to the hustings as a salesman driving his flock into the market."[330]

Kerry exemplifies another notorious practice of the eighteenth and nineteenth centuries: the canting of farms, a kind of auction in which leases are bought and sold. Enter the figure of the middleman, the successful purchaser of the lease canted, whom Arthur Young encounters in his *Tour of Ireland* in September 1776:

"what they call land pirates, or men who offer the highest rent, and who, in order to pay this rent, must, and do re-let all the cabin lands at an extravagant rise, which is assigning over all the cabins to be devoured by the farmer".[331]

The canting of farms is carried out in North Kerry on the Hare estates with terribly traumatic consequences for the old tenantry, who are summarily evicted by the middlemen because considered non-productive or having defaulted on rent.

Some estates are sinking under debt, and not all debt can be blamed on inefficient management and poor rent returns from farm subdivision. Many estates are burdened by jointures (dowries) and annuity payments, for example the Denny estate around Tralee, which has to pay a jointure to the young widow of Sir Barry Denny who survives her husband fifty years after his death in the duel at Oakpark in 1794. The Ventry estate is placed in chancery in 1826, a complete turn-around from the days of prosperity in the decade prior to the Union when the first Lord Ventry's activities in property acquisition were legendary. The turn-around probably owes something to the expensive divorce of his son, William Townsend Mullins, 2nd Baron, whose application for the dissolution of his second marriage is heard before the English and Irish houses of Lords just before the Union. (He married thirdly.)[332] In 1807 his father, the first Lord Ventry, recovers a loan to the Denny estate of £20,286 by forcing the Denny executors to sell lands at Cappaclogh (Camp, Dingle

---

330 *Reports from Committees*, vol. 7, 13 May–18 June 1824, *Disturbances in Ireland*, testimony of Mr Justice Day, given 2 June 1824.
331 Arthur Young, *Tour of Ireland 1776-9* (2 vols. London/New York, 1892), p. 369.
332 *Dub. Eve. Post*, 27 March 1798 reports a bill concerning Thomas' brother, William Townsend Mullins, 2nd Baron, before the Irish House of Lords, to recognise his English divorce after the dissolution of his second marriage

Peninsula).[333] Sir Edward Denny and his wife are already planning their departure from Tralee to live permanently in Worcestershire when Lady Denny's father, Judge Day, draws up the private Denny Act of Parliament of 1806, naming as trustees the Judge and his cousins Dick Herbert (Cahernane, Killarney) and Stephen Edward Rice (Mount Trenchard), with powers to sell parts of the estate in order to satisfy creditors. The Act[334] refers to "the several persons entitled to incumbrances upon said premises, which incumbrances amount to the sum of forty-nine thousand and ten pounds, seventeen shillings and fivepence halfpenny". The Judge controls Tralee's parliamantary return to Westminster, a lucrative income for the estate right up to the victory of Maurice O'Connell in 1832. Not for nothing does he claim to be "the man who has saved the House of Denny from dissolution".[335]

Many absentees are addicted to the high life in London and to the Grand Tour in Europe. Francis Thomas, 3rd Earl of Kerry has very expensive aesthetic pursuits which cause him to squander the Lixnaw estate of the FitzMaurices during his residence in England and France, forcing him to sell out in 1782 to Hare, later barons Ennismore and earls of Listowel. Maria Edgeworth, made Francis Thomas FitzMaurice, third Earl of Kerry, the subject of her novel *Ennui* (1809). The novel is the confession of a Lord Glenthorne (Francis Thomas, 3rd Earl) who has never visited his Irish estate but lives in London and travels in Europe in search of art and high society. The novel follows his adventures when he comes one day to Lixnaw. One of the minor characters is named Bland, and there is a footnote about the nurse (Joan Harman) who, centuries before, made her way to Europe to inform the FitzMaurice heir of his succession to the estate and the danger to the estate from an upstart relative: [336]

> "I was lord over an immense territory, annexed to the ancient castle of Glenthorn; - a noble pile of antiquity! Worth ten degenerate castles of modern days. It was placed in a bold romantic situation; at least as far as I could judge of it by a picture, said to be a striking likeness, which hung in my hall at Sherwood Park in England. I was born in Ireland, and nursed, as I was told, in an Irish

333 Registry of Deeds, 580 477 399 170, date 1807.
334 "An Act for vesting the settled estates of Sir Edward Denny Baronet, of Tralee, in the County of Kerry, in Trustees, to be sold for the payment of certain incumbrances affecting the same, under the directions of the Court of Chancery in Ireland, and for other purposes therein mentioned."
335 FitzGerald papers; Day, Loughlinstown House, 13 July 1824, to Maurice FitzGerald.
336 Edgeworth was a regular visitor to the Earl of Shelburne at Bowood, where she would have heard all about Francis Thomas from his cousin the Marquess of Lansdowne. (Information Patrick Pilkington)

cabin; for my father had an idea that this would make me hardy: he left me with my Irish nurse till I was two years old, and from that time forward neither he nor I ever revisited Ireland."

Responding to the Crisis: Public work schemes and coordinated relief

The large farmers survive the Famine. Since the eighteenth century they have prospered in the provision trade and earned additional income from the spinning and weaving of their wives and daughters. Those who starve are the poorer tenantry, including labourers and cottiers, who depend almost entirely on the potato. When the potato blight first strikes in 1845 it destroys approximately one third of the crop; in the following two years it destroys three quarters – and then the seed potatoes are eaten. The Famine lasts into the following decade; the immediate effects include a million people dead in Ireland and a million and a half forced to emigrate to America.

Prime Minister Sir Robert Peel establishes temporary relief schemes, taking care not to trespass on the workings of the Poor Law system. In Nov. 1845 he makes a secret purchase of £100,000 worth of Indian corn from America, which arrives at Cork in early 1846. Public work schemes are announced in March 1846 as the means to distribute cash to purchase food: works include fisheries, harbours, drainage, improvement of estates, and construction and repair of roads; only the construction and repair of roads will receive government subvention – 50% of the cost – the rest, and all the other schemes, to be financed with a rate struck by the grand juries.

The great Killarney landlords, Henry Arthur Herbert of Muckross (namesake of his grandfather) and Lord Kenmare, find themselves moderately well prepared for the crisis, having tackled the evils of the middleman system. Of the two, Henry Arthur Herbert (1815-66, succeeded to the estate in 1836) "stands out as the more progressive in terms of management, vision and encouragement".[337] Prepared to agree to the removal (eviction) of families of occupying tenants, Herbert has consolidated holdings: he "radically altered the composition of any new lease granted ... by strictly applying a series of covenants, which in effect meant that Herbert was very much in control"; he has curtailed the burning of land to produce lime and ashes for fertiliser, introduced turnips and

337 Shane G. Lehane, *The Great Famine in the Poor Law Unions of Dingle and Killarney, Co. Kerry* (M.A. Thesis, University College Cork 2005), p.15. Herbert commences the building a the new Muckross House, which will be ready in time for Queen Victoria's visit in 1861.

green vegetables, inaugurated an agricultural society and an agricultural show, and awarded lease renewals on the basis of "intelligence, industry and motivation".[338]

The central Relief Commission is already in operation since late 1845 and presides over local committees. Lord Kenmare will chair the committee in Kerry. In April 1846 the Killarney committee purchases a shipment of Indian corn from merchants in Cork, which the poor find "peculiarly palatable, very nutritious and extremely firm".[339] The committee purchases another shipment from Stack & Moore of Liverpool. It arrives at Ballykissane Pier, Killorglin, on the last day of May. Ironically, Peel's decision to remove the Corn Laws and free up trade to help reduce food prices for the industrial poor of England will impact negatively on Ireland during the rule of his successor. The Corn Laws are repealed in July 1846 and Peel shortly after loses power to a Whig administration headed by Lord John Russell.

Lord John Russell's tenure as prime minister is the peak of Victorian laissez faire economics, and his first year in power coincides with the recurrence of the potato blight for the second year running. Henceforth relief will be confined to public work schemes alone (with half-starving men presenting to offer their labour). The schemes will undergo a drastic reorganisation. Where central government heretofore financed 50% of the road work, now all moneys must be raised locally; loans may be available from the government, but they will have to be repaid. There will be no further importation of corn, and no interference with the principles of free trade. Local committees must sell corn meal at current local market prices, and from August the government food depots will be closed (some special food depots will remain in the most distressed regions) along the western and southern coasts.[340] Government inspectors are introduced to supervise – in effect, downgrade – local voluntary relief committees. Killarney immediately refuses to comply. Lord Kenmare, wearing his hat as Lieutenant of the county, forms a local Kerry relief committee, which is soon in dispute with the government inspector.

Soup and Souperism: Temporary Relief of Desperate Persons (Ireland) Act of 1847

The Bible Crusade in Kerry makes its own distinctive contribution during the Famine. In 1844 Fr Denis Leyne Brasbie is transferred as curate from Boherbue to the parish of Ballyferriter in the far west of Kerry to help counter the Protestant Bible Crusade then operating from communities in Dingle, Ballyferriter

---

338 Lehane, p. 22, 24, 16-17.
339 Ibid., p. 90.
340 Ibid., p.100.

and Ventry. Lord Ventry has been promoting the Crusade in both places, investing in houses and offering other inducements. Within a month or two the new curate has converted publicly to the Anglican faith.

"The Protestant campaign", according to Mícheál Ó Mainnín, "really started in Dingle in 1833 when the Rev. Charles Gayer came as private chaplain to Lord Ventry." However, Parson Thomas Chute Goodman of Dingle, to whom Gayer was appointed curate, has sufficient knowledge of the region to refrain from participating in the new mission, Goodman's father having been Parson in Dingle from 1780; and the Catholic mission to Dingle of the Vincentian fathers in 1846 plays a significant part in helping to undo the achievements of the Crusade.[341]

However, starving people may be easily induced to change faith. Soup kitchens appear when the government intervenes again. The government understands by the spring of 1847 that the public work schemes are not operating effectively. Increased fatalities and distress, plus the neglect of agriculture, have made necessary the passing of the Temporary Relief Act in late February 1847. Public works are immediately reduced by 20%, then abolished by 1 May. The new Act, effective to August and September of the same year, will distribute relief free. Soup will be dispensed only to the destitute – those with no land or very little land. Those who operate the scheme are usually members of the Established Church who use the people's distress to enforce a change of religion. The scheme satisfies Russell's plan to leave market forces and local initiative deal with the problem of Irish distress. Complaints are heard immediately that the "disemployment" of men in the Dingle peninsula is generating a new wave of distress, and assisting the creation of a stronger farmer class.

In order to rid itself of responsibility for conditions in Ireland, and in anticipation of another potato failure in 1847, the government returns responsibility to the Poor Law guardians with the Irish Poor Law Extension Act (1847). This time the guardians, rather than the workhouses only, will manage distress and react to distress outside as well as inside the workhouses. There is a feeling in official circles that the Famine can be taken as having passed. Local ratepayers will finance the relief operation, for which responsibility is placed squarely on to the shoulders of the guardians. The Act contains the infamous Quarter-Acre clause, also known as the Gregory clause, requiring those who occupy farms of less than a quarter of an acre to give up their holdings as the precondition of entering the work house.

---

341 Mícheál Ó Mainnín, "A Post-Mortem on the Protestant Crusade in Dingle", in *J.K.A.H.S.*, 1996, pp. 99-118, pp.100, 102.

Evictions in the context of Assisted Emigration

The treatment by historians of the subject of assisted emigration has often attached an undue blame to landlords and agents; but a good land agent when confronted with a tangle of interconnected human and social difficulties, on top of estate indebtedness, could consider assisted passage overseas a very viable and humane option. Emigrant nostalgia has been fed by literature on the subject and songs from the likes of Lady Dufferin (her *The Irish Emigrant*), not forgetting the gramophone recordings of the great tenor John McCormack whose success was enormous among the Irish race world wide.

In the decades immediately prior to the Famine Tralee merchants Hickson and Donovan dominate the hardware trade in Kerry; they import timber from Quebec, which as a consequence becomes an important destination for Kerry emigrants. Most of Kerry's emigrant ships go to Quebec with a few going to St Johns, New Brunswick and Nova Scotia.[342]

Long before the Famine we find the future 3rd Marquess of Lansdowne (Henry Petty-FitzMaurice) writing, that it is "absolutely necessary to dispose of several cottage tenants, though the task is distressing from the predilection they have for the situation to which they are accustomed".[343] Some of the best landlords are of the opposite political persuasion: resident Tory and unionist, the political outlook exemplified by Archdeacon Arthur Blennerhassett Rowan; the Archdeacon responded vigorously to the Famine emergency.

Liberal Unionists (who like many of the Tories are resident landlords though Whig in sympathy), have been commended by historians for their very positive approach to estate clearances and emigration. We find a cluster of Liberal Unionists on the southern bank of the Shannon in West Limerick. Sprung from the lower reaches of the aristocracy they are the neighbouring and inter-related families of O'Brien, Rice (Mount Trenchard) and De Vere (Curraghchase, near Adare). The O'Briens of Cahermoyle (near Newcastle West) produce William Smith-O'Brien. He is MP County Limerick from 1835, one of O'Connell's anti-Tories and a vociferous opponent of Peel's policies for Ireland. Later he sheds his unionism to ally again with O'Connell in his struggle for disunion and the restoration of the Irish Parliament. (His daughter, Charlotte Grace O'Brien, 1845-1909, will display an equally gritty independence of class when she exposes the conditions at

---

342 Helen O'Carroll, "Tralee Emigrant Ships", in *The Famine in Kerry* (*K.A.H.S.* 1997), pp. 16-22.
343 Lord Henry Petty to Francis Horner MP, Kenmare, 30 September 1805, in Marquis of Lansdowne, *Glenerought and the Petty-FitzMaurices* (London 1937), pp. 117.

the lodging houses at Queenstown – today's Cobh – and the dock slums of New York.) Not too distant from Smith O'Brien is Aubrey de Vere (1814-1902), of Curraghchase. In 1847 at the height of the Famine De Vere's brother Stephen travels between decks with the steerage passengers from London to Quebec to inspect conditions on the coffin ships and conditions in Canada on arrival. There he inspects the quarantine station of Gross Isle. The report of his efforts bears fruit when London and Canadian reforms follow.

Thomas Spring Rice (1790-1866) MP, of Mount Trenchard (Foynes), already mentioned for his prominence in efforts to establish the National School system, pioneers assisted emigration to Australia during and after the Famine, at the same time clearing his own estate of over-crowding. He entered Parliament when he defeated the Limerick Tory interest in 1820; there he debated repeal with O'Connell, all the time working from Limerick and in the committee rooms at Westminster for the alleviation of Irish distress. In the 1830s Spring Rice opposed the introduction of the Poor Law, suggesting instead state-assisted emigration:

> "I have the worst possible opinion of the existing system of poor relief in Ireland. I consider it quite unsuitable to the circumstances of the country, and would with pleasure see all the workhouses thrown down if a better system were to follow."

He argued "that Ireland should not be forced into an English mould and punished for centuries of British mismanagement and interference".[344]

> "The sword of conquest passed through our land but a century and a half back – insurrections in 1798 and 1803 – partial outbreaks at later times – tithes collected at the bayonet point – Penal Laws continued till 1820, and then reluctantly repealed – these things have destroyed our country – have degraded our people, and you, English, now shrink from your responsibilities; you keep gabbing about the incompetency of the Celtic race and the injustice of Irish landlords; … remember as Wilberforce said, that England owes us a debt for the wrongs of centuries. Endeavour to repay it, not by pauperising us, but by raising us above our present condition."[345]

---

344 Jennifer Ridden, *Making Good Citizens*, pp.133, 134, 137.
345 Spring Rice on Charles Trevalyan's Irish policy in 1846, quoted in Ridden, p.138.

Now he hounds the government to promote assisted emigration to Australia, himself paying the costs of passage for emigrants from his own estate. (The Spring Rices drift to outright republican sympathy; a later family member, Mary Spring Rice will participate in the importation of arms on the yacht Asgard at Howth, near Dublin, in the build-up to the 1916 Rebellion.)

After the Famine, assisted emigration is practised in a very uncompromising fashion by William Steuart Trench (1808-72), agent for the fifth Marquess Lansdowne, Governor of Canada, later Viceroy of India. From his office in Kenmare town Trench conducts an extraordinarily detailed census of the Lansdowne estate in late 1849 in order to arm himself with the facts before taking the measures necessary to run the estate efficiently. Trench's survey, like his assisted emigration, aims at stamping out the practice of subdivision. He insists on permission from the agent to marry. Even then a condition is attached: a brother must emigrate. And marriage without permission (bringing the inevitable new household on a plot adjacent to the old home) will ensure that the whole family is turned out. He requires an emigrating family to tumble down the cottage before departing for America. The actions of another Kerry agent in promoting emigration betray an obvious sadism: "We do not want to have an agent over us who is proverbial as the exterminator", stated one critic of the infamous George Sandes, agent for a number of landlords in North Kerry.

Sandes, of Greenville, Listowel, appears to have exceptional powers from absentee landlord Benn-Walsh since the time of his appointment as Benn-Walsh's agent in 1858,[346] with the result that the methods he employs from his first years engender great bitterness among the tenantry, their priests and the Kerry newspapers. He achieves even greater notoriety in 1875 when he appears in the Court of Queen's Bench to sue one of the tenant farmers for slander; he fails to win his case or even recover his costs. Matters only get worse after 1880 when the land war is in progress, and he continues to wreak havoc with the lives of the poor until his removal.

Perhaps the most famous Kerry land agent of the post-Famine era is Sam Hussey, author of *Reminiscences of an Irish land Agent* (London (1904). Hussey's situation is remarkable, for, while being a very visible representative of the British establishment of his day, he is related by marriage to the knights of Kerry and a direct descendant of the very brave Walter Hussey who laid siege to Tralee Castle in 1641 before being himself besieged by the forces of Cromwell years later at

346 Bryan MacMahon, "George Sandes of Listowel, Land Agent, Magistrate and Torror of North Kerry", in *J.K.A.H. S.*, vol.3, 2003, pp.5-56.

Castlegregory and Minard Castle. Rev. Arthur Blennerhassett Rowan is said to have taken the one remaining stone from Walter Hussey's castle and inserted it in the wall at Edenburn, Sam Hussey's residence. [347]

The Oxford Movement and Kerry

One further point of interest about these Liberal Unionists is how they participate in an important contemporary revolt against their own Established Church. Aubrey de Vere, friend of Wordsworth, Carlyle and John Henry Newman, his brother Stephen de Vere and Charlotte Grace O'Brien convert to Roman Catholicism after the example and inspiration of John Henry, later Cardinal, Newman. Newman wrote *Tracts for Our Times* which cost him his professorship at Oxford and launched the Tractarian and Oxford Movements. Augustus Welby Pugin, architect of Killarney Cathedral, was one of his followers, and the Victorian Gothic is the architectural expression of the movement's fascination with the Middle Ages. Another of the leading converts to Catholicism is Hurrell Froude: his brother is historian James Anthony Froude who begins to write his *History of the English in Ireland in the Eighteenth Century* when he takes Derreen, near Kenmare.

In 1845 Peel, that great political pragmatist and convert to Catholic Emancipation, introduces two measures to undo remaining Catholic disabilities: the augmentation of the Maynooth grant for the training of priests from £9000 to £26,000, and a provision for university education for Catholics in Ireland (the Academical Institutions, Ireland, Bill). The Queen's Colleges come into existence – later the university colleges at Cork, Galway and Belfast. Peel's plan however meets resistance from within the Catholic hierarchy, notably Archbishop MacHale of Tuam. O'Connell supports MacHale, referring to the new institutions as "Godless Colleges"; the two condemn the absence of a Catholic theology faculty, and government control of appointments.

Rome denounces the new Colleges and supports the foundation of a Catholic university. John Henry Newman comes to Dublin as rector of the Catholic University, which becomes the alternative to the "Godless Colleges". Newman's College has a fatal draw-back: it does not have degree-awarding status. However, one of the clauses of Peel's Bill can permit the delegation of college appointments to the hierarchy-controlled boards. In 1865 Catholic MP O'Donoghue of the Glens advocates extending to the Queen's Colleges the right to award degrees to the Catholic University, which is what eventually happens.

347 Friar O'Sullivan, Muckross Abbey, "Ancient History of the Kingdom of Kerry", in *Journal of the Cork Historical and Archaeological Society* 1899, pp. 18-37, p.29.

Cultural Conservation Post-Famine

The departure of a million and a half or so Irish people to America means the loss of huge numbers of native Gaelic speakers from the western half of Ireland. And more than the language is lost: where heretofore the valleys and hillsides teemed with music, song and lore, including the rural crafts taught to the young by their elders down the generations, there is now the eerie silence of abandonment and desolation. The new National Schools, founded before the Famine, operate on a prejudice against the Irish language; they also sound the death knell of the hedge schools (pay schools), which proliferated in Kerry. The National schools win acceptance when the parish priest is installed as manager. The schools use the notorious "tally stick" to record incidents of the use of Irish by pupils and to administer chastisement accordingly. (We will find the reverse in schools of the twentieth century when coercion is the fate of those unwilling to learn Irish.) Daniel O'Connell had little use for the Irish language or a concept of nationhood founded on a Celtic identity. In this regard he is not so much a nineteenth-century revolutionary as a disciple of the eighteenth-century Enlightenment, to promote which he favoured the anglicisation of his country.

This new mind-set ignores the value placed on Irish culture by the generation after Kinsale, the generation of the Four Masters and the Irish colleges on the Continent. Sir William Herbert of the Munster Plantation had high hopes for his plans to evangelise Kerry for the Church of England, at the same time bring industry and commerce to the region: "The action that we have undertaken is to plant in these desolate parts piety, justice, civility, quietness, good order and industry".[348] To assist evengelisation Herbert planned the use of Irish translations of the Prayer Book. Sir Richard Boyle's son, Robert, a famous scientist, also saw the language as key, and had collaborators in the likes of Narcissus Marsh (today's Marsh's Library, Dublin) and Bishop Jones of Meath.

Two great scholars of tenant farmer background, Eoin O'Curry, of Kilbaha, near Loop Head in West Clare, and Kilkenny native John O'Donovan are employed on the Ordnance Survey under Thomas Larcom during the 1830s and 40s in response to the recommendation of the parliamentary commission chaired by Spring Rice. The survey involves collecting, in Kerry as elsewhere, not only the topographical material for map making but everything of antiquarian value. Aware of the work of O'Curry and O'Donovan, Dr Charles Graves (1812-99) of TCD and the Royal Irish Academy (later bishop of Limerick) helps sign up O'Curry and O'Donovan

348 Quoted in *The Tralee Chronicle*, 25 June 1878.

to transcribe, translate and assist in the publication of first modern edition of the *Annals of the Four Masters*.[349]

Bishop Graves's grand-father was Dean of Ardfert in the 1780s, living at Sackville, near Ardfert village. The Bishop's son is Alfred Perceval Graves (b. 1846), H.M. Inspector of Schools in Manchester, whose son is the poet Robert Graves, who wrote that all of European literature begins with the figure of Amergin and the coastal region of South Kerry.

Bishop David Moriarty's friendship with Eoin O'Curry and John Henry Newman helped O'Curry's appointment to Cardinal Newman's Catholic University in Dublin; Moriarty's friendship with Aubrey de Vere is evidence of a shared interest in the Gothic revival, Anglo-Catholicism, Tractarianism and the Oxford Movement. All of these influences speak of a revolt against the utilitarianism of Daniel O'Connell's generation and a real interest in the revival of the Irish language and the preservation of the medieval Christian commonwealth of Kerry. Killarney Cathedral continues the symbol of their friership.

Dr Charles Graves (Bishop of Limerick, Ardfert and Aghadoe 1866-99), summer resident at Parknasilla (Sneem), antiquarian and friend of Kerry antiquarian Rev. Arthur Blennerhassett Rowan (above right)

The Young Ireland movement, to be considered next, coincides with the youth of two brothers of Glenosheen, near Kilfinane (Kilmallock), Patrick Weston Joyce and Robert Dwyer Joyce, conservators of the Irish tradition and admirers of Young Ireland. Patrick Weston Joyce, a leading educationist and place

349 Graves is later involved in the collection and publication of manuscripts for the *Historic Manuscripts Commission*.

names expert, will pen an idyllic account of a pre-Famine upbringing, and turn his hand to collecting songs during his holidays. His *Ancient Irish Music* is published in 1873) to be followed by his *Irish Music and Song, Irish Peasant Songs in the English Language* and *Old Irish Folk Music and Songs*. In the West of Kerry, Rev. James Goodman (1828-96), son of the rector of Dingle, assembles a valuable archive of Irish airs, most of it while stationed in Ardgroom, Co. Cork.

Young Ireland Insurrection ends at "Widow McCormack's Cabbage Garden"

We revert for a moment to the campaign against the Act of Union. During the Repeal agitation O'Connell acquired some unexpected support from a group of student activists in Trinity College, Dublin. They included the visionary poet and song writer Thomas Davis, of Mallow (1814 - 45), John Blake Dillon, and a colleague with a talent for organisation, Charles Gavan Duffy. They became known as Young Ireland. They founded *The Nation* (Gavan Duffy its editor) which became the vehicle for the movement's literature and its plan to re-empower the Irish people with a knowledge of their past. Speranza, mother of the literary genius Oscar Wilde, is a contributor. So also is Tralee man William Pembroke Mulchinock, later famous as the writer of the song *The Rose of Tralee*. Aubrey de Vere and his literary circle of West Limerick contribute.

William Mulchinock submits his early poems to *The Nation*, inspired, it is believed, by the writings of Thomas Davis. In 1849, the year after the Young Ireland Rebellion, Mulchinock sets out for America with his wife and family. His wife is Alice Keogh from Ballinasloe, Galway. He tries to pursue a career in journalism. Unfortunately the marriage collapses and after some years he returns home alone. The song of *The Rose of Tralee* is inspired by a poor girl, Mary O'Connor from Brogue Lane, who, despite the social disparity, wins Mulchinock's heart. According to one account, she works in the dairy at Cloghers House. The claim that Mulchinock departs for India for a few years shortly after he meets Mary O'Connor is considered doubtful, and that he returns to find that Mary has died. India is but one of a number of uncertainties in the story of the Rose. Another is the location of the "pure crystal fountain" of the song. Like the Rose, William Mulchinock dies young, said to end his days in loneliness.

Davis' writings have placed a new emphasis on Irish culture, and they contribute to the literary revival of the twentieth century at the time of Yeats, Kerry's George FitzMaurice and many others. Young Ireland harbours a growing distaste for

O'Connell's utilitarianism. The failure of O'Connell's monster meetings only adds to their disillusionment. They disagree with O'Connell's identification of Ireland with Catholicism, and with O'Connell's opposition to Peel's legislation of 1845 to set up the Queen's Colleges; O'Connell has called them "Godless Colleges". O'Connell is considered too close to the principal opponent of the Colleges, Archbishop John McHale (the "Lion of Tuam"), too close to the apparently insatiable demands of the Irish Catholic Church.

Some of these young revolutionaries believe that Ireland will never solve her problems without total independence from England. After Davis's death, Charles Gavan Duffy and William Smith O'Brien secede from O'Connell and Repeal. Going a step further is Newry man John Mitchel who unites the historic struggle for the land with a revived struggle for the Republic. Mitchel is influenced by Fintan Lalor and his Tenant Protection Society to push for the creation of independent landed proprietors in lieu of tenantry. Mitchel will retain the option of armed insurrection to achieve the Republic. When Young Ireland rejects his programme he founds his own organisation, is arrested, tried and transported to Tasmania for fourteen years. His *Jail Journal* – begun on this journey to the Southern hemisphere - will become a staple of Kerry reading and republican thought. His style is the kind of "savage indignation" that distinguished Swift: castigation of England for conniving with nature to create an artificial Famine in order to starve Ireland; castigation of British commerce, and of the European Enlightenment of which the greed and cruelty of British rule are the extension.

The Young Ireland prisoners will continue Emmet's practice of refusing to recognise the court. Men like Mitchel and Thomas Francis Meagher will attack a justice system in the pocket of the administration; and, in common with a young O'Connell and the later Fenians, they will castigate the packing of juries. The public will respond with sympathy to the obvious high-mindedness of the prisoners and the quality of their speeches before sentencing. Their sentencing will turn them into martyrs, and later the public will hear the sufferings in English jails of such as Michael Davitt, and penal practices like the picking okum.

France once again supplies the inspiration for action: 1848 is the Year of Revolutions in which King Louis Philippe is removed. Kossuth leads a rising of the people of Hungary against the rule of Austrian empire.

William Smith O'Brien, Terence Bellew MacManus and Thomas Francis Meagher ("Meagher of the Sword" for his fiery eloquence) try to raise the half-starved people when they embark on an expedition from Wexford into Kilkenny and Tipperary. Their efforts earn the ridicule of their enemies when they end in the siege of some policemen at the Widow McCormack's house at Ballingarry, Co. Tipperary. Smith O'Brien and Meagher are tried at Clonmel and transported to Van Diemen's Land. Mitchel hears of the fiasco, and later they are all united in Van Diemen's Land. Mitchel and Meagher escape to America, where they enter politics and journalism and help to foster the growth of Fenianism.

William Smith O'Brien, of Cahermoyle (near Newcastlewest), descended from Irish high kings through the O'Briens of Dromoland

Of activity in Kerry, Richard O'Gorman, a barrister from Clare, appears to have attempted to exploit the notorious disaffection of the hill country around Athea – the disturbed mountain region between Rathkeale and Listowel. His efforts are not rewarded with any great success, and he is such an object of vigilance that he is kept on the move until he eventually departs for America. Maurice Leyne of Tralee becomes part of the Young Ireland rebellion over in Tipperary. His obituary tells us: "In all the hardships, dangers and distress of that hopeless event he played his part gallantly and was at last arrested with Meagher and O'Donoghue near Holy Cross." Arrested with Meagher, he is not charged, for want of evidence. He dies of typus fever at 34 and is buried in Thurles. His father was a cousin of Daniel O'Connell and trained as a physician, as did Maurice Leyne's grandfather (three generations of Leyne), on the continent.

The Rebellion at an end, there is a return to constitutional politics and the genesis of an independent Irish parliamentary party at Westminster around opposition to the Ecclesiastical Titles Bill (the Pope has set up Catholic dioceses in England and appointed an archbishop); but when two Irish MPs, Sadleir and Keogh, defect on being offered appointments under government, the constitutional movement in Irish politics is again discredited. Having demonstrated a lack of discipline and cohesion, historians will call these Irish MPs "the Pope's Brass Band".

The Later Nineteenth Century

"Tralee (1860) brought within the range of the telegraph, the railway; of a seven day journey to the Irish capital & of weekly steam communication with London direct."

Rev. A.B. Rowan, *Tralee and Its Provosts,*
by the Last of its Provosts, 1860

The Fenians: "Hell is not Hot Enough nor Eternity long enough to Punish the Miscreants" (Bishop David Moriarty of Kerry)

The American Irish will call the movement the Fenian Brotherhood, an allusion to the mythological force led by Fionn MacCool which policed Ireland just before the arrival of St Patrick and which fought a famous battle on the strand of Ventry against Daire Donn, King of the World. Other antecedent groups include the Phoenix Society, and the Brothers of St Patrick who attack Kilmallock police barracks in the year of the Fenian Rising. A name very often given the movement in Ireland is the Irish Republican Brotherhood (I.R.B.).

The mysterious figure at the head of the Fenian movement is James Stephens, a native of Kilkenny. Wounded at Ballingarry, he flees to Paris where he teaches English. Another refugee from Ballingarry, the handsome and imaginative John O'Mahony of Mitchelstown, shares his Paris exile for a number of years but in 1854 crosses the Atlantic to America. The American ingredient is seriously introduced into Irish politics at this time, for it is there that the expanding population of Irish emigrants will provide the vital support for the next armed struggle in Ireland.

Stephens is back from Paris in 1856 and begins his great walking circuit of the country to organize the regions. En route to Kenmare Stephens's party calls to Skibbereen where the revolutionary Phoenix Society exists to pursue the same ideal and is ready for take over by the more country-wide network of Stephens. Its leading figure is Jeremiah O'Donovan Rossa (from Rosscarbery) who has swept through Kerry in a recruiting drive.

In 1858 Stephens's walking marathon takes him to Kenmare:

"We were now in the dominion of Lord Lansdowne, governed by his Agent Trench, one of the meanest and most contemptible petty tyrants that ever held authority over poor mortals. His vigilance never slumbered, consequently there was more caution displayed here on that account. This I learned from a man who sat beside me, and who had arrived later than the others. I could not help noticing that an uneasy feeling possessed him, and asked was there anything the matter with him, he looked so woebegone.
'No', said he; 'but this is new to me, and this is a terrible place'.
'This house?' said I.
'No', said he; 'I mean the town; you can't move without you are watched and talked of'.
He then told me of the espionage that was exercised and some of the rules this agent had laid down for observance by the community. If any one should go to a wake, no

matter how great the friend, or near the relative, you must first get the agent's consent. Tenants were not permitted to marry without his sanction. Such were some of the rules in this part of Kerry. This beautiful place was cursed by this haughty tyrant, blustering and crimping all the joys and comforts, social and economic all round." [350]

In the same year (1858) the Parish Priest of Kenmare, Fr John O'Sullivan, assures Trench of his support. He writes to Lansdowne, that "as long as Mr Trench or any other landlord (sic) leaves me the free exercise of my rights with the people, I will not directly or indirectly interfere in their dealings with their tenants". [351]

A revolution in steam transport on the high seas and the railways facilitates the work of revolution. The propaganda value of funerals is recognised. Terence Bellew MacManus's funeral in 1861 attracts the kind of crowds witnessed in the next revolution at the funerals of O'Donovan Rossa and Kerry's Thomas Ashe. The participation of priests (though not the bishops) is conspicuous. The famous Father Lavelle says the prayers at the graveside of MacManus (Stephens giving the oration) while the official church keeps a disapproving distance.

The literature of Fenianism glorifies the Gaelic past and the frugal lifestyle of the rural poor. Charles Kickham's novel Knocknagow becomes hugely popular, taking its place at Kerry firesides and going into twenty-eight editions between 1873 and 1944. Its simple village world possesses a greater nobility than the artificial world of the oppressor, and all eyes are turned to the feats of athletic youth performed by "Matt the Thrasher", performed to the slogan "For the credit of the little village". Kickham's funeral becomes a huge demonstration of Fenian support.

The propaganda value of transportation and imprisonment is recognised. John Boyle O'Reilly of near Drogheda is transported to Australia in 1867 and later escapes on a whaler to America where he works in *The Boston Pilot*. With John Devoy he arranges the purchase of a whaleship, the Catalpa, which rescues a group of Fenians in Western Australia. (President Kennedy reminded his Irish audience of John Boyle O'Reilly during his visit to Ireland in 1963.) The sheer world-wide scale of the Fenian project distinguishes it from earlier revolutions, which involved only France and America. Britain's empire has undergone an exponential growth in the

350 Joseph Denieffe, *A Personal Narrative of the Irish Revolutionary Brotherhood* (Shannon 1969), p.33.
351 Fr O'Sullivan, 27 February 1858, in Gerard J. Lyne, *The Lansdowne Estate in Kerry Under the Agency of William Steuart Trench 1849-72*, p.349.

nineteenth century (the empire "on which the sun never sets"). Fenians are struck by the commitment of Britain to liberal values elsewhere, and the repression which marks her rule in Ireland. Foreign Minister Lord Palmerston is in the tradition of George Canning, a great Liberal and interventionist who supports revolutions against repressive regimes like the Spanish and the Turks, meanwhile Ireland remains impoverished and subjugated.

Stephens's work of organisation is helped by the fact that many of the Fenians are products of the National School System set up by the efforts of Chief Secretary Stanley back in 1831. In contrast to the risings of 1848 and 1798, we see a move away from untrained peasant participation towards a sophisticated and secret organisation usually in the hands of office workers, teachers, journalists, and the like. Secrecy is considered essential, which is why the movement is organised on Circles in which members know only the identity of their immediate colleagues. Fenians also put aside any dilemmas about the use of fire arms and gunpowder – and they will take their bombing campaign to England.

The American Civil War (1861-65) helps the movement's transition to armed revolution. Demobilised Irish soldiers return across the Atlantic from the end of the war, arriving furtively in Ireland or assembling more openly in London. While still in America some have joined front organisations such as the Emmet Monument Association, organisations subsumed eventually into the Fenians.

A recent new resident down at Parkanasilla, Bishop Charles Graves of Limerick, discusses the American Civil War with his neighbour, the local parish priest Fr Michael Walsh (PP Sneem 1829-1866). Fr Walsh likes to follow the campaigns of the American Civil War on a map. The two have another common interest in the general area of Irish antiquities and the Irish language. Graves numbers Rev. Arthur Blennerhassett Rowan and Rowan's protégé Richard Hitchcock among his antiquarian friends. Fr Walsh will become a kind of sagart aroon (loveable priest) in the song "Father O'Flynn" composed by the bishop's son, Alfred Perceval Graves.

In 1865 the government swoops. The result is a series of high profile trials, those of Thomas Clarke Luby (later a biographer of O'Connell) and the noble John O'Leary from Tipperary town among them. Poet William Butler Yeats will be impressed by the nobility of Mitchel and O'Leary. O'Leary, a figure in a flowing white beard, is still alive in Yeats's youth and becomes the subject of Yeats's lines, "Romantic Ireland's dead and gone/It's with O'Leary in the grave".

The Fenian rising finally takes place in 1867. Kerry

rises prematurely. What activity there is takes place in the south of the county, with the Bishop's condemnation to follow. Later in the year come the executions of the "Manchester Martyrs", Allen, Larkin and O'Brien, captured after the shooting and killing of a policeman during an attempt to rescue a Fenian prisoner.

Bishop David Moriarty's denunciation of the Kerry Fenians, in which he thunders "we must acknowledge that eternity is not long enough, nor hell hot enough to push such miscreants", is quite representative of the Irish hierarchy.[352] The great exception is John MacHale, Archbishop of Tuam (aka "The Lion of the Fold of Judah", or "The Lion of Tuam"). A devotional revolution is in progress since the Famine, driven by Cardinal Paul Cullen. Cullen promotes the Romanisation of the Irish church at this time, features of which include regular benedictions, missions, and the requirement on priests to wear the Roman collar. In Kerry, Bishop Moriarty introduces great Redemptorist missions, though he dissents from Cullen's adverse view of popular devotional practices among the Irish poor, including Cullen's attempts to put a stop to house stations, which Cullen considers occasions of drunkenness and licentiousness.

Priest and historian Fr Kieran O'Shea has revealed Moriarty as a man of very broad education well able to confront the nationalists of his day. Having attended school with the sons of Kerry's Protestant gentlemen at Ardfert Classical academy, Moriarty proceeded for his secondary education to Boulogne Sur Mer, before going on to the Irish College in Paris to serve as vice-rector, dean and professor of scripture. His time at Boulogne Sur Mer coincided with the revolution of 1830 (when Charles X Bourbon was deposed), and he was in Rome for the Revolution of Young Italy in 1848, when a colleague was shot through the heart. Back in Ireland he is installed at All Hallows in Dublin. He is introduced to John Henry Newman while raising funds in England for All Hallows; a deep friendship evolves that lasts to Moriarty's death.[353] Moriarty's great hostility to international Liberalism is founded on its hostility to Catholicism, and Catholic education in particular. Experience has soured him against contemporary French society, leaving him very positively disposed to certain counter-trends in England. He is an enthusiastic supporter of Newman's Catholic University, at the same time condemning the Queen's Colleges, "those Godless and graceless institutions

---

352 "Denunciatory Address of the Bishop", reported in the *Tralee Chronicle*, 19 February 1867.

353 Rev. Kieran O'Shea, "David Moriarty (1814-77)", in *J.K.A.H.S.*, 1970, pp. 84-98, pp. 82-93.

which represent the indifferentism or infidelity of modern society".[354] Fenianism coincides with the revival of international Catholicism under Pius IX (Pio Nono), contemporary with the rise of French Freemasonry and the opposition of French Liberals to the Church's educational programme. When Pius IX's Index of 1864 warns Catholics against certain Liberal tendencies (anticipating his declaration of Papal Infallibility of 1870) Bishop Moriarty is pushing ahead with a programme of Catholic school and church construction in Kerry.

Bishop Moriarty's achievements in education and church building are very impressive indeed, and the unionist in him envisages further British support for his programme. His foundations include St Mary's Seminary in Tralee in 1855 and St Brendan's in Killarney in 1860, and the re-establishment of the Dominicans in Tralee and the Franciscans in Killarney, in the 1850s and 60s.[355] He has no argument with the state system of National Schools, established through the efforts of Chief Secretary Lord Stanley in 1831, as there is provision for the take-over of the system by the Catholics in the person of the local parish priest. Now the Fenian scare threatens a fresh educational initiative of Mr Gladstone: the endowment of Catholic education from the funds released at the Disestablishment of the Church of Ireland. There is support aplenty for this endowment among liberal Protestants, but also opposition from the local Tory constituency: Mary Agnes Hicksom writes to the *Kerry Sentinel* "against the proposed application of the church's surplus to the endowment of a department of the Roman Catholic Church, and the destruction of the Queen's Colleges".[356]

The Bishop's work in education receives unexpected assistance from an outstanding Tralee philanthropist and Catholic convert, John Mulchinock (1781-1863), whose obituary in the *Tralee Chronicle* observed that "there were few pious purposes whether local or national which had not the advantage of his support".[357] Uncle of the famous William Pembroke Mulchinock, author of *The Rose of Tralee*, he makes his fortune early in life after going abroad. Returned to Tralee he becomes involved in the linen and woollen trade, and builds Cloghers House for his residence. He becomes the owner of a number of shops in the town, and purchases a large tract of the Bateman estate in the Encumbered Estates Court (legislation 1849). He converts to Catholicism and endows the Mercy order of nuns by providing the site at Baloonagh for a convent and school (foundation stone laid on 22 May 1855).

354 Ibid., 94.
355 O'Shea, "David Moriarty", *J.K.A.H.S.*, 1971, pp. 107-127, pp. 113-119.
356 *Kerry Evening Post*, 24 July 1880.
357 *Tralee Chronicle*, 2 October 1863.

He repeats the gesture with the gift to the Christian Brothers of a site and appropriate funding for a school for boys. He dies at his residence, Cloghers House, 29 September 1863.

Fenianism has a sequel in 1884 with a renewed bombing campaign in England. William Francis Lomasney, born in Detroit of Fermoy parents, sets out with two others to blow up one of the bridges over the River Thames in London in December 1884. The dynamite explodes, killing Lomasney, his brother and the third member of the party. By the time of this phase of Fenianism, the Liberals under PM William Gladstone have introduced Irish Land legislation and a Home Rule bill.

William Gladstone: "My mission is to pacify Ireland". Home Rule and winning the Farms of Kerry

Two very visible revolutions in the Irish countryside accompany the destruction of the Anglo-Irish ascendancy and the world of deference surrounding it. One is the overthrow of the system of rent collection under pressure from the land agitators and the Land War. The second is the disappearance of the mounted gentleman with the advent of the trains, barbed wire fencing, and other iron and machine innovations of the Industrial Revolution.

Most observers recognise that the defeat of the Fenians can only postpone temporarily the necessary measures to ameliorate the deep-seated problems of the Irish countryside. With the advent of William Ewart Gladstone as Prime Minister these are now addressed. This extraordinary man of leonine profile and unsurpassed oratory, became a disciple of Peel at the time of the break-away from the Tories over the Corn Laws, and forever after left behind his staunch defense of the Established Church and the old electoral system. In 1869 he piloted through Parliament the disestablishment of the Church of Ireland and the transfer of some of its funds to secular purposes. In 1870 came the first of the Land Acts, under which tenant farmers were to receive compensation for improvements to their farms, or compensation in the event of eviction. It proved unworkable in important respects, including its failure to foresee the simple strategy of raising the rent. It marks a beginning, though like many an initiative to stem a revolution, it only encourages new demands for even greater change.

The Land War is driven by Michael Davitt who founds the Land League in Mayo in response to the threatened famine of 1879 and the increase in the number of evictions. The release of Fenian prisoners at this time helps the spirit of revolt, particularly when the harsh conditions under which they have been held becomes known, including the treatment of O'Donovan Rossa. The League adopts the strategy of social ostracisation against individual landlords or their agents, and against individual farmers who fail to cooperate with the campaign of ostracisation, or boycotting, as it has come to be called. The term derives from its first victim, the Mayo land agent Captain Boycott. This is also the era of the Moonlighters who are a continuation of the Whiteboys, the more regional response to rural oppression. Operating usually under cover of darkness, Moonlighters bring their distinctive contribution of shooting and maiming (meted out for a variety of offences, including the taking of farms), and maiming and houghing of cattle. On the nights when they are out they signal to each other in the old fashioned way with fires on the hillsides. Barrington tells us that the first group of Moonlighters is formed in Castleisland in 1879.

Davitt unites his movement with the Home Rule campaign under its new and innovative leader, Charles Stewart Parnell: their joint action becomes known as the "New Departure", a kind of watering down of Fenianism and the isolation of physical force men like John O'Leary in favour of a strategy of constitutional politics – at least for now. It is a very strange alliance. Davitt's family emigrated from Mayo to Lancashire when he was a child, the boy working in one of the cotton mills, where he lost an arm. Parnell is a Wicklow landlord and an MP at Westminster. His mother was an American whose father fought against the British in the war of 1812. Parnell's paternal ancestors supported pro-Ireland policies as members of the Dublin Parliament, including Catholic Emancipation. The great mystique of Parnell impresses contemporaries, as it continues to impress posterity, the handsome though diffident figure who "imposed himself upon his world by a self-confidence so intense as to be regarded later by his fellow-countrymen as almost superhuman".[358]

Home Rule means the restoration of the Irish Parliament, but unlike the 1782 settlement ("Grattan's Parliament") there will be no British executive in Dublin, but the link with Britain will remain in the monarchy. In contrast with Parnell, Davitt has served years of imprisonment in England for bombing offences in pursuit of his dream of an independent Irish Republic. Can Davitt and Parnell work together? A rumour has it that Parnell is prepared to go beyond Home Rule and embrace the Republic; therefore Home Rule is not considered unreasonable in a Britain toying with a future government of the Empire on the basis of federated nations. Joe Chamberlain, the powerful mayor of Birmingham, has no difficulty with granting an Irish Parliament jurisdiction over

358 F.S.L. Lyons, *Ireland Since the Famine* (1971), 1975 edn. p.156.

a range of government departments responsible for specific administrative decisions. The problem will arise when and if Home Rule under Parnell comes to mean more, something akin to an Irish Republic.

Gladstone's Conversion to Home Rule: the decade of Parnell

William Gladstone returns as Prime Minister in 1880. He will bring in a new land Bill as a response to the Land War begun in 1779 and orchestrated by Davitt's Land League. The Act of 1881 grants the 3 Fs – Fair rent, Fixity of tenure, Free sale. The purchase of farms is provided for, but the loan is an inadequate percentage of the total cost of purchase, making it of little use; land courts are to decide a fair rent – either landlord or tenant may apply – and so a kind of dual ownership is recognised; but those in arrears are not covered by the Act.

Charles Stewart Parnell,
courtesy National Gallery of Ireland

In Kerry the baronies of the north of the county are again the theatre of greatest action. The 1881 Act proves largely useless against the continuing abuses by one Kerry land agent, George Sandes, who simply raises the rent in order to effect a change of tenancy. The waiting new tenant is often careless of the distress being endured by his evicted predecessor. But Kerry's tenant farmers, with important allies the priests and the press, are ready to fight evictions; and the Land League is now a sophisticated country-wide organisation.

The sadistic Sandes, agent for most of the leading landlords of North Kerry at this time, inspires a great demonstration in Ballydonoghue in May 1881 when 10,000 people attend. The priests demonstrate a willingness to throw down the gauntlet, the majority of them more used to expressing publicly feelings of outrage about the eviction of a large family and the taking of its cattle; the *Kerry Sentinel* weighs in with "a disgrace in any Christian land, and amongst any civilised people".[359] But accounts leave us in no doubt that the laity also produces leaders, men who have probably inherited the radical streak from their predecessors' involvement in secret societies.

Parnell remains dissatisfied after the 1881 legislation, and he issues a No Rent Manifesto against a background of countinuing unrest in the countryside. After Parnell makes a speech containing a personal attack on Gladstone, the government has Parnell and Dillon put in prison in Kilmainham. Parnell is released as part of a deal known as the Kilmainham Treaty, but the situation unrest continues to deteriorate. When a new chief secretary and a his companion are knifed to death the evening of their arrival in Dublin (the Phoenix Park murders, by a group known as the Invincibles), Parnell is horrified and privately considers resignation.

The Ashbourne Act, 1885, provides for grants of the full purchase price, repayable at low rates of interest. By the time of the Act, the landlords are losing the will to fight: already they have lost their power over electors since the widening of the franchise in 1867 and the granting of the household franchise in 1884.

All this time Parnell has not forgotten Home Rule. The National League has replaced the Land League, banned by the government, and it helps deliver 86 MPs for Parnell's Home Rule party in the general election of 1885. The distinction between the activities of the two movements is blurred, particularly in the hands of a figure such as Edward Harrington, editor of the *Kerry Sentinel,* who gives vital support to the tenant farmers

---

359 Bryan MacMahon, "George Sandes of Listowel, Land Agent, Magistrate and Torror of North Kerry" in *J.K.A.S.,* vol. 3, 2003, pp.5-56, p.24.

and to the party of Parnell. Harrington, from Castletownbere, becomes one of Parnell's 86 MPs when he wins a seat in the general election. His brother Timothy is the secretary of the National League at central office in Dublin, while Edward is president of the Tralee branch. The League sets up its own judicature to pronounce on individuals who grab land (take a farm after an eviction) or who assist an eviction. The League sets down the level of rent to be paid, and the League also gains control of some of the Board of Guardians.

In 1886 with his greatly enhanced number of MPs, Parnell becomes kingmaker, placing Gladstone in power at the expense of the Conservatives. Gladstone introduces a Bill to give Ireland Home Rule, the principal provision of which is a parliamentary assembly in Dublin with powers over domestic affairs, Westminster to continue to control foreign and colonial affairs, military and naval expenditure, customs, and the Post Office. It will mean the end to the presence of Irish MPs at Westminster. A split now opens in the Liberal party. Joseph Chamberlain senses something about to take place which is far more radical than his federated Empire proposal:

> "The scheme involves the absolute destruction of the historical constitution of the United Kingdom."[360]

Meanwhile, Randolf Churchill's famous piece of demagogery, "Ulster will fight and Ulster will be right", exploits the potential of an agitated Ulster as the greatest insurance against Home Rule. The split foreshadows the demise of the Liberal party in British politics and the rise of Labour in the twentieth century – all on account of Ireland. Unionism is born, and Ulster becomes a factor in British-Irish politics. A powerful Liberal Unionist grouping under Chamberlain joins the Conservatives: Gladstone's first Home Rule Bill is defeated and Gladstone is turned out. The year is 1886 and Lord Salisbury succeeds as Prime Minister.

We need to recall the expansion of the British Empire in the nineteenth century, as well as the vision of British foreign policy. In the hands of foreign minister Lord Palmerston (owner of an estate around Sligo town) British foreign policy was tailored to the needs of liberation movements in Europe and the wider world. On the other hand, Home Rule for Ireland became problematic, viewed an odious prospect by many of the Anglo-Irish ascendancy and by the likes of historian James Anthony Froude. Froude lived at Derreen House, Kenmare in 1869/1870, where he began to write his *History of the English in Ireland in the Eighteenth Century* (published 1874). Or take the military commander Herbert Kitchener, born in North

---

360 Enoch Powell, *Joseph Chamberlain* (London 1977), p.74.

Kerry, who makes his name in Egypt, a country Britain needs to control in order to extend the railway line to link Europe and Asia; Kitchener will play a leading part in the conquest of neighbouring Sudan. His highest profile among the public will come later when he appears on the poster for army recruitment during the First World War.

The Catholic Church has come over now to the side of the people, having broken with the Romanising and pro-government direction of the hierarchy in the post-Famine of Cardinal Cullen of Dublin and Bishop Moriarty of Kerry. The great figure of the present era is Thomas William Croke (1832-1902), Archbishop of Cashel (whose statue stands the Square of the centre of the town of Thurles). Croke's paternal grand-mother owned a general store in Tralee at the corner of the Mall and the Square; and Croke spoke all his life with a Kerry accent, the legacy of holidays in Kerry during his childhood.[361] Archbishop of Cashel in 1875, he takes the side of the Land League during the Land War. He distances himself from Parnell in urging acceptance of the 1881 Land Act, and likewise from William O'Brien (native of Mallow) on the No Rent Manifesto which follows.[362] When, together with many of the priests and the hierarchy, Croke continues his efforts on the side of the League, including participation in the Parnell Testimonial Fund to bail Parnell out of his estate debts, he is summonded to Rome in 1883. Pope Leo XIII has been the recipient of a stream of propaganda against Croke from the English envoy, but when the tries to admonish the Archbishop ,the Archbishop gives as good as he gets:

> "Well, Holy Father, all I need say in that connection is this: If Garibaldi had the same amount of support from the priests and people of Italy behind him that I have had in the stand I have taken against Irish landlordism and English injustice in Ireland, it no longer surprises me to find your Holiness a prisoner in the Vatican". [363]

We can easily credit the tumultuous reception that greets Croke when he returns to Cashel, and the popularity of his choice to become the first patron of the Gaelic Athletic Association in 1884. The G.A.A. proves an extraordinary success and in a brief number of years spreads far and wide its network of football and hurling clubs. Some see its potential outside of sport: It provides a home for many Fenians who flock to the movement in years before politics are taken out of the movement. Kerry

361 Mark Tierney, *Croke of Cashel, The Life of Archbishop Thomas William Croke 1832-1902* (Dublin 1976), p.5.
362 *Croke of Cashel*, pp. 108-116, 128-130.
363 *Croke of Cashel*, p. 149.

is gripped from the beginning by the enthusiasm for Gaelic games, though there is no evidence of Gaelic football at this time, only one of its precursors, the game of Caid; the county will achieve conspicuous success in football in the twentieth century, but for now hurling and field sports reign supreme.

The land war is renewed by the League from 1886 to 1890. To this phase belongs the "Plan of Campaign". "The Plan" involves a kind of industrial action on rents similar to the successful action of trades union in England: a committee decides the rent to be paid, makes this offer to the landlord, which, if rejected, becomes an estate fund in the hands of the League. The most famous operation of the Plan is on the Smith-Barry estate around Tipperary town where the tenants build New Tipperary in protest.

There is general unanimity among modern commentators that in 1886 (the Moonlighters now in their heyday) Kerry is the most disturbed county in Ireland. (Clare will compete for that honour at the end of the decade.) We are told that by mid 1886 there are "on the Kenmare estate eight National League branches adjudicating on tenants's grievances"; elsewhere, that "by the late 1880s the county becomes notorious for its high level of agrarian crime". [364] In 1886 Dingle has become "perhaps the most active centre of boycotting at present in this country"; in the Poor Law election of that year to return a board of guardians, Lord Ventry is unseated as chairman.[365] But divisions have begun to appear in the campaign. Some politicians favour the League but not the extreme use of the boycott. Among the rural community the cottiers, including labourers and carriers, never enjoyed the best of relations with the tenant farmers. (The 1884 Reform Act enfranchised the smallest tenants and labourers; the question is, Will the League examine the oppression of this community by the tenant farmer?) [366]

The governing elite in Kerry is divided. When Sir Redvers Buller is in Kerry from September 1886 as a resident magistrate he becomes "sickened to the heart" by the "demoralisation of the peasantry". He removes some of the systems which protect agents, such as police participation in evictions and police security around agents, noting that legislation favours property, with the consequence that "the bulk of landlords do nothing for their tenants but extract as much rent as they can by every means in their power …".[367]

---

364 Barrington, *Discovering Kerry*, p. 120; MacMahon, "George Sandes of Listowel", *J.K.A.H.S*, 2003, p.25.
365 Sean Lucey, *National League in Dingle*, p.34
366 Lucey, *National League in Dingle*, pp.13-33 passim.
367 B. MacMahon, "Sir Redvers Buller in Kerry, 1886" in *The Kerry Magazine*, no.14, 2003.

The Plan of Campaign is the rock on which the League founders. The nation-wide Plan is driven by Tim Healy and William O'Brien, Parnell's principal lieutenants – soon to be his bitter opponents. But the Plan does not enjoy the support of Parnell. In Kerry it operates on only five estates, one of these being the Earl of Cork's at Ballyferriter in the far West, and even here the priest brokers a settlement and the Plan is denied a victory. The system fights back with the Crimes Act of 1887, a piece of legislation associated with Chief Secretary Arthur Balfour (nephew of the Prime Minister Lord Salisbury and known as "Bloody Balfour") - and this time Redvers Buller is compelled to play his part. Dingle is proclaimed in September, and individual members are targetted for arrest. The League is compelled to reverse its policy on boycotting. (Better leave boycotting to the Moonlighters and not embarrass Parnell.) The 1888 Poor Law elections reduce the representation of League members on the Dingle Board of Guardians by half, and though unsuccessful in the contest for the chair, Lord Ventry regains control. [368]

Meanwhile Parnell's star is in the ascendant. He emerges triumphant from an attempt to smear him in the *London Times*. What happended is this. The *Times* ran a series of articles in March 1887 under the headline "Parnellism and Crime", claiming among other discoveries a letter by Parnell in which he expressed regret at having had to condemn the Phoenix Park murders. Later, a certain Richard Piggot admits his part in the forgery of the allegations contained in the articles, absconds to Europe and commits suicide in Spain in February 1889. Parnell and his supporters feel vindicated.

Later in the same year one of his supporters, a Captain O'Shea, files for divorce and cites Parnell as co-respondent. The case is tried in November 1890 and Parnell is fighting for his political life. The campaign to ditch Parnell causes a fatal split in the Home Rule Party when Gladstone announces that he will not negotiate while Parnell retains leadership of the Home Rule party. The Fall of Parnell divides the country; dividing families – in Kerry as elsewhere – for a generation or more. The resultant division proves fatal to the cause of Home Rule at a time when its achievement has seemed just around the corner. North Kerry MP Michael J. Flavin MP expresses the view that Parnell should go. Even the founder of the Land League, Michael Davitt, calls for Parnell's resignation, as do the Fenians.

---

368 Lucey, *National League in Dingle*, pp.40-45.

The Catholic Church will be blamed for its share in the impasse after it calls for Parnell's removal. The Church in Kerry lays it on the line when 67 priests sign a petition in January 1891 against Parnell's continued leadership. To now Archbishop Croke has made no secret of his support for Parnell and for the Plan of Campaign. His stance has placed him again at odds with the Vatican and Leo XIII, though by the late 1880s the Irish hierarchy is better represented in Rome and the Pope is able to balance what he hears from the envoys of the British government. All changes when the Parnell scandal breaks and Gladstone demands Parnell's replacement before he can contemplate re-introducing a Home Rule bill. Some six weeks after the Kerry priests' petition, Croke urges his own priests to convene their parishoners, "and lay before them in plain terms ... in what and how shamefully he (Parnell) has sinned against the Christian code, without having ever uttered a word of repentance".[369]

Parnell refuses to resign and sets out on a tour of the country to recover any vestiges of remaining support. He makes speeches in which he casts terrible anathemas at the church for failing to back him. It is a desperate and health-destroying effort to shore up his position and save his leadership. He visits Kerry where his host is Pierce O'Mahony of Kilmorna House, near Listowel. Parnell is said to have spoken to a crowd fron the window of the present Listowel Arms Hotel. But a revived career is not to be. His health is ruined, and in October 1891 he dies in Brighton in the arms of Kitty O'Shea.

The perceived betrayal of Parnell will make a deep impression on the writer James Joyce and inform a number of his stories, as it will the stories and plays of other writers. The Parnell split will consume political energies for years into the immediate future. In the year of his death the Conservative government introduces the Congested Districts Board as part of its policy of "killing Home Rule with kindness", under which overpopulated regions are to benefit from state funding to assist cottage industries and local construction projects.

---

369 *Croke of Cashel*, p. 243.

*Sergt. James Talbot (1868-1938), Royal Irish Constabulary, native of Tralee,
who served all his career in Cos. Kilkenny and Wexford. A noted sportsman,
he excelled at the 16lb. and 56lb. hammer events. He retired from the R.I.C. in
1915. His wife (m 1913) is Margaret Tuohy, Wexford.*

The Twentieth Century

" ... whose firesides would be forums
for the wisdom of serene old age"

(Eamon deValera, radio address 17 March 1943)

Anticipating the Twentieth Century:
founding of the Gaelic League

The division of opinion around the Parnell issue, and the postponement of Home Rule when Home Rule appeared inevitable, have generated widespread disillusionment with politics, contributing to a feeling of apathy throughout the Irish world. Then, in 1893, the Gaelic League is founded. Its enthusiasm for the preservation and propagation of the Irish language excites people from all walks of life and all political and religious affiliations. Its first president is Douglas Hyde, son of a Roscommon Protestant clergyman and direct descendant of Rev. Arthur Hyde, Rector of Killarney in 1810.

Though the West of Kerry preserves the Gaelic way of life and the Gaelic language well into the second half of the twentieth century, scholars begin to flock there when they realise the inroads being made by modern society and emigration. Native writers such as Blasket Islanders Peig Sayers and Tomás Ó Criomhthain are willing to write autobiographies that preserve an account of the hardships and tragedies, and the joys, of a life lived by generations of their ancestors.

Political activity becomes subsumed in League organisation, but not for long. Hyde soon fights and loses the struggle to keep the League out of politics: some of its leading figures, Pearse, for example, are members of the I.R.B. One of the leaders, Eoin MacNeill, inspires the Howth gun-running (below) with an article in the League's organ *An Claidheamh Soluis* about the need to rearm the South as the Ulster Volunteers have just rearmed the North with their importation of guns at Larne.

The centenary of the 1798 Rebellion reinvigorates nationalism. Inspiration is drawn from events in the Hungarian division of the Austro-Hungarian empire, and from South Africa where the Dutch (Boers) have taken on the British in the Boer War. (Support for the Boers against the British appears to ignore the plight of the native South Africans.) In Hungary the elected MPs have refused to attend the Imperial Parliament, instead setting up their own assembly in 1867. Arthur Griffith, a Dubliner with Fenian leanings, is impressed at this display of successful peaceful resistance; he now works, through a movement called Sinn Fein (meaning Ourselves Alone, 1905 the date generally given for its inception), to reduce the republican component in Irish nationalism and redirect nationalism to the support of Irish land and industry. He envisages for Ireland something akin to the Hungarian constitutional arrangement with Austria under a Dual Monarchy; the 1782 Grattan constitution is to be a non-negotiable starting point.

Many physical force republicans dissent from such a plan, but unity is patched up after a modestly successful showing by a Sinn Fein candidate in a challenge for a parliamentary seat in 1908 – in Leitrim.

The Sinn Fein economic programme can be seen as a restatement of Swift's protests concerning discrimination against Irish trade. Now they go another step: the recently formed (1895) county councils of Ireland should form the nucleus of an independent Irish authority to protect Irish trade.

John Redmond, from Wooden Bridge in Wicklow, reunites the Parnellites for a time. Their day comes when they hold the balance of power after the general elections of 1910. A 1911 Act of Parliament reduces the Lords' veto power to a two-year postponement of legislation. The way is clear for the Home Rule Bill of 1912. It passes and is expected to become law in 1914. However in 1912 Edward Carson persuades the northern Unionists to sign the Ulster Covenant to resist Home Rule, and when the Great War intervenes Home Rule was postponed. The failure of Home Rule and the introduction of conscription provokes the Easter Rising of 1916 during Britain's war with the Kaisar. The British press inaccurately names the rising the "Sinn Fein" rising. But its leaders are the I.R.B.

Easter Rising, 1916.

One of the events antecedent to the Easter Rising is the Howth (near Dublin) Gun Running of July 1914, in which Mary Ellen Spring Rice of Mount Trenchard is a participant with Erskine Childers and his wife. Previous to this the Ulster Volunteers have imported a shipment of guns at Larne in a similar gun running exercise. These events hasten the militarisation of the Ireland/England conflict just as Worl War One looms: Home Rule, finally passed in 1912 and due to take effect in 1914, has been placed put on the back burner. War breaks out in Europe on the assassination of Franz Ferdinand, heir to the throne of the Austo-Hungarian Empire. The outbreak of war postpones Home Rule – with fatal effect.

John Redmond, the Home Rule party leader, urges the Irish Volunteers to join the British army. Eoin MacNeill, leader of the Irish Volunteers, opposes his call. A meeting at the Rink, Tralee, on 13 October 1914 strongly supports MacNeill, despite the urging of some Kerry Redmondites, notably Tom O'Donnell, MP West Kerry. O'Donnell's continuing canvas for Kerryment to join the forces has the support of the North Kerry MP Michael J. Flavin.[370] Kerry has the lowest enlistment

---

370 T.Ryle Dwyer, *Tans, Terror and the Troubles, Kerry's Real Fighting Story 1913-23* (Cork 2001), p.43.

in the entire country, and Kerry will have the lowest casualty figures, in marked contrast to Ulster.[371]

Sir Roger Casement, of Cushendall, Co. Antrim, lands from a German ship, the Aud, at Banna Strand in the early hours of Good Friday, 1916. He has spent a year in Germany seeking help for an Irish rising and attempting to win over Irish prisoners of war. There are 20,000 rifles of inferior quality on the Aud, all that Germany can spare. The ship is off the Kerry coast all of Thursday awaiting the signal to land. No signal appears.

Casement has behind him a distinguished career in the British consular service. He has been knighted for his investigative journalism in exposing the plight of the poor rubber gatherers of the Belgian Congo and the outrages suffered by the poor natives in the Amazon.

The Volunteers – really the I.R.B – have planned a rising for 23 April, Easter Sunday (presenting MacNeill with a fait accomplit). In Kerry a ship with arms from Germany is expected, but it is of vital importance that Dublin rise first. McNeill, apprised of the rising, is appalled at the prospect. On Sunday the Irish Independent carries his notice cancelling all "manoeuvres" that day. But the rising will take place the following day, Easter Monday, without official authorisation and without the participation of the countryside. The seizure of the General Post Office in Dublin by Padraig Pearse and his colleagues will turn Dublin upside down for a week. At the end of Easter Week the centre city will be in ruins, and fifteen men will be sentenced to death by court martial and shot.

Casement, having failed to secure realistic assistance in Germany, is believed to have considered an Irish rising hopeless, and wished to do all in his power to prevent it. He lands with Robert Monteith from the Aud, and after a few hours of exhausted rest they are detained and brought to Tralee by two police men. Meanwhile the Aud departs; the British have been apprised by their spies of its true identity, and after evading a number of attempts to arrest it at sea the captain scuttles the Aud in Cork Harbour.

In Tralee RIC Barracks Casement becomes more guest than prisoner of the Head Constable, John Kearney. Kearney has nationalist sympathies. He expects an attack on the barracks this night to release Casement. Our evidence now points to a willingness on his part to cooperate with any rescue by the local I.R.B. : the door is left open, the children are sent to bed early, Casement is kept in the living quarters rather than in a cell, and Kearney and Casement spend the night in conversation. But nobody arrives to rescue Casement. Casement asks to see a

371 Martin, Thomas F., *The Kingdom in the Empire*, p. 84-5.

priest: Fr Ryan, Dominican, is brought to him. The suggestion is that Casement wishes Fr Ryan to reach the Volunteers with the message to cancel the rising. The priest contacts Austin Stack.

Austin Stack is head of the I.R.B. in Kerry and widely known as a county footballer and nationalist (he participated in Kerry's first All Ireland football triumph). His father was a Fenian. He has been apprised of plans for the rising and has made all the preliminary arrangements, including cooperation from the railway men and setting up a radio station. Now he appears intent to follow Pierse's instructions to the letter to keep Kerry out of the rising until Dublin has risen first. This instruction and the apparent support for republicanism in the military barracks at Balllymullen (as well as among the R.I.C.) may explain the surreal pattern of Stack's movements during the few days of Casement's presence. Stack, having heard from Fr Ryan, goes to Tralee Barracks. His pockets are filled with letters of a highly incriminating nature. It is believed that he wishes to be arrested. Whatever Stack and the I.R.B. are doing, Casement, who has been taken very openly from Banna, is never rescued in Tralee. He is tried for treason in London, convicted, and executed at Pentonville Prison on 3 August 1916. His bones will be returned to Ireland in 1966 for reburial at Glasnevin Cemetery in Dublin.

Said to be among the first casualties of struggle for independence is Captain Daniel Sheehan, Monagae, drowned at Ballykissane Pier (near Killorglin) 20 April 1916 when going to Cahirciveen to dismantle wireless equipment in the Marconi school which they plan to use to contact the Aud, the German gunship.

During the Easter Rising "The O'Rahilly", from Ballylongford, is gunned down in Dublin during the street fighting. Killed also in Dublin at about the same time is Patrick Shortis of Ballybunion. Captain Con Colbert, of Castlemahon in West Limerick, fights in the General Post Office that Easter of 1916, and is executed by firing squad.

The War of Independence

The execution of the leaders of the Irish Rebellion of Easter 1916 proves a disaster for British rule in Ireland: the executions lead directly to the War of Independence from 1919 to the end of 1921, followed by the Treaty which sets up the Free State in the southern twenty-six counties of Ireland. The Free State later becomes the Republic through a series of unilateral actions by De Valera that remove Britain from the constitution; and yet the Republic will be but the part-fulfilment of the dream of separatists since the era of the French Revolution, as North of Ireland continues under British jurisdiction under the terms of the Treaty signed by the Irish leaders to end the War in December 1921.

Let us return to the aftermath of the executions of the leaders of the Easter Rising. When America enters the World War on the side of Britain in 1917 it is considered politic to release the remaining Irish leaders from jail in England. But the introduction of conscription in 1918 causes the Irish Parliamentary Party, after the Hungarian precedent, to withdraw from Parliament; at the same time the conscription emergency boosts the revolutionary organisations in Ireland, and it is they, rather than the Home Rule party, who swing the support of the country behind them. An attack on the RIC barracks at Gortatclea, east of Tralee, on the night of 13 April 1918 is considered the beginning of hostilities in the Irish War of Independence (though the better-known attack by Dan Breen at Soloheadbeg in Tipperary in January 1919 is the incident often cited by historians as the beginning of the conflict).

World War One ends on 11 November 1918 (Armistice Day). A general election follows in which sweeps the country. candidates are unopposed in Kerry: those elected are, Austin Stack in West Kerry, James Crowley in North Kerry, Piaras Beaslaí in East Kerry and Fionán Lynch in South Kerry.

January 1919 sees the first meeting of Dáil Eireann (the illegal Irish Parliament that implements the Sinn Fein's policy of withdrawal from Westminster). The local elections of January 1920 witness another sweep for Sinn Fein: 72 of the 127 town and city councils have Sinn Fein majorities, and 28 of the 33 county authorities. The result means regime change on a sweeping scale. Immediately the local authorities give their allegiance to Dáil Éireann, open their own bank accounts and demand the use of the money collected in rates. Some rewriting of history occurs. Since the creation of the local authorities in 1898 the parliamentary party has been in charge, and for months after the Easter Rebellion its members continue to make honourable mention of local recruits killed in the trenches. This now changes, and in parts of Ireland there is a destruction of the minutes of meetings to remove those parts containing honourable mention of young men killed in the trenches during World War One.

Numerous officers of the Royal Irish Constabulary resign in 1920, causing the British to introduce poorly trained replacements from the jails of England, many of them ex-servicemen from the World War. With not enough uniforms to go round they wear military khaki in combination with R.I.C. uniform. They become known as the Black and Tans, after a breed of dog. Bands of Black and Tans terrorise the countryside and towns of Ireland during 1920. Vacant R.I.C. barracks are torched during the spring and early summer of that year. The great leader of the fight against the Tans is Michael Collins, who is also Minister for Finance in the Provisional government. More locally, some of leaders of these attacks on R.I.C. barracks are future founders of political dynasties in the Parliament (Dáil) of the Irish state soon to come into existence – TDs (MPs) Tom MacEllistrim in Kerry, and James Collins in West Limerick, for example. In June 1920 there is a mutiny at the Listowel barracks of the R.I.C. led by Constable Jeremiah Mee. He promptly offers his services to Michael Collins.

Across the Shannon, Clare has become almost ungovernable with the I.R.A. cashing in on the old rural campaign. There has been a good deal of recent dissatisfaction among the smallholders at the creation of ranches for better-off farmers during the distribution of farms under the land acts. Now large farms are taken over and cattle are driven off. In the new year, 1921, outrages continue in Kerry. On 23 February the village of Ballylongford is burned, then on 14 April 1921 Sir Arthur Vicars is taken out and murdered outside Kilmorna House, some miles east of Listowel. Vicars used to hold the position of Ulster King of Arms but since 1912 he has resided at Kilmorna House, the home of his step-relatives, the Gun family. (It was 1907, during his tenure as Ulster King of Arms, that the Irish crown jewels were stolen; they have never been recovered.)[372] Not long after the murder of Sir Arthur Vicars, Captain Patrick Dalton, Athea, is killed in action at Gortaglanna, Knockanure on 12 May 1921.

The Irish delegates to the Treaty negotiations, conducted at the end of the year in London, include Arthur Griffith, the most eminent leader of the Irish struggle before the Rebellion (who remained almost completely invisible during Easter Week), and the legendary Michael Collins, native of West Cork, the most prominent organiser of the Irish in the War of Independence which followed the Rising. Collins is a very young man, and he and the other negotiators face a British team of vast experience which includes David Lloyd George and Winston Churchill. The Treaty they sign divides the island leaving six of the Northern counties still under Britain (though with a promise that this situation will be reviewed by a boundary commission); the southern twenty-six counties are to continue

372 J. Anthony Gaughan, *Listowel and its Vicinity* (Kingdom Books 1973), pp. 322-328.

still within the British Commonwealth. When they return to Dublin the Treaty is immediately denounced by the President of the Republic, Eamon De Valera. At the end of the Treaty Debates in the Dáil, when the motion is put and the Treaty carried, De Valera leads his followers out of the chamber. The Irish Civil War soon begins when the government of Griffith and Collins borrows guns from the British to shell the Four Courts, which has been taken over by a faction of the Republicans. In the course of the fratricidal strife which follows, Kerry witnesses a number of terrible outrages of Irishman on Irishman, most notably the Ballyseedy Massacre, when a number of the Free State soldiers tie a group of Republicans to explosives and detonated them; all are killed except one who survives with hardly a scratch. The following is an account of the botched capture of a group of Republicans at Clashmealcon Caves under the cliffs which overlook Ballybunion strand above Causeway. It is one of the last tragedies of the Civil War before the war ends in May 1923:

> "Timothy ('Aero') Lyons and his Republican companions were in hiding in Dumfort's cave overlooking the Shannon estuary when Free State troops discovered them. Two Free State soldiers, Volunteer O'Neill and Lieutenant Pearson, were killed while attacking the cave, and then it was decided to starve the men out ... Thomas McGrath and Patrick O'Shea were drowned while attempting to escape. Lyons surrendered, but while he was being lifted up from the cave, the rope broke and he fell on to the rocks; he was then shot by the troops above. The other three men ... were hanged in Tralee on 25 April, 1923. A petition from local people to spare the men was refused, with Major-General O Dalaigh, C.O.C. Kerry Command, claiming that the Republicans had prevented attempts to assist one of the Free State soldiers."[373]

A very acrimonious division of opinion around the Treaty will persist in Ireland for generations, creating in the process the two main political parties, Fianna Fail (a party composed of those who walked out of the chamber when the Dail majority ratified the Treaty, but who returned in 1927 and became the government in 1932) and Fine Gael, the inheritors of the old Home Rule tradition and more diposed to a link with Britain.

---

373 Bryan MacMahon, *The Story of Ballyheigue* (Ballyheigue 1994), p. 155.

Epilogue: the Twentieth Century

Kerry's support for Irish separatism draws on a very long tradition, one that long predates the modern republican tradition dating from the French Revolution, through 1798, to the men of 1848, the Fenians and the men of 1916; it reaches back at least to when the Munster Geraldines offered the Emperor of Germany the crown of Ireland. Kerry's allegiance to the Catholic faith needs qualification also: her people looked to Rome and the continental monarchies during the centuries of persecution and during the devotional revolutions of the nineteenth and twentieth centuries, otherwise, even in an individual like Archbishop Croke, there has been a noticeable indifference to Roman strictures; and for much of the twentieth century artists and others have felt particularly uncomfortable when repressive censorship became identified with Catholic power in the new Irish state.

When the Civil War ended, the Sinn Fein party under De Valera, continued outside of Dáil Eireann (Irish Parliament) in the same situation of self-exclusion which existed when the fighting began. In 1926 De Valera proposed that Sinn Fein end this policy and enter the Dáil to try and promote its policies from there. Sinn Fein refused, so De Valera founded what would become the largest political party in southern Ireland: Fianna Fail. The new party contested the general election, becoming the second largest party in the Dail. It became the largest party in the 1932 general election and De Valera became President of the Executive Council (prime minister). No sooner elected to power, he began to dismantle the constitution agreed under the Treaty with Great Britain, gradually removing all references to the King and degrading the position of the Governor General. His first decade is marked by the economic war with Britain: De Valera withheld the annuity payments due to landlords who had sold their estates under the Land Acts, and Britain responded with a ban on the import of Irish cattle. In 1938 a settlement was reached when De Valera agreed a cash amount in return for Britain's restoration of the Southern Ireland ports retained when Britain left the country at the end of the War of Independence. Poverty and emigration are enduring memories of the nineteen thirties, forties and fifties, symbolised by the crowded platforms at the trains stations, and the hiring fairs in Tralee where young men and girls from Cromane and Callinafercy sold their labour to the strong farmers of North Kerry outside St John's Catholic Church.

Today, De Valera's Ireland is often reviewed – many believe unjustly – as a bleak and somewhat suffocating environment, particularly restrictive for poets and those of artistic sensibility, and for married women. The ideals of De Valera came to seem unrealistic of achievement as the country suffered under mass emigration and economic war. The hoped-for reunification of the island underestimated the contrary wishes of the North of Ireland Protestants; the revival of the Irish language and Irish culture, often linked to the hegemony of Gaelic games, became a huge burden on the educational system. It is true that these aspirations helped considerably to bond communities in the South of Ireland: the Eucharistic Congress of 1932 was an impressive demonstration of the historic fidelity to the Catholic faith, and the extraordinary success of Kerry in Gaelic football (with four All Ireland senior championships in a row 1929-32) helped assuage the feelings of bitterness in Kerry after the Civil War, not least through the comraderie among players. Attendance at Catholic ceremonies was higher than ever, helped by the Legion of Mary and other societies associated with purity campaigns in the wake of of World War I when troops returning from the trenches brought the threat of venereal disease and societal breakdown. There was a consciousness of Ireland as a Catholic society determined to chart a course distinct from that of, for example, France, where the attack on Catholic education was well known to Bishop David Moriarty in the previous century. It would take a second world war and the dawning of the 1950s to loosen decisively the bonds of family and church, the effects of which on the next generation, in the aftermath of the advent of television in 1960 and the church's second Vatican Council, are being now assessed; then too would be revealed the sexual abuse apparently unnoticed, certainly unreported, in Irish society, the origins and scale of which have not as yet been entirely understood.

There were early signs that Articles two and three of De Valera's constitution of 1938, which claimed jurisdiction over the six norther counties of Northern Ireland, were making no impression on the Protestants there except to strengthen their resolve to remain unannexed by the South. The execution of Charlie Kerins of Tralee proved the equal resolve of De Valera's southern government to defeat any splinter I.R.A. groups still active, together with any fresh campaigns to destabilise the northern state. Meanwhile, a new generation of students at the South's primary schools, many of them bound for emigration to England and America, were suffering under the imposition of the Irish language as part of state policy in education. Little or nothing was done to relieve teachers or students of this burden until the 1970s when a non-De Valera coalition government removed the obligation to pass Irish or fail the entire Leaving Certificate examination at the end of second level.

From 1969 the tensions in the North of Ireland spilled over into the violence that appeared nightly on our television news, with what effect on Irish life south of the border we find it difficult to gauge; and soon there were new challenges which our ancestors could never have foreseen, many of them the results of the collapse of the traditional family under the onslaught of the consumer society. As we draw the story of Kerry to a close, the power sharing Assembly has resumed its work of government in the North of Ireland. May this book make some small contribution to an understanding of how we faced the challenge of coexistence in another corner of Ireland.

Appendix

Jacobite Parliament 1689 (from William King, *The State of the Protestants of Ireland under the Late King James's Government,* London 1691)

County Members
Nicholas Browne, Esq., Sir Thomas Crosby, Knight

Ardfert
Roger M'Elligott, Colonel McGillycuddy

Dingle
Edward Rice FitzJames of Ballinleggin, Esq, and John Hussey of Cuhullin, Co. Limerick

Tralee
Maurice Hussey, John Browne of Aradagh

Parliament of 1692 (from *Journals of the Irish House of Commons*)

County Members
Hon. Thomas Fitzmaurice, Armiger, Edward Denny, Armiger

Ardfert
Andrew Young, Christopher Dominick

Dingle
Hon. William Fitzmaurice, Armiger, Frederick Mullins senior, Armiger

Tralee
John Blennerhassett de Ballysheddy, Armiger, James Waller, Armiger

Bibliography

Bagwell, Richard, *Ireland Under the Stuarts,* 5 vols. London 19-9-16

Bowen, Elizabeth, *Bowen's Court* (London/New York/Toronto, 1942)

Bradshaw, Brendan, *The Dissolution of the Religious Orders in Ireland under Henry VIII* (Cambridge 1974)

Brady, D.D., W. Maziere, *The MacGillycuddy papers, A Selection fro the family archives of "The MacGillycuddy of the Reeks" with an introductory memoir, being a contribution to the history of the county of Kerry* (London 1867)

Butler, William F.T., *Gleanings from Irish History* (London 1925)

Burke, Sir Bernard, *A Genealogical and Heraldic history of the Landed Gentry of Great Britain and Ireland,* 2 vols, 1894

Burke's *Peerage and Baronetage* 1999

Cloncurry, Valentine Lawless, Lord, *The Life and Times of Valentine Lord Cloncurry* (Dublin 1849)

Conlan, Patrick, OFM, *Franciscan Ireland* (Cork 1978)

Corish, *The Catholic Community in the Seventeenth and Eighteenth Century* (Dublin 1981)

Cork, "Memoir of the Great Earl of Cork from a Manuscript in the Library of Francis C. Crossle, Esq., M.B., Newry", in *Journal of the Cork Historical and Archaeological Society,* May 1892, vol. no.5, pp.87-93

Corkery, Daniel, *The Hidden Ireland,* 1924

Cusack, M.F. *A History of the Kingdom of Kerry* (London, Boston, Dublin 1871)

Denny, Rev. Henry Lyttelton Lyster, M.A., F.S.G., *A Handbook of County Kerry Family History* (the County Kerry Society 1923)

Denny, Rev. Henry Lyttelton Lyster, M.A., "Biography of Sir Edward Denny, Knight Banneret, of Bishop's Stortford, Herts., Gentleman of the Privy chamber to Queen Elizabeth, Governor of Kerry and Desmond" in the *Transactions of the East Herts Archaeological Society,* vol. 2 part 3, pp. 247-260 (originally prepared for the *Hertfordshire Dictionary of Biography*), *Kerry Evening Post* of 22 and 26 September 1906

Devlin and Howard B. Clarke (eds.) *European Encounters, Essays in Memory of Albert Lovett* (Dublin 2002) pp. 97-117

Dickson, David, *Old World Colony, Cork and South Munster 1630-1830* (Cork 2005)

Donovan, Tom, "Some Transported Rebels of 1798" in *The Old Limerick Journal 1998*

Downey, Declan, "Irish-European Integration, The Legacy of Charles V", in Judith Devlin and Howard B. Clarke (eds.) *European Encounters, Essays in Memory of Albert Lovell* (Dublin 2002).

Dunlop, Robert, *Ireland Under the Commonwealth* (2 vols. Manchester 1913)

Dwyer, T.Ryle, *Tans, Terror and the Troubles, Kerry's Real Fighting Story 1913-23* (Cork 2001)

Elliott, Marianne, *Wolfe Tone, Prophet of Irish Independence* (Yale 1989)

Fagan, Patrick, *The Stuart Papers,* Dublin 1995

Faulkner, Rev. Anselm, O.F.M., "General John Sigismund Maguire and the Kerry Connection", in *J.K.A.H.S.* no. 15-16, 1982-3pp. 61-70.

Froude, J.A., *The Two Chiefs of Dunboy,* London 1891

Gaughan, J. Anthony, *Listowel and its Vicinity* (Kingdom Books 1973)

Gaughan, J. Anthony, *The Knights of Glin* (Kingdom Books 1978)

Graves, Alfred Perceval, *To Return to All That* (London/Toronto, 1930)

Grosart Rev. Alexander B., D.D., L.C.D. FSA. (Scot), *The Lismore Papers: Selections from the Private or Public (or State) Correspondence of Sir Richard Boyle never before printed*, 1886, 5 vols.

Hayes, Richard, *A Biographical Dictionary of Irishmen in France* (Dublin 1949).

Herbert, *Retrospections of Dorothea Herbert 1770-1806*, first published 1929-30

Herbert. *Herbert Correspondence*, ed. W. J. Smith, University of Wales Press, 1963, 1968

Herbert, William (Keaveney and Madden eds.), *Croftus Sive De Hibernia Liber*, Irish Manuscripts Commission 1992

Hickson, Mary Agnes, *Selections from Old Kerry Records, 1st and 2nd series* (London 1872, 1874)

Hodson, Major V.C.P., *List of the Officers of the Bengal Army*. (London 1928)

Johnston-Liik, Edith, *History of the Irish Parliament* 1692-1800 (Ulster Historical Foundation 2002)

Kelly, Liam, Lucid, Geraldine and O'Sullivan, Maria, *Blennerville, Gateway to Tralee's Past*, Tralee 1989

Kerney Walsh, Micheline, *Destruction by Peace: Hugh O'Neill After Kinsale* (Armagh 1986)

King, Jeremiah, *History of Kerry, or History of the Parishes in the County*, 1908-14, 1st edn

King, William, *The State of the Protestants of Ireland under the Late King James's Government* (London 1691)

Lansdowne, Marquis, *Glanerought and the Petty-FitzMaurices* (Oxford 1937)

Lansdowne, Marquis, *The Petty-Southwell Correspondence 1676-1687*, edited from the Bowood Papers (London 1928)

Lehane, Shane G., *The Great Famine in the Poor Law Unions of Dingle and Killarney, Co. Kerry* (M.A. Thesis, University College Cork 2005)

Ludlow, Edmund, *The Memoirs of Edmund Ludlow, Lieutenant-General of the Horse in the Army of the Commonwealth of England 1625-1692*, by C. H. Firth, M.A., 2 vols, Oxford 1894, first published 1698

Lynch, Kathleen M., *Roger Boyle, First Earl of Orrory* (Tennessee 1965),

Lyne, Gerard J. *The Lansdowne Estate in Kerry Under the Agency of William Steuart Trench 1849-72* (Dublin 2001)

Lyons, F.S.L., *Ireland Since the Famine* (London 1971)

MacCarthy Glas, Daniel, *The Life and Letters of Florence MacCarthy Mor* (London 1867, reprint Cork 1975)

MacCarthy, Robert, *The Trinity College Estates 1800-1923* (Dundalk 1992)

McCarthy Morrogh, Michael, *The Munster Plantation* (Oxford 1986)

McCormack, Anthony M., *The Earldom of Desmond 1463-1583* (Dublin 2005)

MacCotter, Paul, "The Ferriters of Kerry", *J. K.A.H.S.*, 2002, pp.55-82

MacCurtain, Sr Benvenuta, "An Irish Agent of the Counter-Reformation, Dominic O'Daly", in *Irish Historical Studies*, Sept. 1967, pp. 391-406

MacCurtain, Sr Margaret (Benvenuta), "The Fall of the House of Desmond", in *J.K.A.H.S.* no. 8, 1975

MacDonagh, Oliver, *O'Connell, The Life of daniel O'Connell* (London 1991), p. 407

MacGillycuddy, Rosemary Brownlow, *A Short History of the Clan McGillycuddy* (Dublin 1991)

MacLysaght, Edward, (ed.), *The Kenmare Manuscripts*, Irish Manuscripts Commission 1942

McDowell, R. B., "The Personnel of the Dublin Society of United Irishmen 1791-4", in *Irish Historical Studies*, vol. 2. 1941-41, pp. 12-53

McMorran, Russell, and O'Keeffe, Maurice, *A Pictorial History of Tralee* (Tralee 2005)

Martin, Thomas F., *The Kingdom in the Empire* (Tralee 2007)

Meghan, P.J., "Stephen De Vere's Voyage to Canada, 1847" in Etienne Rynne (ed.) *North Munster Studies, Essays in Commemoration of Monsignor Michael Moloney* (Thomond Archaeological Society, 1967)

Memorials of the Dead, *Journal of the Association for the Preservation of the Memorials of the Dead in Ireland* 1895-1928

Mooney, Canice, O.F.M., *Boetius MacEgan of Ross* (Killiney 1950)

Nicholls, K.W., *Gaelic and Gaelicised Ireland in the Middle Ages* (Dublin 2003)

O'Brien, Donough, *History of the O'Briens from Brian Boroimhe, AD 1000-1945* (Cairo 1949)

O'Callaghan, John Cornelius, *History of the Irish Brigades in the Service of France,* 1870

O'Carroll, Gerald, *Mr Justice Robert Day (1746-1841): the Diaries and the Addresses to Grand Juries (1793-1829)* (Tralee 2004)

O'Carroll, Helen, *The FitzMaurices Lords of Kerry and Barons of Lixnaw,* Lixnaw 1993

O Ciardha, Eamon, *Ireland and the Jacobite Cause 1685-1766, A Fatal Attachment* (Dublin 2002)

O Concubhair, Padraig, *They Kept the Hills of Kerry, 1848 by Fealeside,* Duagh 1998

O'Connell, Mrs Morgan John, *The Last Colonel of the Irish Brigade,* 2 vols. (London 1892)

O'Connell, Maurice R., and Leyne, Gerard, *The Correspondence of Daniel O'Connell,* 8 vols., Dublin 1973-81

Ó Faoláin, Seán, *King of the Beggars* (1938)

O'Flanagan, Roderick, *The Old Munster Circuit, Tales, Trials and Tradition* (London 1880)

Ó Lúing, Seán, "Richard Griffith and the Roads of Kerry", in *Journal of the Kerry Archaeological and Historical Society* 1976, pp. 92-124

O'Shea, Rev. Kieran, "David Moriarty (1814-77)" (4 parts) in *Journal of the Kerry Archaeological and Historical Society,* 1970, pp. 71, 72, 73

O'Sullivan, Donal J., *District Inspector John A. Kearney, The R.I.C. Man who Befriended Roger Casement* (printed Victoria, B.C., Canada 2005)

O'Sullivan, Friar (of Muckross Abbey), "Ancient History of the Kingdom of Kerry", in *Journal of the Cork Historical and Archaeological Society* 1899

O'Sullivan – Amhlaoibh O Sullleabhain - 1827-1831, *The Diary of Humphrey O'Sullivan,* ed. Tomas de Bhaldraithe, Mercier 1979

Orpen, Goddard Henry, *The Orpen Family,* London 1930

Prendergast, John P., *The Cromwellian Settlement of Ireland* (London 1865)

Rowan, Rev Arthur Blennerhassett Rowan, *Tralee and its Provosts Sixty Years On, with introduction by The Last of its Provosts* (private collection, only 24 copies printed)

Rutland, *Correspondence between the Right Honourable William Pitt and Charles Duke of Rutland Lord Lieutenant of Ireland* (Edinburgh, London 1890)

Lansdowne, Marquis of, *Glenerought and the Petty-FitzMaurices* (London 1937)

Simms, J.G., *Jacobite Ireland* (Dublin 1969)

Smith, Charles, *Antient and Present State of the County of Kerry* (Dublin 1856)

Spenser, Edmund, *View of the State of Ireland* (1596)

Stafford, Thomas, *Pacata Hibernia, or A History of the Wars in Ireland during the Reign of Queen Elizabeth, especially within the province of Munster under the Government of Sir George Carew, and compiled by his direction and appointment,* edited and with an introduction and notes by Standish O'Grady, 2 vols., London 1896

Stevens. *Journal of John Stevens containing a Brief account of the War in Ireland 1689-91* (ed. The Rev. Robert H. Murray, Litt.D. Oxford Clarendon Press 1912, p.187).

Stokes, Canon A. E., "Thomas Coningsby", in *Dictionary of National Biography* (Oxford 2004)

Tierney, Mark, *Croke of Cashel, The Life of Archbishop Thomas William Croke 1832-1902* (Dublin 1976)

Walsh, Katherine, "Franciscan Friaries in Pre-Reformation Kerry", in *Journal of the Kerry Archaeological and Historical Society*, no. 9, 1976

Walsh, T.J., *Nano Nagle and the Presentation Sisters* (Dublin 1959)

Walsh, T.J., *The Irish Continental College Movement* (Dublin and Cork 1973)

Young, Arthur, *Tour of Ireland 1776-9* (2 vols. London/New Youk, 1892)

INDEX OF PEOPLE AND PLACES

Descent of leading families from the "Rebel" Earl of Desmond

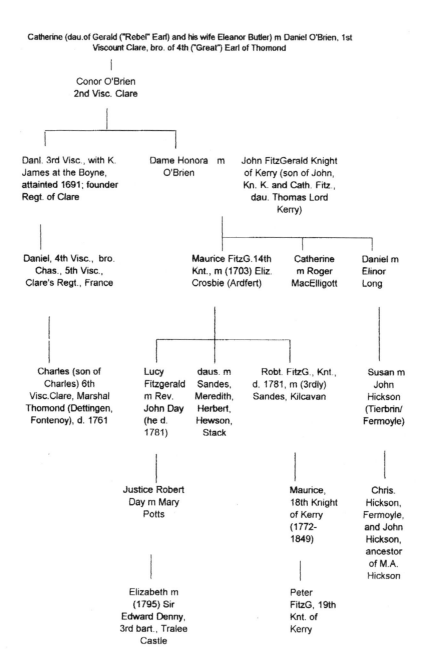

Catherine (dau.of Gerald ("Rebel" Earl) and his wife Eleanor Butler) m Daniel O'Brien, 1st Viscount Clare, bro. of 4th ("Great") Earl of Thomond

Conor O'Brien
2nd Visc. Clare

Danl. 3rd Visc., with K. James at the Boyne, attainted 1691; founder Regt. of Clare

Dame Honora   m   John FitzGerald Knight
O'Brien   of Kerry (son of John, Kn. K. and Cath. Fitz., dau. Thomas Lord Kerry)

Daniel, 4th Visc., bro. Chas., 5th Visc., Clare's Regt., France

Maurice FitzG.14th Knt., m (1703) Eliz. Crosbie (Ardfert)

Catherine m Roger MacElligott

Daniel m Elinor Long

Charles (son of Charles) 6th Visc.Clare, Marshal Thomond (Dettingen, Fontenoy), d. 1761

Lucy Fitzgerald m Rev. John Day (he d. 1781)

daus. m Sandes, Meredith, Herbert, Hewson, Stack

Robt. FitzG., Knt., d. 1781, m (3rdly) Sandes, Kilcavan

Susan m John Hickson (Tierbrin/ Fermoyle)

Justice Robert Day m Mary Potts

Maurice, 18th Knight of Kerry (1772-1849)

Chris. Hickson, Fermoyle, and John Hickson, ancestor of M.A. Hickson

Elizabeth m (1795) Sir Edward Denny, 3rd bart., Tralee Castle

Peter FitzG, 19th Knt. of Kerry

Browne (Killarney), planters of Kerry under Elizabeth, later (Jacobite) viscounts Kenmare. Pedigree one.

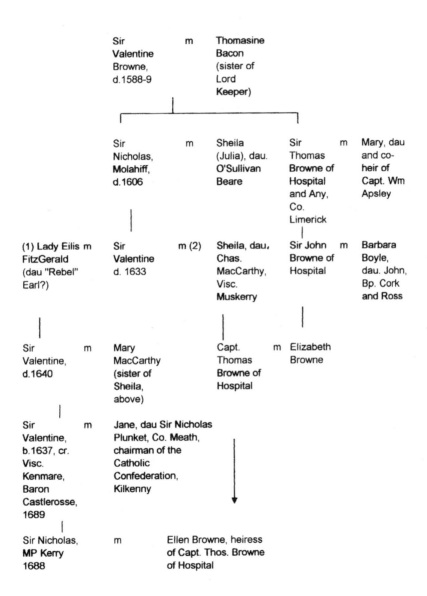

Jacobite viscounts to Georgian earls:
18th century Brownes (lords Kenmare) and intermarriage with the Herberts

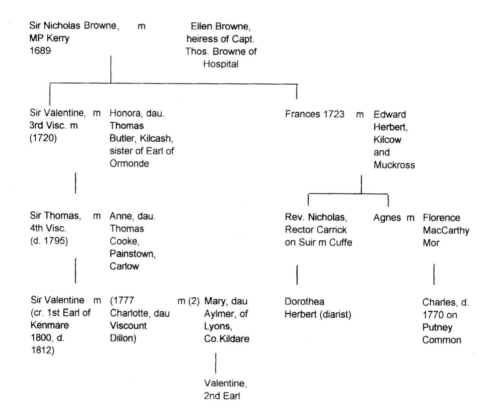

Sir Nicholas Browne,　m　Ellen Browne,
MP Kerry　　　　　　　heiress of Capt.
1689　　　　　　　　　Thos. Browne of
　　　　　　　　　　　Hospital

Sir Valentine,　m　Honora, dau.　　　　Frances 1723　m　Edward
3rd Visc. m　　　Thomas　　　　　　　　　　　　　　Herbert,
(1720)　　　　　Butler, Kilcash,　　　　　　　　　　Kilcow
　　　　　　　　sister of Earl of　　　　　　　　　　and
　　　　　　　　Ormonde　　　　　　　　　　　　　Muckross

Sir Thomas,　m　Anne, dau.　　　　　Rev. Nicholas,　　Agnes　m　Florence
4th Visc.　　　Thomas　　　　　　　Rector Carrick　　　　　　MacCarthy
(d. 1795)　　　Cooke,　　　　　　　on Suir m Cuffe　　　　　　Mor
　　　　　　　Painstown,
　　　　　　　Carlow

Sir Valentine　m　(1777　　　　m (2) Mary, dau　Dorothea　　　　　Charles, d.
(cr. 1st Earl of　Charlotte, dau　Aylmer, of　Herbert (diarist)　1770 on
Kenmare　　　Viscount　　　Lyons,　　　　　　　　　　　Putney
1800, d.　　　Dillon)　　　　Co.Kildare　　　　　　　　　Common
1812)

　　　　　　　　　　　　　Valentine,
　　　　　　　　　　　　　2nd Earl

Denny, from Munster Plantation
to Williamite/Jacobite Wars

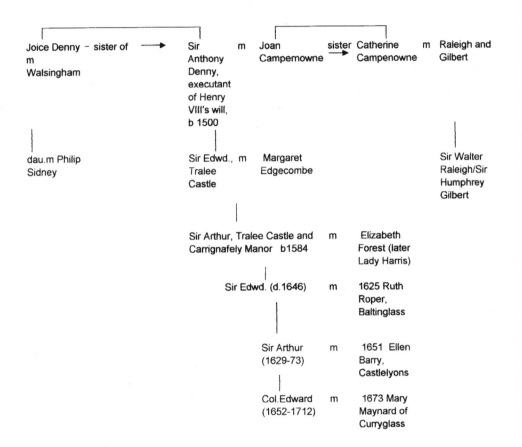

Joice Denny – sister of → Sir   m   Joan   sister   Catherine   m   Raleigh and
m   Anthony   Campemowne → Campenowne   Gilbert
Walsingham   Denny,
                   executant
                   of Henry
                   VIII's will,
                   b 1500

dau.m Philip   Sir Edwd.,   m   Margaret   Sir Walter
Sidney   Tralee   Edgecombe   Raleigh/Sir
                   Castle   Humphrey
                                                     Gilbert

Sir Arthur, Tralee Castle and   m   Elizabeth
Carrignafely Manor   b1584   Forest (later
                                          Lady Harris)

Sir Edwd. (d.1646)   m   1625 Ruth
                                 Roper,
                                 Baltinglass

Sir Arthur   m   1651 Ellen
(1629-73)   Barry,
                                 Castlelyons

Col.Edward   m   1673 Mary
(1652-1712)   Maynard of
                                 Curryglass

Denny: the eighteenth and nineteenth centuries

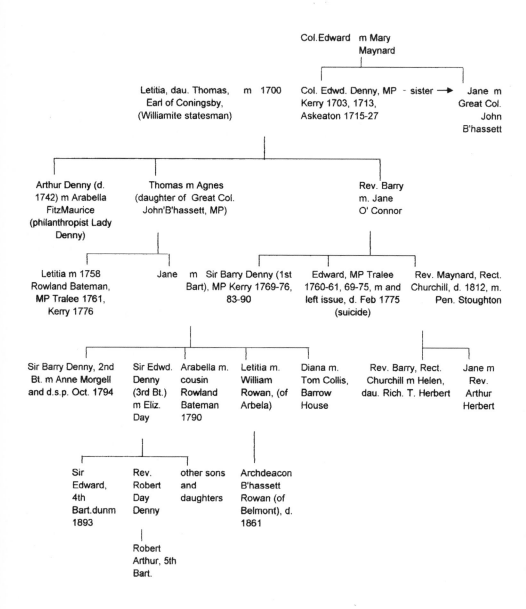

Cromwellian Waller/Petty intermarriage
with Fitzmaurice, barons Lixnaw, earls of Kerry

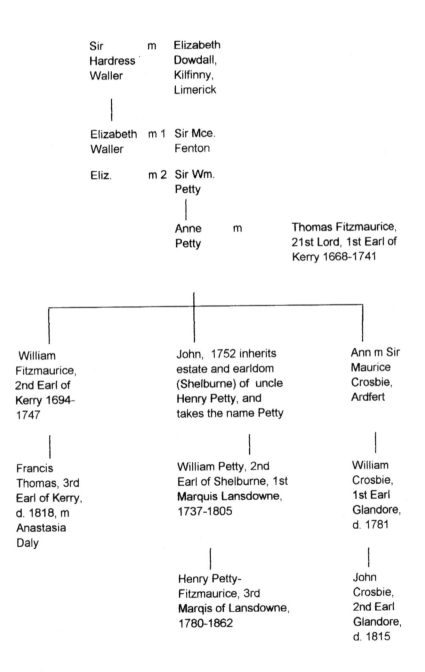

Sir   m   Elizabeth
Hardress   Dowdall,
Waller   Kilfinny,
              Limerick

Elizabeth   m 1   Sir Mce.
Waller   Fenton

Eliz.   m 2   Sir Wm.
               Petty

         Anne   m   Thomas Fitzmaurice,
         Petty   21st Lord, 1st Earl of
                                  Kerry 1668-1741

William Fitzmaurice, 2nd Earl of Kerry 1694–1747	John, 1752 inherits estate and earldom (Shelburne) of uncle Henry Petty, and takes the name Petty	Ann m Sir Maurice Crosbie, Ardfert
Francis Thomas, 3rd Earl of Kerry, d. 1818, m Anastasia Daly	William Petty, 2nd Earl of Shelburne, 1st Marquis Lansdowne, 1737-1805	William Crosbie, 1st Earl Glandore, d. 1781
	Henry Petty-Fitzmaurice, 3rd Marqis of Lansdowne, 1780-1862	John Crosbie, 2nd Earl Glandore, d. 1815

Blennerhassetts of the Williamite Wars,
and ancestry of Harman Blennerhassett

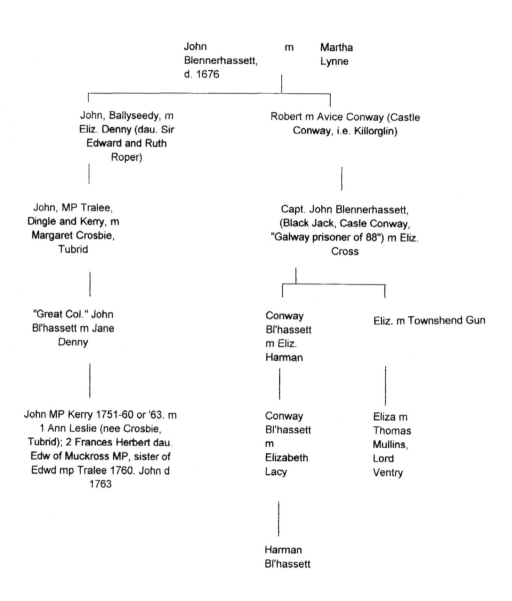

John Blennerhassett, d. 1676   m   Martha Lynne

John, Ballyseedy, m Eliz. Denny (dau. Sir Edward and Ruth Roper)

Robert m Avice Conway (Castle Conway, i.e. Killorglin)

John, MP Tralee, Dingle and Kerry, m Margaret Crosbie, Tubrid

Capt. John Blennerhassett, (Black Jack, Casle Conway, "Galway prisoner of 88") m Eliz. Cross

"Great Col." John Bl'hassett m Jane Denny

Conway Bl'hassett m Eliz. Harman

Eliz. m Townshend Gun

John MP Kerry 1751-60 or '63. m 1 Ann Leslie (nee Crosbie, Tubrid); 2 Frances Herbert dau. Edw of Muckross MP, sister of Edwd mp Tralee 1760. John d 1763

Conway Bl'hassett m Elizabeth Lacy

Eliza m Thomas Mullins, Lord Ventry

Harman Bl'hassett

Stuart and Bourbon Jacobite alliance

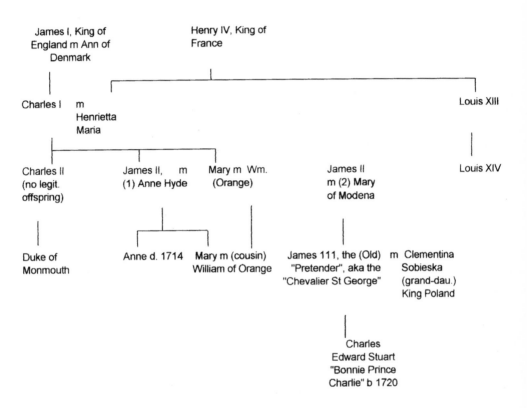

Province of Munster and (inset) the Baronies of Kerry

Inset (the Baronies of Kerry):
Iraghtconnor
Clanmaurice
Trughanacmy
Corkaguiney
Magunihy
Dunkerron North
Iveragh
Dunkerron South
Glanerought

Main map:
Galway Bay
Shannon R
Aran Islands
Bunratty
Kilrush
Carrigaholt
Kilkenny
Thurles
Limerick
Ballybunion
Ballingarry Castle
Glin
Askeaton
Rathkeale
Hospital
Cashel
Listowel
N'castlewest
Kilmallock
Cahir
Lixnaw
Charleville
Suir R
Clonmel
Tralee
C'maine
C'island
Buttevant
Waterford City
Blasket Is.
Dingle
N'market
Kanturk
Mallow
Fermoy
Lismore
Dingle Bay
Killarney
Blackwater R.
Duncannon Fort
Valentia Is.
Milstreet
Kilgarvan
Macroom
Sneem
Cork
Kilmackillogue Harbour
Bandon
Kinsale
Beare Is.
Baltimore
Bantry Bay
Castletownshend